PRAISE FOR THE SECOND EDITION OF *THE MINDFUL INTERNATIONAL MANAGER*

"Managers in all areas are under pressure to act with increasing certainty in a business environment that is increasingly *uncertain*. As this book demonstrates with rigorous but accessible advice, mindfulness is one of the keys to resolving this paradox. If managers can be more aware of their own behaviour and the behaviour of others, they will be better able to take advantages of the possibilities open to them. This book provides managers with practical advice and case studies and, above all, with food for thought for those who want to improve their international effectiveness."
Ian McMaster, Editor-in-chief, Business Spotlight magazine

"...conversational and immediately accessible to anyone who is new to the content... great care has been taken in these pages to talk the way people talk in the real world and to relate theory to practice."
Craig Storti, writer and cross-cultural trainer, author of The Art of Crossing Cultures, Speaking of India *and many more long- and best-sellers*

"This is not only a valuable handbook for managers who work in international or intercultural contexts; it is also ideal for preparing those who are soon to do so. Comfort and Franklin's lucid exposition of key concepts, their judicious use of relevant case studies and their emphasis on best practice combine to make this an optimal textbook for my graduate students in international courses of study. Short Q & A's with managers who grapple with intercultural issues provide springboards into discussion, and the situational judgement commentaries lead students on a journey of guided discovery of their own values and behaviour. This book definitely belongs in students' backpacks as well as in managers' briefcases."
James R Chamberlain, Director, Language Centre of the Bonn-Rhein-Sieg University of Applied Sciences, Germany

PRAISE FOR THE FIRST EDITION OF *THE MINDFUL INTERNATIONAL MANAGER*

"...a first-rate book... really useful, even for managers with a lot of international experience."
Ludger Opgenhoff, former Marketing Director Europe, DHL Express and Professor of International Management, Gelsenkirchen University of Applied Sciences, Germany

"The book presents readers with information on skills and competencies the successful international manager needs and also invites them to complete cases and exercises designed to encourage reflection on their own behavior. This book has a variety of uses. While best placed in the context of executive training and development, it could also be a supplemental text in a communications class ...provides an excellent overview for any manager dealing with diverse cultures or international assignments, and it can easily be read and understood without the guidance of an instructor."
Lizabeth A Barclay, Oakland University, USA, Business Communication Quarterly, *75 (3), pp 343–46*

"...busy managers who are not going to sit still for too much theory and pages of academese are the real winners here... It is very practical and includes five detailed case studies that bring the concepts to life in situations almost any manager can relate to. *The Mindful International Manager* is a lucid, brief, extremely accessible book that presents more useful, practical insights in its 130-plus pages than many books two and three times its length."
Craig Storti, author of The Art of Crossing Cultures

"This book is an invitation to reflect and its strength lies in blending 'mindfulness' with intercultural communication. This does not lead to a deeper knowledge of specific cultures, but it does create an awareness of intercultural cooperation and communication. This is already extremely valuable."
Personal Zeitschrift für Human Resource Management, *2009, 2*

"...a very accessible and practical guide that supports managers in their complex international work...remarkable chapters on feedback and conflict."
Vincent Merk, Eindhoven Technical University, Netherlands, former president, Society for Intercultural Education, Training and Research, Europe

"A wide range of situations are considered and, unlike so many other writers, Comfort and Franklin consider culture as more than merely 'national' culture."
People Management

"*The Mindful International Manger* is the perfect handbook for individuals that interact with and manage diverse workforces... provides an easy to understand breakdown of cultural variation in the workplace and provides best practices built soundly on intercultural theories... Comfort and Franklin have created a useful management guide which individuals may use to improve productivity within the work environment by focusing on creating a universal work culture built on the strengths and competencies of employees."
SIETAR Baltimore

"An attractive presentation and considerable white space make the book easy to read, particularly for the many of us who have now consumed more print in pixels than in ink. The authors, both interculturalists of experience and stature, have taken care to make the book interactive, encouraging us to apply the ideas contained to our own person and our experiences. It frequently asks us to assess the degree to which we find ourselves culturally inclined to or engaged in ranges of behaviour, belief, concepts and practices."
George Simons, www.diversophy.com

"It is thorough in exploring how differences and difficulties can be handled effectively with the right knowledge, skills and attitudes – examining a number of issues from feedback to conflict and offering techniques and options for a better outcome."
CPO Agenda

"...weaves theory and practice together – with the emphasis on the latter – so that both experienced and inexperienced managers can be guided through the many challenges of working internationally."
Gabriele Eilert-Ebke, formerly of Corporate Learning, Henkel AG & Co.Kgaa, Dusseldorf

"Consultant Jeremy Comfort and Professor Peter Franklin provide basic pointers on how to become 'mindful' of aspects of culture that, if ignored, could derail your business... getAbstract recommends its concise and informative tips to frequent business travellers, expatriate employees, managers leading culturally diverse teams and anyone looking to get a better grip on doing business globally."
getAbstract.com

"*The Mindful International Manager* addresses a more experienced management population, who has perhaps been managing for a number of years and is now being increasingly exposed to international project teams or working abroad. As such, it has more in-depth (and very realistic) case studies with suggested solutions, and carefully distinguishes between national culture, organisational culture and personality or individual preferences. I really liked the way each chapter was structured: an explanation of cultural differences and similarities, then a description of the key competencies required to handle these differences, followed by a guidance to develop best practice."
Sanda Ionescu, The Culture Broker

"The book carefully analyses what it means to be interculturally competent and helps the reader to understand the role of culture in such key areas as organization and change management, management style, communication, feedback and dealing with conflict, as well as taking advantage of diversity. It is based on the extensive knowledge of the authors and experience of international managers. It encourages observation and reflection, rather than quick-fix solutions. Above all, it goes out of its way to avoid harmful stereotyping."
Robert Gibson, Siemens AG, Munich, Germany

SECOND EDITION

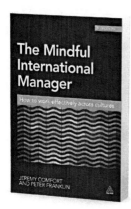

The Mindful International Manager

How to work effectively across cultures

Jeremy Comfort
and
Peter Franklin

KoganPage

LONDON PHILADELPHIA NEW DELHI

First published in Great Britain and the United States in 2011 by Kogan Page Limited
Second edition published 2014

2nd Floor, 45 Gee Street	1518 Walnut Street, Suite 1100	4737/23 Ansari Road
London EC1V 3RS	Philadelphia PA 19102	Daryaganj
United Kingdom	USA	New Delhi 110002
www.koganpage.com		India

© Jeremy Comfort and Peter Franklin, 2011, 2014

The right of Jeremy Comfort and Peter Franklin to be identified as the authors of this work has been asserted by them in accordance with the Copyright, Designs and Patents Act 1988.

ISBN   978 0 7494 6982 5
E-ISBN   978 0 7494 6983 2

British Library Cataloguing-in-Publication Data

A CIP record for this book is available from the British Library.

Library of Congress Cataloging-in-Publication Data

Comfort, Jeremy.
   The mindful international manager : how to work effectively across cultures / Peter Franklin, Jeremy Comfort.
      pages cm
   Revised edition of: The mindful international manager : how to work effectively across cultures / Jeremy Comfort and Peter Franklin. 2011.
   Includes bibliographical references and index.
   ISBN 978-0-7494-6982-5 – ISBN 978-0-7494-6983-2 (ebk) 1. International business enterprises–Management. 2. Management–Cross-cultural studies. 3. Intercultural communication. 4. International business enterprises–Personnel management. I. Franklin, Peter, 1955- II. Title.
   HD62.4.C627 2014
   658'.049–dc23

                                                                                    2013035791

Typeset by Graphicraft Limited, Hong Kong
Printed production managed by Jellyfish
Printed and bound by CPI Group (UK) Ltd, Croydon, CR0 4YY

CONTENTS

Acknowledgements xi
Foreword by Craig Storti xii

Introduction 1

01 Managing internationally 10

Core competence 10
Surfacing expectations 14
Understanding your own cultures 15
Profiling your own cultures 16
Best practice: Focused on goals, flexible on approaches 20
Case study 1: Nora Lundquist 22

02 Cultures 24

Competing values? 24
Power and status in national and organizational cultures 26
Time in national and organizational cultures 30
Communication style in national and organizational cultures 32
Individualism and group-orientation in national and organizational
   cultures 35
Performance orientation in national and organizational
   cultures 37
Taking the outsider's perspective on your own culture 39
Profiling other cultures 42
Best practice: Building a common culture 43

03 Individuals 46

Stereotypes 46
Personality and behaviour – at work and at home 49
Personality 50
Connecting the individual and culture 52
Personality and your international profile combined 55
Best practice: Get to know your colleagues 58
Best practice: The role of leadership 59
Case study 2: Laurence Berger 61

04   Situations   63

Situations   63
Situational judgement   63
Culture, personality and situation   64
Shared values and decision-making skills   65
Scenarios   65

05   Direction   69

The relationship between setting direction and uncertainty   69
Direction and vision   71
Results and relationships   72
Communication styles   73
Communicating direction: Big picture or detail? Push or pull?   73
Long- and short-term orientation   75
Past, present and future   77
Best practice: Top-down or bottom-up or something else?   79
Case study 3: Phil Carey   81

06   Organization and change   84

Attitudes towards change   84
Making change happen   87
Changing organizational structure   87
Change and cross-cultural mergers and acquisitions   89
Working in international projects   90
Working without a leader   91
Best practice: The four Ps   92
Case study 4: Pierre Menton   94

07   Roles   96

Management roles and styles   96
Supportive and directive styles   97
International roles and local roles   98
The role of the expert and the role of the manager   99
The role of the influencer   101
The role of the connector   103
The role of the facilitator   105
Best practice: Defining roles   108
Case study 5: Sun Mei Ling   110

08 Support 112

Why support is so important 112
Ways of developing yourself 113
Ways of supporting your colleagues 114
Ways of developing your team 116
Case study 6: Nguyen Binh 122

09 Feedback 124

Formal and informal feedback 124
Culture and feedback 125
Face and feedback 127
Personality and feedback 128
Building a feedback culture 129
Types of feedback 130
Best practice: Balancing transparency and harmony 131
Case study 7: Claudia Borges 133

10 Representing 135

The importance of representing 135
The skills of representing 136
Factors that influence representing 137
Representing internationally 139
Tuning into body language 140
Representing through socializing and building relationships 142
Best practice: Representing yourself, your team, your
    company 146
Case study 8: Talal Hamieh 146

11 Conflict 149

Causes of conflict 149
Attitudes towards conflict 152
Culturally influenced attitudes towards conflict 154
Preventing conflict through effective and appropriate
    communication 156
Preventing conflict through understanding the context 158
Resolving conflicts: Some options 159
Best practice: Yourself, the others and trust 161
Case study 9: Gisela Schaefer 162

12   Cooperation 164

The basis for cooperation   164
Regulating cooperation   166
Building a common culture to leverage diversity   168
Best practice: Cooperating in virtual teams   170
Best practice: Cooperating in international teams   173
Case study 10: Bracken International   176

13   Leading 179

Managers and leaders – managing and leading   179
Power as the basis for leadership   181
The heart of leadership   181
'Doing' leadership   182
Being a leader   182
How leadership may differ from culture to culture   184
What leaders have in common across cultures   188
Case study 11: Leila Mehmet   191

Case study answers   193
Situational judgement commentaries   200
Profiles of the managers quoted   204
Glossary   206
References   224
Index   228

ACKNOWLEDGEMENTS

It has been a pleasure to work together on this second edition. Two years after the publication of the first edition, our experience of working with international managers has grown. The revisions and additions have been made in response to their needs in an ever more complex world.

We are very grateful to those countless people working across cultures who over the years have enriched our workshops and courses with their experiences and insights and, in that way, unwittingly contributed to the book. Without the stimulation they provided this book would have been much poorer.

We would like to thank the managers who were kind enough to give us interviews to be used in this book. We have acknowledged them and the organizations they work for by name in the text and short biographies of them are included at the back of the book. In this connection, we would also like to thank Bob Dignen, Director of York Associates, who was responsible for conducting the interviews.

We also express our thanks to all those fellow interculturalists and other writers, researchers and scholars whose insights we have benefited from and used. Their names appear in the text itself and the particular books and articles we refer to are contained in the list of references at the end of the book.

Special thanks go to Nigel Ewington and his colleagues at WorldWork Ltd for allowing us to make such liberal use of their International Competency Set; and to Janet Leonard and her colleagues at TMS Development International Ltd for allowing us to use the Team Management Profile.

We are also very grateful to Julia Swales at Kogan Page for suggesting we create this expanded edition, for supporting our work, and for her patience.

Last but by no means least, we would like to thank Lilian Meyer for her tireless work formatting the manuscript and removing the typos and Manuela Breucker for checking the references. Any remaining errors are ours.

Jeremy Comfort and Peter Franklin

FOREWORD

Mindfulness has an impressive pedigree, going back to the time of the Buddha, who famously declared:

> Phenomena (words and deeds) are preceded by mind.
> Mind is their chief; they are made of mind.

In Buddhism mindfulness – more accurately, *Right* Mindfulness – occupies a supremely elevated status as one of the constituents of the Noble Eightfold Path, the path that leads to enlightenment. More precisely, mindfulness refers to awareness of one's mental states, which means that if mind does indeed precede all actions, then before we do or say anything we are aware of our impending conduct.

If we shift our focus to the world of culture and management, mindful international managers are aware of their own culturally influenced values and behaviours but also of the – possibly very different – values and practices of their colleagues and partners from other cultures. They are in a position to reflect on and judge the *appropriateness* of their impending actions in a different cultural context and, if necessary, come up with new, culturally more appropriate actions for the situation.

Which brings us to the real value of Jeremy Comfort and Peter Franklin's new edition: it gives the international manager the basic tools he needs to make that critical determination of whether or not what he is about to do – in a wide variety of business and workplace contexts – whether or not his impending actions are going to be appropriate and effective in dealing with someone from a different culture. Just being mindful of the actions you are about to take is a valuable skill, but if you have no framework for judging the probable efficacy of the impulses thus revealed, you haven't helped yourself very much. This book gives you that framework.

The framework has expanded from the first edition to include new chapters and additional case studies. Messrs. Comfort and Franklin have sifted through the growing body of intercultural knowledge and made a judicious selection of concepts with special relevance to the world of business. If that sounds like faint praise, it is not; in a book such as this, a succinct overview of a complex field, selection is critical.

Along with two other factors: (1) prose that is conversational and immediately accessible to anyone who is new to the content; and (2) specific examples illustrating how the key cultural concepts play out in common business settings. Great care has been taken in these pages to talk the way people talk in the real world and to relate theory to practice.

Messrs. Comfort and Franklin can't tell you everything you'll need to know about being mindful – about all the cultural differences you should be aware of at the critical moment between thought and action – but in truth, they don't have to. They introduce you to the most important *categories* of difference, with numerous examples, and astute international managers can extrapolate from there.

In the end the central lesson *The Mindful International Manager* teaches is one you may already know: you can't always trust your instincts. But you may not have known just how unreliable your instincts can be.

Craig Storti

Introduction

This part of the book answers these questions:

- Who is this book for? Who exactly is the 'international manager'?
- What is the context of managing internationally?
- What is meant by working mindfully across cultures?
- What is 'mindfulness' and what is mindful interaction?
- How does the international manager act and communicate mindfully?
- How can the international manager become more effective?
- How can you influence and monitor your own development as an international manager?
- What makes this book different from other books about working internationally?
- Who are the writers of the book?

Who is this book for? Who exactly is the 'international manager'?

The international manager could be based in his/her home country but travelling to other countries or could be an expat, somebody sent on an assignment to another country to live and work there for a number of years. The international manager could also be a 'global nomad', somebody moving from an expat position in one country to another in the same or a different country with the same or a different employer so often that they lose contact with their country of origin, even if they ever had only one. Increasingly, international managers work virtually from their local or home office, communicating globally via video conference, teleconference, email etc.

The international manager could be leading a team 'at home'; some of the team's members may be from different countries but are located in the same place; or the team could be a virtual team spread across the world with colleagues who rarely meet face-to-face. They may have people reporting directly to them or indeed may have no direct reports but need to influence colleagues without using hierarchical authority. They may work in a line management role or mainly in projects.

The international manager could be working in the private sector in a large multinational; in a medium-sized company which has a strong home base but works internationally; or in a small family-owned or family-run company trying to build its business globally. They could also be working in the public sector for government ministries and embassies or for other state institutions, forging links with partners abroad, or for NGOs working, for example, in the field of development aid.

In short, there are fewer and fewer managers who can restrict their work to a local and familiar environment. More and more, managers are confronted with the task of taking advantage of the enormous opportunities which our connected world offers us.

What is the context of managing internationally?

The acronym VUCA, often used by organizations when considering strategy, helps to summarize the context in which international managers work:

Volatility. The world is volatile in the sense that changes happen suddenly and dramatically. Change is one of the few constants in international management. This can mean that there are numerous, large swings in market trends around the globe; companies rise and fall; others need to reinvent themselves; new sectors appear and then disappear and new markets develop. Volatility can be political in nature, as seen in violent clashes in countries in political transition, or economic, as seen in the euro crisis and its impact on countries in the eurozone, particularly those in southern Europe.

Uncertainty. There is a paradoxical relationship of tension between the need for planning in order to *handle* uncertainty and the need for flexibility in order to *respond to* uncertainty. The larger and more internationally active the organization, the more it needs to structure, plan and standardize; but, to survive, it also needs to respond quickly to change. In some parts of the world, it is almost impossible to predict or plan because it is very uncertain what is going to happen, even the next day. This uncertainty is thus especially felt in organizations working internationally. Some managers are used to living with this uncertainty; others find that uncertainty leads to a threatening feeling of insecurity – especially about jobs and whether they or their role will become redundant.

We can also be uncertain about the meaning of messages we receive from our foreign colleagues. Much international communication is less than complete – this can lead to much misunderstanding. Such misunderstanding can be caused by language problems; it can also occur because we do not share the same culture and market context. If we shared the same context, we would be better able to fill in the gaps in messages and give meaning to implicit messages.

Complexity. The context of managing internationally can be experienced as more complex than working at home for many reasons. The world can be regarded as more complex because it is more connected and therefore we can analyse situations on more and more levels. Working in a flat and networked organization, for example, means we can learn about many new fields and maybe be expected to take these into account when making decisions. Working internationally is also complex because of different time zones, the coordination of agendas and sometimes the unreliability of communication technology. A major reason why managing internationally is complex is because managers are confronted with contexts in which their unspoken values, unconscious norms and accustomed management practices – in short the effects of their home culture – are not shared to the same extent by the organizations and people they are working with. At home, our culture helps us to manage the complex context we live and work in, but this mechanism for managing complexity does not work so well internationally where we are likely to encounter a multiplicity of cultures.

Ambiguity. When we are working in familiar contexts – for example at home with colleagues we know well – we can be clear about where we stand. We may feel what is right or wrong is fairly obvious. We may feel it is clear who we can work with and who we can't. However, when we are working in different cultures with a range of people whom we don't know so well, the situation may become blurred and ambiguous. It's not so easy to understand why people do things or maybe don't do them.

The VUCA acronym underlines the *challenge* of working internationally. But it does not express the *opportunities* it offers. International managers have the chance to explore new cultures, learn new languages and, above all, work with people from many different backgrounds. As long as they develop and apply the competencies that are effective and appropriate for their work (and are described in this book), this diversity can build and sustain their motivation and their managerial qualities and skills over a long career.

What is meant by working mindfully across cultures?

All managers work under pressure to perform to high standards and achieve results. Organizations reinforce result-driven behaviour by identifying KPIs

(Key Performance Indicators) by which they can be judged – maybe bottom-line profit, additional sales, new customers, customer satisfaction, cost control etc. Good managers understand that they can achieve these results by doing a good job but also by building strong relationships with their colleagues and partners. Good relationships are based on mutual understanding and respect. And understanding comes from an ability to observe and reflect on one's own behaviour and that of your colleagues. Stepping back and focussing on this behaviour and the *context* and *process* of working together – as well as focussing on the result – is at the heart of mindfulness.

What is 'mindfulness'?

In our understanding of the term, mindfulness is a state of awareness in which it is possible consciously or unconsciously to exploit the knowledge, skills and attitudes you need to interact effectively and appropriately across cultures.

With roots in Buddhism, mindfulness is a concept that various disciplines such as psychology, communication studies and applied linguistics have adapted and used to describe an essential fundamental of successful communication, also across cultures.

> Mindfulness means being aware of our own and others' behaviour in the situation, and paying focused attention to the process of communication taking place between us and dissimilar others... attending to one's internal assumptions, cognitions, and emotions, and simultaneously attuning to the other's assumptions, cognitions, and emotions.
>
> *Ting-Toomey 1999: 16,267*

> When we are mindful, we can make conscious choices as to what we need to do in the particular situation in order to communicate effectively.
>
> *Gudykunst 2004: 253*

> The key qualities of a mindful state of being [are]: (1) creation of new categories; (2) openness to new information; and (3) awareness of more than one perspective.
>
> *Langer 1989: 72*

Ting-Toomey (1999) and Gudykunst (2004) brought the concept of mindfulness to intercultural communication studies from psychology, where it was first elaborated on by Langer (1989, 1997). In the management field, Thomas and Inkson (2003) underline the significance of mindfulness.

What is mindful interaction?

Central to all management is interaction – joint, goal-oriented behaviour which is expressed in actions and communication. International managers interact with others in order to perform their management tasks and to achieve their goals with others. When people communicate, they do not simply transfer messages to and fro. Rather, they *express meaning* and also have to *interpret*, or *give meaning* to, a large part of what others say. This is necessary because it is impossible to express everything explicitly in language, even if you are speaking your native language. Thus we can say that *together* with those they communicate with, international managers *co-construct meaning* and *create mutual understanding*.

They do this by using...

- their skill in the – often foreign – language they are communicating in;
- their ability to interpret non-verbal signals;
- their knowledge of the person they are communicating with;
- their knowledge of the world and the particular situation in which they find themselves;
- and, not least, their knowledge of the culture and cultures of the people involved.

When managers communicate across cultures, this *co-construction of meaning* and *creation of understanding* can be very difficult and is often dysfunctional, because they...

- may not be using their mother tongue and may therefore have difficulty understanding the other person and expressing themselves fully;
- may not yet have built up a relationship with the other person to support the creation of understanding;
- may be using a set of cultural knowledge to help them give meaning to what is said which is *different* from that of the other person;
- may be unaware that they are doing this;
- may be unaware of how this knowledge sets the norm for behaviour in their own culture but not necessarily for behaviour in the culture of the other person.

For these reasons, we can say metaphorically that two people from different cultures who communicate with each other construct meaning on two different building-sites! The meaning given to the message by each person on these two different building-sites is rarely exactly the same and this is how miscommunication can occur. This may make it important for the mindful international manager explicitly to *negotiate meaning*, ie to explore more carefully what the other person meant (see next section).

Mindful international managers are aware of these threats to successful communication and of the resulting need for *mindful interaction*. That is to say, they focus not just on the *outcome* of their interaction but also on the *context* of the communication. This context is made up of the *cultures* of those communicating (see especially Chapter 2 of this book) and of their *personalities* (see Chapter 3) as well as the *situation* in which they find themselves (see Chapter 4). They also focus on the *process* of communication, ie they...

- pay particular attention to *how* they themselves and the person they are talking to communicate;
- are sensitive to the need to ensure understanding; and
- are able to adapt the language they use and their communication style flexibly to achieve this.

Mindful international managers have developed the competencies that we present in this book to support this dual focus on *context* and *process*.

How does the international manager act and communicate mindfully?

Mindful international managers:

- focus with understanding on the *context* and *process* of communication and cooperation as well as on their outcome;
- *construct understanding* and *negotiate meaning* when communicating with people with backgrounds different from their own, for example by:
  - listening actively
  - modifying their language to make it more comprehensible
  - paraphrasing
  - summarizing
  - testing their own understanding
  - repairing misunderstanding and
  - interpreting non-verbal behaviour;
- pay attention to their own cultural and individual assumptions, values and norms;
- realize that these are only one set of guiding principles for action among many others;
- pay attention to what they can see of the cultural and individual assumptions, values and norms of the people with whom they are working;
- pay attention to the personality of the person they are communicating with;
- try to see the different cultures and situations they are in through the eyes and with the feelings of the people they are working with;
- take account of these different perspectives and feelings in their own actions and in their evaluations of people from different cultures.

How can the international manager become more effective?

The book not only *explains* cultural and individual differences in management values and behaviour. It also helps you to *handle* these differences. It helps you to become more mindful.

It gives you the *knowledge* you need to *understand* the context and process of international management but it also describes the *skills* and *competencies* you need to work effectively across cultures.

In the first four chapters we develop your mindfulness by expanding your understanding in the following ways:

Chapter 1: Differences between working locally and internationally.

Chapter 2: The impact of culture on your behaviour and that of your foreign partners.

Chapter 3: The impact of personality on your behaviour and that of your foreign partners.

Chapter 4: How situations can be understood differently.

In the next nine chapters we develop your skills and competencies:

Chapter 5: Direction – how you can align your diverse colleagues to a common objective.

Chapter 6: Organization and change – how you can structure your teams, departments and projects to adapt flexibly to a rapidly changing environment.

Chapter 7: Roles – how you can switch roles flexibly to get the best out of your teams and partners.

Chapter 8: Support – how you can support and develop your people across cultures.

Chapter 9: Feedback – how you can use feedback to maintain and improve performance.

Chapter 10: Representing – how you can promote and communicate effectively about the achievements of your people and yourself.

Chapter 11: Conflict – how you can deal with resistance and conflict from colleagues in different locations and cultures.

Chapter 12: Cooperation – how you can build and maintain cooperation with colleagues, especially when working virtually.

Chapter 13: Leadership – how leading across cultures needs different leadership qualities.

How can you influence and monitor your own development as an international manager?

The book includes numerous exercises to encourage you to reflect upon your own personal values and work practices and those of the organizational and national cultures you belong to. They also help you to become aware of and understand the values and practices of the people from other cultures that you are working with.

The book contains 11 short case studies which are the intermediate step between the 'theory' of the book and your own management 'reality'. They give you the opportunity to apply the insights contained in the book and compare your interpretation with the authors'.

The book also identifies key competencies which you can track. These are taken from the Worldwork International Competency Set for working effectively in international contexts. Based on research and the practical experience of people operating internationally, Worldwork Ltd, London, has identified 10 key competencies covering 22 different factors, which enable people to become effective in unfamiliar cultural settings.

This competency set, which we refer to throughout the book, forms the framework for The International Profiler questionnaire and feedback tool that has been developed to help managers and professionals understand where they typically put the emphasis when working internationally. It helps to raise their awareness of potential areas in which they may require future development, and suggests actions they can take to fill the gaps. Full details can be found at **www.worldwork.biz**.

What makes this book different from other books about working internationally?

This book:

- places managers and the management situations they have to handle in their daily work at the centre of the stage;
- quotes the experiences and insights of practising international managers;
- not only describes differences and difficulties but also describes what knowledge, skills, attitudes and qualities you need to handle them effectively;
- does not suggest that the challenges facing a manager working internationally are exclusively caused by differences in national or

ethnic culture but also deals with the influence of organizational culture and emphasizes the importance of the personality and preferences of the individual manager;

- avoids harmful stereotypes;
- is written in a style that is easy for non-native speakers of English to understand – using short sentences and simple vocabulary;
- tries to avoid jargon. Where jargon is unavoidable, it is relatively transparent and easy to understand. When not, a glossary of terms and difficult words at the end of the book may help.

Who are the writers of the book?

We believe it is important for the reader to be aware of the context in which this book was written. The authors are Jeremy Comfort and Peter Franklin. They were both brought up and educated in Great Britain and have both had international and intercultural careers, living and/or working outside the United Kingdom (mainly in Europe but also in China) and with people from all over the world. Despite this international context to their lives, the book inevitably reflects their particular view of the world and also the largely Western orientation of the knowledge and insights they possess about culture, communication and management. Readers should be aware of this 'culture-centredness' when reading the book. Members of other cultures may well see the world differently from the authors.

Jeremy Comfort founded York Associates in the UK more than 30 years ago with the mission to develop people internationally. He has trained and coached hundreds of individuals and teams who face the ever more complex challenges of working internationally. He works closely with a number of international businesses including Nestlé and Henkel. Jeremy is responsible for creating the Developing People Internationally approach, an innovative set of training materials, out of which this book has grown.

Peter Franklin is a professor at Konstanz University of Applied Sciences in Germany, where his teaching and research activities concern culture and communication in international management. He also teaches on MBA programmes in China, Switzerland and the UK. Peter works with corporate clients such as Siemens and Daimler to develop the competencies described in this book. He is also editor of the Internet knowledge community dialogin, The Delta Intercultural Academy, located at **www.dialogin.com**.

Managing internationally

This chapter focuses on:

- Why the international manager needs to communicate more transparently when working internationally than when working at home.
- What steps the international manager needs to take to make teams work well.
- Why it is important to understand the impact of culture on your behaviour and on the way you manage.
- How your behaviour and the way you manage can be affected by culturally influenced values, beliefs and attitudes.
- How culture functions as an orientation system and gives its members identity and a sense of belonging.
- How we are all members of a number of different cultures at the same time.
- Applying the chapter's insights to a team management case study in the field of international cooperation.

Core competence

Balancing the achievement of results and the maintenance of relationships is the core competence of the international manager. All managers achieve results through the people they manage and influence – be they bosses, direct reports, colleagues or fellow team-members. Building and cultivating relationships effectively in order to achieve results across cultures is even more challenging than operating just in your own culture. Mindful international managers understand the challenges and are ready to deal with them.

At home, in a domestic environment, a lot of what we expect of the people we manage is unspoken – it is taken for granted. For example, a manager might say to someone in their team, 'I'd like that report by next Monday', and the team member understands what they are saying about the finished state of the report and the urgency of the deadline. The team member understands because the manager said it many times before and everyone in the team has a shared understanding of what is needed in this situation.

Of course, this does not mean that the report will arrive on time and in the right state! That also depends on the competence and motivation of the person writing the report. In a domestic context, we often do not display our expectations of performance because we feel people understand them. The familiar context and the shared culture help to get the message across. In the international context, the context may be unfamiliar and the culture is not shared. So a different approach is necessary.

Working effectively in the international context

One of the most common contexts in which managers first encounter the challenges of working across cultures is the international team, often consisting of members located across the globe and meeting face-to-face only from time to time. This context will serve in this book as the setting for the international manager's work. However, much of what we say about the work of managers in international teams is not restricted to teams but can be applied to other kinds of international work setting: the international project, the multicultural group working co-located in one country, the subsidiary abroad.

Domestic, mono-cultural teams often perform better than international, geographically dispersed or virtual teams, relying on this unspoken and shared understanding. But well-managed international teams have the potential to do better than domestic teams. Both experience and research (for example, Distefano and Maznevski, 2000) indicate that international teams are more creative, generating more ideas than their mono-cultural counterparts and more criteria to judge the quality of their ideas. In another study, Stahl *et al* (2010) suggest members of international teams achieve a higher degree of satisfaction with their team work than members of domestic teams. So it may be in the interest of the mindful international manager leading or working in an international team to ensure that this creativity is leveraged in the team.

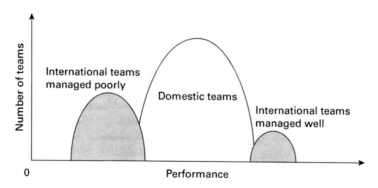

Adapted from Distefano and Maznevski (2000)

In numerous publications (for example, Lane *et al*, 2009), Maznevski proposes a three-stage model to make sure diverse international teams fulfil their potential:

1 Mapping

We need to spend time understanding the differences we observe and experience in our interaction with others in the team:

- cultural values (see Chapter 2);
- leadership styles (see Chapters 5 and 13);
- personality (see Chapter 3).

Spending time on this first vital step is not easy, especially if you are used to working with a local team that can get down to business immediately. However, projects and teams that do not map the differences will almost certainly run into problems later. Conflicts will arise and frictional loss will occur. Tools to help you map the differences are introduced in the relevant chapters.

2 Bridging

The second step concerns communicating across the differences. There is a danger that, having uncovered the diversity of your team, you are overwhelmed by the differences and retreat into your local way of doing things. The international manager needs to be confident and motivated to open up and take account of the differences. You first need to *decentre* – in other words accept the differences without finding fault – and then *recentre* to agree on a shared way of working based on what you have in common.

3 Integrating

This step guides you to an effective way of working with a diverse team: supporting team members (see Chapter 8), giving feedback (see Chapter 9), resolving conflicts (see Chapter 11) and getting the best out of the ideas and experiences of your team members (see Chapter 12).

A route map for international team management

The Developing People Internationally (DPI) model (on which this book is based) has been devised to give managers a route map to guide them through the challenges of working across cultures. The challenges (see Introduction, VUCA) mean that you need to be more systematic and transparent in the processes you use to build high-performing international teams.

Having mapped the differences and understood yourself and the others (see Chapters 2, 3 and 4), the virtuous circle continues by making sure you and your team or colleagues can answer the key questions about results and outcomes. You and your colleagues need to know where you are going (see Chapter 5: Direction), how you are going to get there (see Chapter 6: Organization and change) and who is going to do what (see Chapter 7: Roles).

The virtuous circle of team management competencies

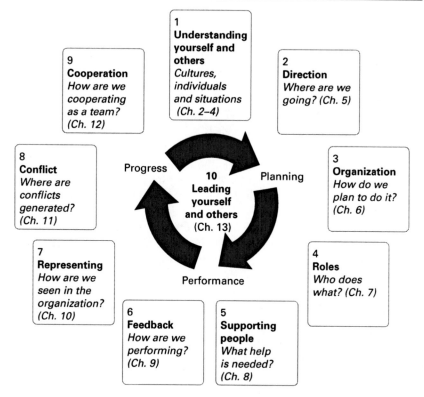

The DPI Model © York Associates 2007

These vital questions should be answered *together with your colleagues* and need to be revisited frequently to check that you are on track.

Getting high performance is not achieved merely through creating clarity about a team's objectives and tasks; it is also dependent on motivation and involvement. So the next three questions that need to be answered are: what help do you need (see Chapter 8: Support), how are you performing (see Chapter 9: Feedback) and how are you seen (see Chapter 10: Representing)?. All managers need to involve and motivate their people. The international manager needs to give even more attention to these three steps. When team members are located in different places across the world, daily personal contact is inevitably lacking and this can often lead to the feeling of not being supported, not being appreciated and not being noticed.

The virtuous circle then acknowledges the likelihood of conflict and Chapter 11 helps you to understand how it can arise and how you can best deal with it in a culturally appropriate way. In Chapter 12 we focus on integrating – maximising the potential creativity in your team and, in particular, facilitating virtual teams. Finally, Chapter 13 looks at the challenges of leading across cultures and the qualities needed to do so mindfully.

Surfacing expectations

When they are working in an international environment, mindful managers do not assume that their teams and other stakeholders understand their expectations. Let us return to the example at the beginning of the chapter and transfer it to an international setting.

A US manager, sitting in her office in Boston, emails an Italian colleague working in Milan. She writes: 'I'd like that report by next Monday'. The US manager intends this to be an urgent request for a finished report. But the Italian may understand this as a wish, not a request. He may not feel the urgency of the deadline at all.

When the report does not arrive, the US manager's prejudice about 'unpunctual Italians' is confirmed. She phones her Italian colleague and expresses her frustration. This confirms the Italian's prejudice about 'pushy Americans'.

Mindful management means that you need to surface your expectations and expose your intentions much more transparently. If the US manager had said: 'I need this report by Monday', she may have still been regarded as pushy by her Italian colleague. But she may also have got the report on time! If you communicate more transparently rather than relying on shared culture to give meaning to your message, your performance and results will compare very well with those of your domestic team. They may even exceed them. In the best of cases, this surfacing of expectations should happen in the mapping phase described above rather than in the course of cooperation, where it can lead to conflict and process loss.

Cultural icebergs

Before managers communicate their specific expectations, it is important for them to reflect on the differences between their own organizational culture and the organizational cultures which their team members may be used to.

Many writers such as French and Bell (1979) have described organizational culture as an iceberg. Others also use the iceberg to describe national or ethnic culture. Ruhly (1976) and Weaver and Uncapher (1981) appear to be among the first. Schein (1985) breaks culture down into three parts:

1 Above the surface: features of the culture that you can see.
   What do you notice first about the company's culture? What do you see when you first enter the building? What processes are in place?

2 Just below the surface: official norms and codes of conduct.
   What does the company communicate about its culture? What are its stated values? How does it expect its people to behave? What is its strategy, its philosophy? What are its goals?

3 Deep below the surface: hidden assumptions and truths.
   What have you discovered about the culture after you have worked there for some time? What are the unspoken beliefs?

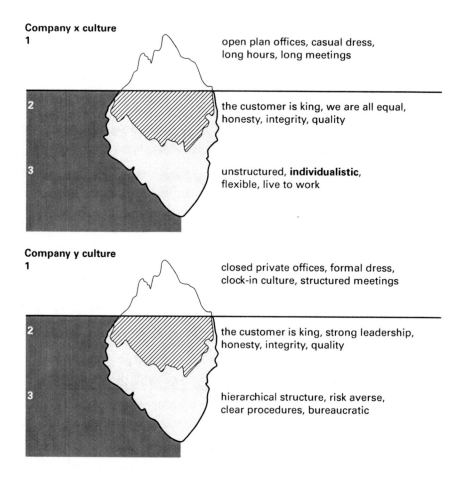

Company x culture

1 — open plan offices, casual dress, long hours, long meetings

2 — the customer is king, we are all equal, honesty, integrity, quality

3 — unstructured, **individualistic**, flexible, live to work

Company y culture

1 — closed private offices, formal dress, clock-in culture, structured meetings

2 — the customer is king, strong leadership, honesty, integrity, quality

3 — hierarchical structure, risk averse, clear procedures, bureaucratic

Understanding your own cultures

As we have seen, in today's world, managers increasingly work in and manage diverse groups. This diversity is created by culture – of various kinds. This variety of cultures may be complex to handle, but when managers use its potential in the right way, it is also a source of creativity and improved performance.

Culture influences the behaviour of groups of people – a group of Brazilians, a group of accountants, or a group belonging to the same extended family. A culture gives group members guidance as to how to think and feel, how to act, and how to evaluate the actions of others; it is an orientation system for behaviour in the group, a guide to handling the complexity of human interaction. A culture also gives to its members a feeling of belonging and identity. It is the glue that holds the group together.

International managers firstly need to understand the various cultures of which they themselves are members and how these cultures influence their behaviour before they can fully understand the cultural influences on their international colleagues, suppliers and clients.

Looking in the mirror

Here are some international managers talking about their perceptions of their own national cultures. Do you see these cultures in the same way?

In France you try to enrich the meeting with imagination, new ideas and in America people are very direct, critical but never against the person, against the fact or the project. In France when you criticize a project, people think you also criticize the person.

Frédéric Thoral (France), Areva, France

In Sweden we have a 'cup of coffee' culture, which means if we have something to talk about in management we put people around the conference table with a cup of coffee. Then we talk about it.

Eric Hallberg (Sweden), TeliaSonera, Sweden

In the USA, there'd be more of a validation, 'You did a good job', patting on the back a little bit. Timothy Taylor (United States), Henkel, Germany

In Italy... a good feeling, good relationships are necessary for good results. Camillo Mazzola (Italy), Henkel, Italy

People think the important thing is to have the client and take the problems later on. I was in Pakistan two weeks ago and everywhere in any kind of business they deal like this. They say 'Yes we can do it'. They never say no. Sherri Warsi (Pakistan), Integrico AB, Sweden

When you have understood your own cultures and how they work, then you are ready to look at the cultures of the people you encounter as international managers.

Profiling your own cultures

Emotional intelligence mainly concerns using insights you have about yourself to give you insights into other people. In a similar way, cultural intelligence, as we use the term, is the ability to use insights you have about the cultures to which you belong to give you insights into the cultures of those people you interact with.

One of the key competencies of mindful international managers is awareness and understanding of their own cultural icebergs. This understanding acts as a bridge to understanding others.

Before you profile your own cultures, you need to understand the various cultures which you may belong to and which impact on your behaviour.

Religious culture

Shared and espoused beliefs about what is right and wrong, good and bad, as well as norms of behaviour are part of every culture. But they are perhaps especially important for people having and practising a certain religious faith. An outsider visiting a place where a certain religion is practised may notice that rest days are different or that people eat or do not eat particular food.

Socio-economic culture

Some shared attitudes and lifestyles may go hand in hand with income, social background and other demographic features. Outsiders may notice that behaviour, for example consumer behaviour, is very different in one social class compared with another. Generational groups (eg the young, the middle-aged, the elderly) may also be seen to favour different brands and technical gadgets.

Sectoral culture

Shared experience of working in a certain sector – whether in the private or public sector or in different parts of the economy such as food, pharmaceuticals or banking – may form the basis for membership of a culture. From the outside you may notice shared dress codes, and the use of shared jargon.

Functional culture

Shared experience of working in a certain function – for example, accountancy, marketing or human resources – as well as shared education and training may lead to membership of a functional culture. The onlooker may notice different attitudes to work and different priorities.

National and ethnic culture

Values, norms and practices shared by members of the same ethnic group or by citizens of the same nation-state make up one of the most familiar types of culture. In many cases, regional, tribal and linguistic sub-groups may also have separate cultural identities within a national culture.

Organizational culture

Another frequently understood type of culture is that formed by the values, norms and practices shared by people working for the same organization. The observer may see that processes – for example, the way meetings are organized or clients are handled – and communication styles are different.

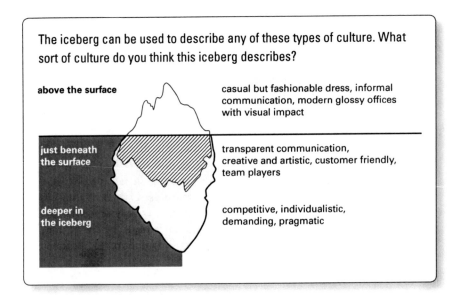

The iceberg can be used to describe any of these types of culture. What sort of culture do you think this iceberg describes?

above the surface — casual but fashionable dress, informal communication, modern glossy offices with visual impact

just beneath the surface — transparent communication, creative and artistic, customer friendly, team players

deeper in the iceberg — competitive, individualistic, demanding, pragmatic

It is obvious that a person belongs to more than just one culture at a time. This can sometimes lead to conflicting preferences, for example when religious culture might suggest one behaviour and socio-economic culture another. But generally multiple membership of different groups is something most people handle as a matter of course and indeed can have advantages for international managers.

Which cultural groups do you feel you belong to?

Write down:

(in the first column) the different cultural groups to which you belong;

(in the second column) some of the values; and

(in the third column) some of the behaviours of the different cultures of which you are a member.

Cultural groups	Values: beliefs and principles my culture (and I) think are important	Norms: behaviours and practices my culture (and I) prefer
My national/ethnic culture, eg, German	eg, honesty 1. _____ 2. _____ 3. _____	eg, direct and explicit communication 1. _____ 2. _____ 3. _____
My organizational culture	eg, high quality 1. _____ 2. _____ 3. _____	eg, continuous improvement process 1. _____ 2. _____ 3. _____
My functional culture, eg, advertising	eg, imagination, creativity 1. _____ 2. _____ 3. _____	eg, tolerance for expression of unconventional ideas 1. _____ 2. _____ 3. _____

Belonging to other cultures

Many people would say they are a member of more than the three cultures you have just been asked to think about.

Consider those other types of culture described on the previous pages and profile another culture which you feel you belong to – religious, socio-economic, sectoral.

	Values: beliefs and principles	Norms: behaviours and practices
My..................culture:	1._____ 2._____ 3._____	1._____ 2._____ 3._____

Best practice: Focused on goals, flexible on approaches

Effective international managers need first of all to be competent in their own environment. They need both the 'hard skills' of management (for example, organization, financial reporting or strategic planning) and the 'soft skills' (for example, the ability to encourage and motivate their team, to focus on goals and to influence senior management). They need to reflect on their own behaviour and performance in these areas.

Key competence: Personal autonomy through focus on goals

Effective international managers are goal-focused and motivated by their objectives. This is especially important because their complex working environment may distract their attention from the objectives. In spite of these difficulties they keep trying to achieve their goals. International managers may have to be more willing to adapt the approaches and methods with which they achieve their goals to local conditions.

Once they start working internationally, managers do not need to throw away all the good practice that has worked for them in their home culture. But the mindful international manager will focus not only on the *outcome* of his or her work but very strongly also on the *process* and the *context*.

You need to reflect first on your own cultural mindset and how this influences you at work. The next chapter will look at some key areas – for example, the ways different cultures see power, time and communication. These underlying attitudes have a big impact on how you behave at work.

Then you need to reflect on how your international partners behave. Mindful international managers need in particular to observe how local managers work and to understand their cultural mindset.

> Look, you need to be what you are. I am Erik and I'm Swedish and I have my own character. But at the same time when I'm setting goals I have to understand what is going on inside the company and the country and I try to find a melody, or tune into what works for this organization and the specific leaders.
>
> *Erik Hallberg (Sweden), TeliaSonera, Sweden*

You need to understand these differences and then perhaps adapt your good practice to the local situation, as in the saying 'When in Rome do as the Romans do'. How far and in what areas you adapt will depend on the situation you are in. You need to consider how far down the road to Rome you go! For example, if you are an expatriate working in a subsidiary or joint venture abroad, you might need to adapt more and in different situations than a frequent business traveller or somebody working at home alongside foreign colleagues.

> In Sweden, people can discuss openly and interactively around the table but in the Baltic States you can't do that. So you have to ask managers questions before big meetings, to get the manager on your side to share the goal.
>
> *Erik Hallberg (Sweden), TeliaSonera, Sweden*

Erik realizes that establishing common goals is key wherever you are. However, you need to be flexible and to adapt your approach to the culture or cultures and to the situation you are dealing with. To do this you need to take account of cultural differences. The mindful international manager is focused not only on the result but also the context and process of communication and cooperation.

Key competence: Flexible behaviour

Effective international managers display not only goal-focus but also flexibility in their behaviour. Being flexible enough to adapt to an appropriate extent is absolutely key to managing the complexity of new cultural contexts. As they are able to behave flexibly, they fit in more easily and people around them feel more comfortable.

International managers are constantly confronted with the relationship of tension which exists between *focussing on the goals* set for them, and the goals they set for others, on the one hand and, on the other, *behaving flexibly* – adapting to local conditions and practices and the expectations of colleagues and clients from different cultures. To get the emphasis right is a difficult balancing act and a key challenge for international managers. Mindfulness of the context and the process helps them to meet this challenge successfully.

CASE STUDY 1   Nora Lundquist

Read the case and then consider the questions below.

The individual

Nora is a 45-year-old economist who has been employed for fifteen years by an international bank in Oslo but who is currently on sabbatical working for BETAID. BETAID is a Norwegian NGO which offers support to development organizations working in the field mainly in the developing world. She has been working in an educational project based in Afghanistan. The aim of the project is to help girls in secondary education. In the bank, Nora leads a small team of well-respected Norwegian economists – three women and one man. She is a serious person who strongly believes that Norway and Norwegians are in a strong position to support development projects – both financially and professionally. She is an introvert but a skilled communicator and a thoughtful leader.

The team

The project team consists of eight educational advisers working most of the time in Afghanistan and four consultants, including Nora. The field team is very diverse in terms of nationality – three local Afghanis, four Europeans and one American. Two of the consultants are from Norway and two from Germany. The project leader is a British educational adviser called Sam Richards. Sam has worked for many years in development projects and has considerable experience in Afghanistan. The whole team meets every quarter but has more regular telcos. Sam is the main point of contact.

The situation

Nora is finding the project a big disappointment. She had hoped to be really involved but finds that she is very much on the margins of the project. In her view, her financial advice is vital for the success of the project but she feels she is not listened to. She finds the meetings very argumentative and rather dominated by the male advisers (two Afghanis and one American). She understands that they want to talk about their experience in the field but she finds the communication to be very anecdotal and not structured at all. She has tried mentioning her dissatisfaction to Sam but he seems to be very absorbed by other issues. She is used to working in a very organized and structured environment where decisions are carefully considered and advice listened to. She finds herself working in what she feels to be a very macho and disorganized project where her values and knowledge do not seem to be respected.

Reflections

'I don't think I can stand this much longer. I had such high hopes for this year and now I feel I am wasting it. Maybe I am too passive but it's not in my character or culture to push people around.' (Nora speaking a few days ago)

'Nora is a very nice woman but she is not suitable for this type of work. You have to be very flexible and put up with all kinds of conflicts. She needs to assert herself in meetings to make sure the others hear what she has to say. I do my best but there are some very strong characters in this project.' (Sam)

Questions to consider

1 What do you think Nora could have done at the start of the project to better integrate herself? Can she do anything now to improve her situation and increase her satisfaction?

2 What do you think Sam should have done at the start of the project to make sure all the team were integrated and performing at their best? Can he do anything now to improve communication in the team?

Suggested answers can be found at the back of the book.

02 **Cultures**

This chapter focuses on:

- The common ways in which all types of culture tend to vary in their values and behaviours.
- How values and behaviours may vary in a person depending on which culture is dominant in a particular activity.
- How individuals may have values and preferences which are different from the cultures of which they are a member.
- How we need to observe and reflect on our own cultures before comparing or commenting on other cultures.
- Why knowledge about other cultures is a key competence for the mindful international manager.

Competing values?

In order to understand better the behaviours and practices you experience when you work across cultures, it is necessary to explore the much larger part of the cultural iceberg below the waterline. Here lie the values, beliefs and attitudes which underpin behaviour.

Some values are more or less universal, for example, the value of giving importance to the family and to the need to protect it. Other shared values are newer, for example, the growing awareness in many parts of the world of the need to protect the planet from climate change and environmental damage. But most of our values have been formed from generations of experience within particular cultural groups.

These values guide the behaviour of members of the group. They help them to deal with the problems and opportunities that the group faces. These problems and opportunities may be similar for all cultural groups but different groups call on different values, attitudes and behaviours to handle them.

Many cultures share some values, but the relative importance they give to these values may vary a great deal. For example, members of many cultures believe in the importance of honesty and the search for truth but members of one culture may tend to be honest about different things and with different people in comparison with members of other cultures. And they may attach less importance to the valuing of honesty and truth and expressing them in behaviour when other values, for example, harmony, appear preferable: you don't say what you honestly think for the sake of keeping the peace!

Which options do you prefer in these situations?

1   You are rushing to an important meeting when you meet a colleague who you worked closely with up until five years ago. You have not seen her since then.

   Do you stop to talk to her or do you greet her but then rush to get to your meeting on time?

   Here the value you place on punctuality and the task in hand could be in conflict with the value you place on relationships.

2   You arrive at the meeting and find that a key participant is not there. He arrives late and has not prepared an update as you, the project leader, requested. He says he has been very busy talking to a potential new client and decided this was more important than the update.

   Do you feel he is unprofessional or flexible?

   Here the value you place on planning and being prepared, plus the respect that you expect for your leadership, may be in conflict with the value you place on flexibility and spontaneity.

3   Your boss keeps his distance from the team and communicates quite formally, saying it is a sign of respect for people he doesn't need to know personally. You think your boss is fair but not very approachable. You believe that communicating informally and reducing the distance between people help to create a more productive working atmosphere.

   Do you feel it would be better if your boss were more one of the team with a more informal style?

   Here the value you place on showing respect may conflict with the value you place on informal relationships at work.

I met the (German) boss of the market research agency and when we shook hands to say goodbye he actually bowed. And that seemed very strange and very formal.

Market research manager (UK), power generation, UK

Power and status in national and organizational cultures

In some societies, hierarchy does not play as important a role as in others. Countries such as Canada and Australia, which have thrown off their colonial past, tend to reject the need for social hierarchies and those with less power in society do not expect and accept that power is distributed unequally. There, *power distance*, as Hofstede (1980, 2001) calls it, tends to be relatively small.

Australians talk about the 'tall-poppy syndrome', a phrase used to explain most Australian's lack of respect for wealth and power. The idea behind this metaphor is that tall poppies should expect to be cut down.

In many countries in the past there was a traditional belief that a person's social rank was fixed at birth and was unlikely to change. This belief is less strong in some parts of the world and perhaps has less hold over young people and city-dwellers in some countries, although it still influences many cultures today. In more traditional societies, there is a belief that people should 'know their place' and not only make the best of it, but dignify their position by accepting their role. Hierarchical societies show greater deference and respect to power and authority.

Q: Is it another world again in China?

A: Yes, but as you know, French business culture is very hierarchical, which is reassuring for the Chinese.

Frédéric Thoral (France), Areva, France

Both Hofstede's classic study (1980, 2001: 107–108) and the more recent GLOBE Study (Carl *et al* 2004: 543), describe how organizational cultures may show the same range of attitudes. In a large, traditional, company with many layers of organization and centralized decision structures, managers may believe they should use the power that the company has given them. They may be regarded as autocrats or father-figures but prefer to see themselves as benevolent decision-makers. They may give orders without consulting their staff and rely on formal rules and larger numbers of supervisory staff to get things done. They may think that status symbols like large company cars and big offices are normal and desirable. There are often large differences between salaries paid at the top and at the bottom of the organization. Information is a source of power and its flow therefore restricted by hierarchy.

On the other hand, people in a young start-up company may feel that power differences should be small. They may think that everybody should have a say in making decisions and be encouraged to take initiatives and that the boss should be a democrat who relies on subordinates. As a result there is less need for supervisory staff. Information flows more openly.

How differences in power distance may express themselves in business and management

Larger power distance cultures	Smaller power distance cultures
Steeper hierarchy, more hierarchical layers	Flatter hierarchy, fewer hierarchical layers
Ideal bosses are benevolent autocrats	Ideal bosses are resourceful democrats
Subordinates expect to be instructed	Subordinates expect to be consulted
More supervisors	Fewer supervisors
Subordinates depend on bosses	Bosses and subordinates depend on each other
Privileges and status symbols for bosses are expected	Privileges and status symbols are disapproved of
Larger salary differentials	Narrower salary differentials
Centralized decision-making; power is concentrated	Decentralized decision-making; power is less concentrated
Information is localized	Information is shared

(Adapted from Hofstede, 2001: 107–108; Carl *et al* 2004: 536)

There are organizational and strategic reasons why large companies may develop many-layered hierarchies. It is a way of handling increasingly complex and diverse businesses. If the national culture in which the company is located is hierarchical as well, then a top-down leadership style may become the norm. On the other hand, a younger company may believe that its entrepreneurial spirit is part of its competitive advantage. So it may want to encourage a more participative management culture and a less deferential way of behaving.

Oh, it's much more hierarchical [in our company in Germany]. It's much more like in-groups – you see it in the cafeteria. There's really a separation between management and non-management. It's very strong, very strong and it's very different from the US. Ok, there is a separation in terms of practicality, but in terms of one-to-one interaction, we have an underlying equality feeling. It's different in character here when you see the tables in the cafeteria, one table for management and one for non-management.
Timothy Taylor (United States), Henkel, Germany

Hierarchy in organizational cultures

How far do you identify with these competing values?

What's the preference of your *organizational* culture?							
More hierarchy	3	2	1	0	1	2	3	less hierarchy
What's your *personal* preference here? Is it different from that of your *organizational* culture?							
More hierarchy	3	2	1	0	1	2	3	less hierarchy

Cultures, both national and organizational, may also differ in how they assign power and status. In the West, especially in business, we like to think that status and power are mainly awarded on the basis of what people *achieve* or have achieved – their knowledge and performance. According to Trompenaars and Hampden-Turner (1997: 105–106), *achievement-orientation* is to be found in the often more Protestant cultures, for example, of north and north-west Europe and the United States.

On the other hand, some cultures tend to *ascribe* power and status according to who a person is, for example, on the basis of age, gender, education or connections. Trompenaars and Hampden-Turner report that such *ascription-orientation* can be found especially in country cultures influenced by Catholicism, Buddhism and Confucianism.

How differences in ascription-orientation and achievement-orientation may express themselves in business and management

Ascription-orientation	Achievement-orientation
Mainly male managers	Male and female managers
Managers qualified by background	Managers qualified by performance
Respect for bosses is expected regardless of how much they know	Respect for bosses is conditional on how much they know and what they have achieved
Titles showing organizational status and influence are used	Titles showing task-related knowledge may be used
Decisions may be challenged by those with more power	Decisions may be challenged by those with more task-related knowledge

(Adapted from Trompenaars and Hampden-Turner, 1997: 118–119)

Managers beginning to work internationally will quickly note that managers all over the world tend more frequently to be male than female – although this tendency may be more marked in some parts of the world than in others.

The GLOBE Study (House *et al*, 2004) explains both these phenomena by demonstrating that *gender egalitarianism* varies across cultures. Gender egalitarianism reflects cultures' beliefs about whether biological sex should determine the roles people play in society in general and therefore in organizations as well. According to the GLOBE Study (Emrich *et al*, 2004: 365), gender egalitarianism in country cultures such as those of Scandinavia and the former Soviet-influenced countries of eastern Europe are likely to have more female managers than those where gender egalitarianism is low, such as South Korea and Arabic countries.

How differences in gender egalitarianism may express themselves in business and management

More gender egalitarianism	Less gender egalitarianism
More women in leadership and management positions	Fewer women in leadership and management positions
Women have higher status in society	Women have lower status in society
More women working	Fewer women working
Men and women have similar educational levels	Women have lower educational levels than men

(Adapted from Emrich *et al*, 2004: 359)

It is interesting and important to note here that the study discovers differences between the scores individual countries achieve for what people believe *should be* the case with respect to gender egalitarianism and what is actually believed to *be practised*. For example, Germany and the United States both score much higher on beliefs about what *should be* the case concerning gender egalitarianism than on beliefs about *actual practice*. This difference is reflected in the current discussion (in large parts of Europe at least) about the urgent need for more female managers and leaders in business and organizations. This discussion has been triggered not only for moral reasons to correct obvious gender discrimination. It has also arisen for practical reasons as organizations see the need to exploit untapped potential and to take action to counter the shortage of management talent that organizations fear will occur in the near future.

Time in national and organizational cultures

Hall (1959, 1966, 1976) was the first to recognize that cultures tend to *view* time differently and therefore *use* time differently.

In more *time-oriented* cultures (or *monochronic* cultures, as Hall called them), for example, in northern Europe and North America, people tend to use time to do only one thing at a time and to get that thing done. They may feel that time is finite and must not be wasted and so they try not to be distracted by other people and tasks. Like money, it seems, time should be spent wisely and can also be saved and wasted. Both work and play must be scheduled, and individuals must plan and prioritize. Time is so valuable in time-oriented cultures that people even attend time-management courses in order to maximize their use of this most precious commodity.

How differences in attitudes to time may express themselves in business and management	
In more time-oriented (monochronic) cultures, people tend to ...	In less time-oriented (polychronic) cultures, people tend to ...
... do one thing at a time	... do many things at the same time
... deal with the task in hand and reject distraction	... accept being distracted and so may tend to deal with tasks as they come up
... attach more value to punctuality	... attach less value to punctuality
... adhere more strictly to schedules	... adhere less strictly to schedules
... be more task-oriented	... be more relationship-oriented

In the Middle East, parts of Asia, Latin America and to some extent in southern Europe, time tends not to rule your life in the same way. To use Hall's term, people can be said to be more *polychronic*. Many things can be done at the same time. People are not so concerned about the precise starting and stopping time of a certain activity. Neither work nor play should be dictated by what is written in your engagement diary. In these cultures, planning and scheduling are less important since you cannot be sure what is going to happen next. You need to be flexible. You also need to respond to people and be available if they want some of your time and so distractions from the task in hand may be willingly accepted.

In business we can see this difference in attitudes towards time clearly in meetings.

How meetings may differ across cultures		
	In more time-oriented cultures	**In less time-oriented cultures**
Meetings tend:		
to start and finish ...	on time	later than announced
to be ...	more structured	less structured
to have ...	a clear agenda that is followed	no agenda or an agenda that may not be followed
to be for ...	making decisions, agreeing actions, moving things on	other purposes as well, such as displaying the leadership competence of those in authority or cultivating relationships
Participants tend:		
to be expected ...	to make controlled contributions that are not too long and are to the point	to be tolerant of contributions that are off the point, or of people doing other things such as looking at their laptops or smart phones
to be expected ...	not to talk at the same time as others	to be tolerant of people talking at the same time or talking on a mobile phone

I think it's partly a cultural thing to do with an attitude towards time. You plan and agree to meet at a certain date and time to organize work for a project, you write it down, and then the person will SMS you hours before the meeting and say 'I can't come but I'll be there tomorrow' when you're not available.

Brian Cracknell (UK), Language Works, Malaysia

Time-orientation in national cultures

How far do you identify with these competing values?

What's the preference of your *national or ethnic* culture?							
More time-oriented	3	2	1	0	1	2	3	Less time-oriented
What's your *personal* preference here? Is it different from that of your national or ethnic culture?							
More time-oriented	3	2	1	0	1	2	3	Less time-oriented

Communication style in national and organizational cultures

Hall (1976) was again the first to investigate the fact that in some cultures, for example the Netherlands or Israel, people tend to place a high value on speaking directly. They feel it is important to be explicit and get to the point; they may not worry too much if they offend people on the way. They may see being direct and explicit as a sign of honesty and an interest in the truth and may regard this as more important than harmonious relationships. They think that conflict will help to clear the air and allow people to move forward. They consider that the important thing in conversation is to emphasize facts in order to create clarity.

> English people like to go around the house, whereas Germans go through the front door... you can just be quite direct and coherent, not beat around the bush.
> *Communications manager (UK), power supply, UK*

In these cultures people pay less attention to implicit messages and to information contained in the context – for example, they tend not to interpret the way their interlocutors are dressed, or their body language, or think about the importance of whom they are related to. For this reason, Hall gave the name *low-context communication* to this communication style. When listening, low-context communicators pay attention to what is actually said explicitly and not to what the speaker may imply or what the listener could infer from the context. They believe that people generally say what they mean and mean what they say.

How differences in communication style may express themselves in business and management	
In low-context communication cultures, people tend to ...	**In high-context communication cultures people tend to ...**
... communicate more directly, explicitly and in detail	... communicate more indirectly, implicitly and vaguely
... say what they mean and mean what they say	... imply what they mean and mean what they imply
... pay attention to the content of the spoken message	... pay attention to the intention of the spoken message
... aim to understand the spoken message	... aim to give meaning to the spoken message by using the whole context of the message
... contrast facts and opinions in the search for truth	... integrate facts and opinions in the search for harmony

In other cultures, for example in Thailand or Saudi Arabia, people tend to place a high value on maintaining harmonious relationships with the people they communicate with, especially in public. They feel it is important to be polite, and that this can be achieved by communicating indirectly and implicitly. They tend to be careful not to make people lose face and indeed may want to give people face. Conflict should be avoided or at least not confronted openly.

Here, business success is built more on relationships than actually what people say or promise. What is important when talking is to create common ground, to give face and to integrate everyone into a harmonious conversation. In these cultures people tend to read the air or sense the atmosphere, as the Japanese put it: 空気を読め. They may pay a lot of attention to the messages implied in the context – the way you dress, the way you sit, your connections and background. For this reason, this type of communication is known as *high-context communication*.

> If I don't actively say I'm okay, other people should be able to understand I'm not okay.
> *Manager (China), car manufacturer, China*

They use their shared knowledge and experience to understand implied messages. The word 'no' will often be avoided. 'Yes' could mean 'I agree', 'I understand', 'I'm not sure', 'I don't know', 'I don't have the authority' or simply 'I want to be polite to you'.

I think for French leaders, things are implicit; we have to read between lines. For Danes and Americans things have to be explicit. And very often I am fed up about the questions because I think they do not understand me. They say to me: 'But Frédéric, tell us what you want exactly.'

Frédéric Thoral (France), Areva, France

Low-context communicators tend to *contrast* facts and opinions in the search for truth whereas high-context communicators tend to *integrate* facts and opinions in the search for harmony.

Communication style in national cultures

How far do you identify with these competing values?

What's the preference of your *national or ethnic* culture?							
More direct, explicit, truth-oriented	3 2 1 0 1 2 3						More indirect, implicit, harmony-oriented
What's your *personal* preference here? Is it different from that of your national or ethnic culture?							
More direct, explicit, honesty-oriented	3 2 1 0 1 2 3						More indirect, implicit, harmony-oriented

---

However, differences between cultures are relative. For Frédéric, French managers are less direct than their Danish and US colleagues. If he were working in Thailand, he would probably find most French managers more direct than most Thai managers.

In Europe, the British are often seen as polite and friendly, and less direct. As a result, it may be difficult for non-Brits (and sometimes even Brits themselves) to know where they stand. This is also because, in international business, the British are generally able to use their native language. Native speakers of English can often be more subtle in their use of language than non-natives, much to the confusion and irritation of non-native speakers. Non-native speakers of English working together use the common language of English perhaps as a fairly rudimentary tool of communication. Neither they nor native speakers of English should take offence if someone uses the language simply and thus very directly. Equally, it is often necessary for native-speakers of British English to express themselves less subtly and indirectly to be sure that they get their message across to non-native speakers of English who may be struggling with the language.

Individualism and group-orientation in national and organizational cultures

Members of different cultures differ in how they see themselves in relation to the other members of the group or groups they belong to. Markus and Kitayama (1991, 1994) found that in some cultures, people see themselves as essentially *independent individuals*. In other cultures, people see themselves more as *interdependent members of a group* with strong obligations to the group and its members.

Hofstede (1980, 2001) and Gelfand *et al* (2004) are among those who have brought the difference between *individualist* and *group-orientated* cultures to the attention of international management. In more group-oriented cultures, such as in Japan or Malaysia, there may be more pressure to conform with group norms and to retain harmony. If your colleagues stay late at work, you tend to stay late at work. If your colleagues never disagree with their boss, you may tend never to disagree with your boss.

In more individualistic cultures, such as in the United States or the United Kingdom, it may be easier for you to behave in ways that are different from the ways your colleagues behave. However, it is important to distinguish once again between national or ethnic cultures, organizational cultures and other types of culture. The United States may be a highly individualistic society but there are many US companies that expect their employees to follow the company line and procedures very rigidly.

How differences in individualism may express themselves in business and management	
In more individualist cultures	**In more group-orientated cultures**
... individuals are autonomous and independent of groups	... individuals are interdependent group-members
... individual goals are more important	... group goals are more important
... management is management of individuals	... management is management of groups
... individuals are rewarded	... groups are rewarded
... individual appraisal and feedback improve performance	... individual appraisal and feedback are a threat to harmony
... there is a belief in individual decisions	... there is a belief in group decisions
... communication tends to be low-context	... communication style tends to be high-context

(Adapted from Hofstede, 2001: 244–245; Gelfand *et al*, 2004: 45)

In individualistic national cultures, individuals are expected to look after themselves and their immediate family. In a working context, individualism means that the focus is on the management and performance of *individuals* – on rewarding and promoting the most successful member(s) of a team, for example.

> It's not teamwork in the concept of the orchestra's music being greater than the individual musicians. Here, there's a lot of ownership, a lot of boundary drawing, defining your piece and taking care of it.
>
> *Timothy Taylor (USA), Henkel, Germany*

In group-oriented cultures, members of the group and of the extended family are expected to look after each other. Networks play a fundamental role both at work and outside. At work, the focus is on the management and performance of the *whole group or team*, rewarding and celebrating group success and not picking individuals out. At home, support networks are large, consisting of extended families across generations; and networks of long-standing, close friends and colleagues. Friends of friends or acquaintances of acquaintances may also be expected to offer support.

> It's a huge room, there are lots of people there, you have no idea what they are paid for, maybe they are close friends. There are very strong networks and you really can't understand. It's a strange and hidden network.
>
> *Thomas Ruckdäschel (Germany), T-Systems, Germany, about working in Jordan*

Cultures do not share the same attitudes towards what is personal and private and what is public and shared. Some cultures, for example in Asia or many African countries, do not expect to protect their private lives as is done in some parts of the Western world. The perfect holiday beach for an individualistic northern European may be in quite an isolated place. For other cultures, the beach is for the extended family and friends, and the more the merrier!

If you are working in Japan, you may be expected to cultivate your relations with the group by socializing with your colleagues after work. As a result, you may see little of your family in the week. Your loyalty to your colleagues and the company you work for is expected to be stronger than your loyalty to the family – at least during the week.

> In German business there is no social element at all. Business in Germany is just business. It's not fun at all. It's completely different in the Arab world.
>
> *Thomas Ruckdäschel (Germany), T-Systems, Germany*

In some national cultures, for example in Norway, work-life balance may be very highly valued. A common belief is that people should not let their work dominate their life, especially to the detriment of their family life.

In some countries, people may separate different areas of their lives clearly. Working life and private life, for example, may remain unconnected compartments. 'Work is work, and schnapps is schnapps' is a well-known saying in Germany underlining the separation of work and social life. In other countries, such as China, work and social life continually overlap.

People never seem to draw the line clearly in anything of anything. It's quite blurred.

Li Chen (China)

Individualism and group-orientation in national cultures

How far do you identify with these competing values?

What's the preference of your *national or ethnic* culture?							
More independent individuals	3	2	1	0	1	2	3 More interdependent group-members

What's your *personal* preference here? Is it different from that of your national or ethnic culture?

More independent individuals	3	2	1	0	1	2	3 More interdependent group-members

---

Performance orientation in national and organization cultures

Another dimension of cultural difference, identified in the GLOBE Study of international leadership (see Javidan *et al*, 2004), is the extent to which a culture encourages and rewards group members for performance improvement and excellence.

While we may recognize large differences in national cultures in this dimension, we can certainly observe that most organizations both in the private and public sectors increasingly strive to embed this value in their culture.

In the United Kingdom, one of the so-called Anglo cultures that score high on performance orientation, the government increasingly seeks to commission private organizations to contribute to the work of the public sector. For example, organizations that believe they can reduce the current high rate at which prisoners released on licence from jail commit crimes again are rewarded for their success. This sort of 'payment by results' is an indication of performance orientation and is becoming more common in areas once the sole responsibility of the public sector. Anglo cultures also encourage competition in school education, ranking schools in terms of their exam results and grading the schools as succeeding or failing.

How differences in performance orientation may express themselves in business and management	
People in higher performance orientation cultures tend to ...	**People in lower performance orientation cultures tend to ...**
... reward performance	... attach importance to quality of life
... value what you do	... value who you are
... attach importance to assertiveness, competitiveness and materialism	... attach importance to seniority and experience
... give emphasis to results rather than people	... give emphasis to loyalty and belonging
... regard feedback as necessary to improve	... see feedback as judgemental and unpleasant
... value a direct and explicit communication style	... value an indirect and implicit communication style
... have a high sense of urgency	... have a low sense of urgency
... attach importance to training and development	... attach importance to societal and family relationships

(Adapted from Javidan, 2004: 245)

Performance orientation is very well-established in many private sector companies, especially those influenced by Anglo practices. Many organizational cultures have put performance reviews or appraisals in place to underpin their performance orientation. These appraisals are usually conducted with the help of a tool to assess and encourage individual performance.

However, there are significant differences as to how much emphasis is put on individual or group/team performance. One simple way to judge this is to look at how incentives are managed – are bonuses related mainly to individual or group performance? Given their individualist values, Western companies are often less skilled in assessing team performance. We can also see evidence of performance orientation in how feedback (see Chapter 9) is delivered. Performance-oriented cultures encourage more direct and critical feedback while also celebrating success – both individual and group – quite loudly.

Performance orientation in organizational and national cultures

How far do you identify with these competing values?

What's the preference of your *organizational* culture?							
More performance-oriented	3	2	1	0	1	2	3	Less performance-oriented
What's the preference of your *national or ethnic culture* here? Is it different from that of your *organizational* culture?							
More performance-oriented	3	2	1	0	1	2	3	Less performance-oriented

Taking the outsider's perspective on your own culture

Cultural intelligence is founded on the ability to observe, talk about and understand one's own culture(s). Only when we are able to do this are we ready to understand and compare other cultures. One way to achieve an understanding of our own culture is to attempt to take the perspective of members of other cultures and to try to identify features of everyday life in our culture that these visitors from other cultures may find challenging or difficult to accept.

How others may see your culture

What could be challenging if members of other cultures came to live and work in your culture? Here are some suggestions. You may be able to explain some of the potential difficulties by considering the differences in values described in the earlier part of this chapter.

Structural

Geography   _____

Climate   _____

Attitudes to government   _____

Attitudes to authority   _____

Attitudes to centralization   _____

Regional differences   _____

History   _____

Religion   _____

Work

Company organization   _____

The importance of hierarchy   _____

Respect for leadership   _____

Delegation   _____

Planning   _____

Cooperation v competition   _____

Team v individual   _____

The working day   _____

Organization and running of meetings   _____

Company communication:

   – written/spoken   _____

   – tone/style   _____

Mobility of personnel   _____

Social

Importance of family   _____

Roles of the sexes   _____

Priorities of personal life and work   _____

Dress   _____

Punctuality   _____

Ways of addressing others   _____

Openness of conversation   _____

Formality   _____

Taboos   _____

Humour   _____

Physical

Space between people   _____

Contact   _____

Handshaking   _____

Gestures   _____

Exposure of body   _____

Facial expressions   _____

Speech: volume, speed   _____

Smells   _____

These everyday behaviours are driven by the values – such as those relating to power, time, communication, individualism, performance – deep in our icebergs. Here are some examples of how some of these behaviours may vary across cultures:

At work

The working day is a significant feature of our culture. Long days with long lunch breaks or shorter days with no lunch break are examples of how the working day may differ across cultures. As is often the case, behaviour at work may be driven by the behaviour of bosses. If you have a boss who stays late and you are in a hierarchical culture, you may feel you have to stay late too. However, it may also be that your organizational culture is very task-oriented with little time given to relationships and so allows you to finish work more quickly without chatting to your colleagues. This sort of culturally influenced practice can be observed in offices where most people have their lunch of sandwiches at their computer.

Connected to the issue of the working day is holiday time. There are enormous variations across the world in the number of days given and taken for holidays. A Japanese businessman told us he took 104 days' holiday a year; at first we were amazed until we realized he was talking about his weekends and this was all he had in the way of holiday.

The developed world has passed laws to regulate working conditions so the law, in theory, controls working hours, breaks and holiday time. However, we soon see the gap between national and local attitudes when we look at specific work-places and find some which follow the letter of the law while others pay little attention to legal requirements.

Away from work

Outside the work-setting there are numerous examples that demonstrate differences in cultural practices – how members of cultures behave 'above the waterline of the iceberg'. Driving habits give us a sudden and sometimes dramatic insight into culture. The challenge for drivers who come from highly regulated cultures finding themselves on the roads in a country like India cannot be overstated.

Socializing after work also gives us an insight into how the culture works. Some people like to keep their working lives very separate from their personal lives and rarely meet with colleagues outside work, while for others, the after-work drink or meal is a vital part of their lives and relationships with colleagues. How much we compartmentalize our lives is at the heart of this issue. We may live in a culture where we believe we can control time and events to suit our individual needs; on the other hand, it is possible that we believe we do not have control and we need to go along with events as they happen.

We can also observe very quickly attitudes towards gender. In so-called masculine cultures, there is much more separation according to gender – women and men lead much more separate lives at work and at home. In these societies, men and women have much clearer and tightly controlled roles in terms of what they do and how much power they have. In more feminine societies the boundaries are less clear – men can stay at home and look after the children and women may reach the top of companies or governments.

Profiling other cultures

Acquiring the kind of information presented in this chapter can mean that mindful managers better understand the differences they have to manage. Extending your knowledge of cultures is a key competence not least because it is easy to develop – through reading or talking to people who can act as cultural informants or taking part in intercultural development programmes.

Converting this knowledge into appropriate behaviour and supportive attitudes usually takes longer and may be more difficult. This is the subject of much of what follows in the rest of the book.

> **Key competence:**
> **Cultural knowledge through information gathering**
>
> Effective international managers are interested in finding out about cultures they are unfamiliar with. They do it through reading and observing behaviour but also by asking third parties or asking members of the cultural group themselves. They also find out more about cultures they already know and about the specific context which is important for their needs.

Best practice: Building a common culture

All these cultural differences could confuse and stress the international manager. Maybe this is why the inexperienced manager often says: 'Aren't we all the same in the end? We're all human beings'. This desire to reduce the complexity in this simple way by denying that differences exist is understandable but will not lead to success.

As a mindful international manager you need first to embrace the diversity – in other words, be open and curious to find out and observe the differences.

> The one point is tolerance of other cultures, to appreciate the different styles.
>
> *Washington Munetsi (South Africa), Nestlé, South Africa*

Having done this, you – together with your international team – need to generate a new culture and get commitment to a set of guidelines or expected behaviours which form the glue that help people to work together. These guidelines work very much like the values and norms that guide behaviour in national and ethnic cultures and like the value statements and codes of conduct in organizational cultures.

> My experience is that in international teams, people often are more attentive, since it seems obvious that differences exist. In national teams, people often underestimate the need for clarification. So, in some senses, international teams may be easier to manage.
>
> *Thorsten Weber (Germany), HLP, Germany*

You need to clarify with your team members what values and attitudes they all share, if any, and which of them should form the common ground for the guidelines.

Steps towards building a common culture

Here are some of the questions you and your team members need to think about, bearing in mind that your answer may lie between the extremes described here. Your answer may also depend on the situation you are in.

Power

Do you believe authority and influence should be given only to the few? Do you thus attach importance to a strongly hierarchical organization in which people know where they are and who they report to?

Or, do you believe power and influence should be shared? Do you thus value a flat, networked organization where it is not or less important what hierarchical position people hold?

Individuals and groups

Do you value being an independent individual motivated to achieve? Are you not especially interested in strong relationships with many people?

Or, do you believe it more important to be a member of a larger group with its dependencies and obligations to many? For example, do you expect to mix with your colleagues socially as well as at work?

Time

Do you value time as a scarce resource to be used economically and with care? Do you therefore expect meetings to be well-prepared, punctual, and to follow an agenda and be action-oriented?

Or, do you attach more importance to using time for many purposes at the same time? Do you therefore expect meetings to be less structured and more discussion and relationship-oriented?

Honesty – harmony

Do you value honesty and the search for truth above all else? Do you therefore expect direct and open feedback, for example?

Or, do you attach great importance to harmonious relationships? Do you therefore prefer, for instance, to encourage face-to-face rather than email communication?

Performance orientation

Do you appreciate a results-driven culture where you and your colleagues are measured and paid according to results?

Or, do you attach more importance to other motivating factors at work such as respect and a sense of belonging?

The guidelines or expected behaviours generated for the new common culture will thus be influenced by the cultural values and preferences of the individual team members. In this way, the guidelines need to be *culture-sensitive*.

At the same time, they should be *culture-blind*: to achieve buy-in from all team members, they need to be generated by *all those in the team* rather than imposed by the team leader or a dominant cultural majority.

But the success of the guidelines will crucially depend on the degree of openness members of the new common culture have for something which for some may be very different from what they are accustomed to.

Key competence:
Openness through acceptance

Accepting behaviour and practices which are different from their own is a quality of effective international managers. They are not intolerant of different practices and do not feel threatened by them. On the contrary, they find difference interesting. They take things and people as they are.

03 Individuals

This chapter focuses on:

- How your actions can be influenced by the situation you are in, the people involved and their cultures.
- How cultural stereotypes can be both useful and harmful.
- How effective international managers need to take account of both culture and personality when working in international groups.
- How getting things done as a manager depends on building relationships with colleagues and staff.
- Applying the insights of this chapter to a case study.

Stereotypes

After you have met a Kazakh, Brazilian or German for the first time, it is all too easy to think that you now understand something about all Kazakhs, Brazilians or Germans and their cultures. But in fact, a person's behaviour and actions are not solely influenced by their culture but result from the interplay of three factors: culture, the person involved, and the situation they find themselves in.

The triangle of behavioural influences

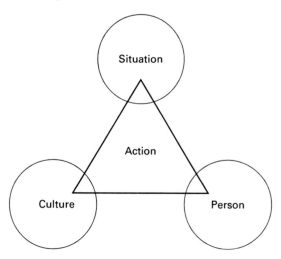

So when you meet a Slovak, Senegalese or Saudi for the first time, you do not necessarily learn something about the national or ethnic culture of this person. You may simply understand something about this individual and his or her personality.

It is in fact sometimes very difficult to distinguish between which features of a person's behaviour are related to their qualities and personality and which are related to their culture. You need to gain much more experience of the culture in question, for example by spending a lot of time watching people from that culture working or playing together. Then it may be possible to decide whether the behaviour and actions you see are mainly influenced by culture or by the individual. Even then, you have to be careful not to over-generalize and assume that all members of that culture are like those you have observed. What you see may be typical only of some of its members.

In building this picture of the other culture, we also have to be careful not to notice only those things that make it different from our own. We perceive an out-group in terms of what makes it different from our own in-group; we may overlook the similarities.

It is therefore very difficult to assess the impact of culture since we are the victims of the triangle of behavioural influences. However, when we watch groups of people from the same culture, we tend to see some patterns of behaviour that repeat themselves. This is where some stereotypes come from. Other stereotypes, generally the less reliable ones, come from factors like minimal knowledge and experience, hearsay, the mass media and out-of-date sources of information, such as schoolbooks and old films.

Stereotypes are fixed, general images that a lot of people believe represent a particular group of people. These images may be accurate in describing what the group is like in reality. Or they may be rudimentary, incomplete and inaccurate.

These inaccurate and less reliable stereotypes can be harmful in a number of ways. In particular, they may result in us seeing only the stereotype when we encounter somebody from a different culture. We may thus ignore the individual, who may in fact be different from the stereotype.

> You have to know stereotypes. For example, when I'm a German in a group, some people approach me in a certain way because they think I'm German and they expect me to act as a German. So I have to know the stereotypes, not so much to change my own behaviour, but to understand why the others behave in a certain way.
>
> *Thorsten Weber (Germany), HLP, Germany*

Some researchers believe that we use stereotypes, regardless of whether they are accurate or inaccurate, to help us to make sense of the world, especially when we have little information about the situation we are in and when we have little time. They reduce the complexity of perceiving, understanding and handling new or unknown situations. For this reason – and because we often unconsciously use stereotypes in dealing with new situations – it is important that our stereotypes are based on knowledge that is accurate and up-to-date.

When stereotypes are accurate in this way and also have other features, as Adler (2002) describes, the mindful manager can use them as a first best guess and a tool for managing cultural complexity. Other research makes clear why stereotypes can be harmful.

A stereotype ...	
can be *helpful* as a tool for managing complexity as long as ...	can be *harmful* because it may ...
you know that it is a stereotype	lead to the ignoring of individuality
it is accurate and based on sound, up-to-date and reliable knowledge	be based on very limited knowledge and experience, hearsay or the mass media
you can modify it on the basis of further knowledge and experience	influence the way we process information and what we remember
it does not evaluate the group but only describes it	fail to take account of new knowledge and experience that contradict the stereotype
you know it describes the group norm and not every member of the group	create expectations and self-fulfilling prophecies

Stereotypes are often only partly accurate because they don't describe all the members of a group. In the best of cases they may describe the norm for the group. A common stereotype could be that Dutch people communicate directly and that Thai people communicate more indirectly. But as you can see from the diagram, some Dutch people are less direct than some Thais, even if the majority of Dutch people are much more direct.

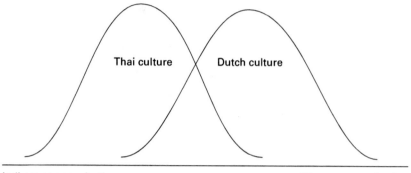

Using stereotypes can lead you to make quick judgements about people when you first meet them. When a Canadian meets a Japanese, the experience may confirm the stereotypes they already have. The Canadian may expect to find the Japanese formal, indirect and rather reserved. The Japanese may expect to find the Canadian informal, direct and outgoing.

If the Canadian and Japanese on one particular occasion do in fact behave in this way, the mindful international manager needs to be aware that their behaviour might be caused more by the situation than any cultural stereotype. For example, the Japanese is speaking English as a foreign language and this is making him seem very quiet and reserved. Or, it could relate more to personality – maybe fellow-Canadians would regard this Canadian as unusually outgoing.

Personality and behaviour – at work and at home

The sociable Canadian whom we met in the last section may not be so outgoing when he is at home. When we are at work, we often adapt to fit in with the cultural norms that we find there. When we are at home, we may show another side of ourselves.

The Johari window, which was originated by Luft and Ingham (1955), shows us how there can be a gap between what we show and know about ourselves and what our colleagues see and know about us.

The Johari window

- The *open* quadrant is where we spend most of the time at work, displaying sides of our personality openly to our colleagues.
- Our colleagues have much less insight into how we behave at home – we may keep this side of our life *hidden* or secret.
- The *blind* spot is where our colleagues see things about us that we do not see ourselves. This could be a weakness or a strength – some potential to perform that we do not recognize ourselves.
- Finally, the *unknown* quadrant is the area for lying on the couch and talking about our childhood to a psychiatrist!

Personality

Mindful international managers need to recognize that behaviour and interaction are not only influenced by culture – the most obvious difference from managing in their home culture – but also by an individual's personality. Personality and thus personal preferences have a considerable impact on performance because generally we do our best work when we are doing what we like. Understanding personal preferences is a good starting point for mindful international managers to get the best out of themselves and their people.

There are many psychometric tools which profile an individual's personality (eg Myers Briggs Type Indicator) or behaviour (eg Belbin's Team Role Inventory). One of them, the Team Management Profile®, which was developed by Margerison and McCann (1992, 1995, 1997), is based on four key dimensions at work:

- relationships (how we like to relate to other people);
- information (how we like to process and deal with information);
- decision making (how we come to our decisions);
- organization (how we organize ourselves and others).

In each case individuals can be placed on a scale:

extrovert   –   introvert
practical   –   creative
analytical   –   beliefs
structured   –   flexible

These results are then processed to give you a dominant team role located on the Team Management Wheel®.

The Team Management Wheel

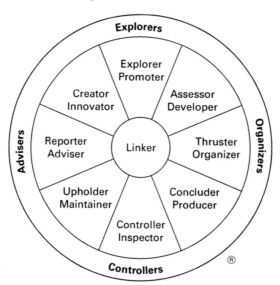

Once you have your profile it is firstly important to reflect on yourself and your preferences – to hold the mirror up to yourself. Preferences are not the same as competencies. For example, you could have an extrovert preference, which means you are quickly bored by details but you could be in a job where you have to deal with details. You can learn to do this better. You may not like it but it doesn't stop you from doing it. However, we perform best when we do a lot of what we like. We also have to remember that, when we are under stress, we tend to lose our awareness of the things that we are not so good at. So the profile helps us to understand our current preferences and indicate areas that we need to develop. It also draws attention to how we relate to people with different profiles.

You probably work with some people who have similar profiles to your own and some with very different ones. Working with people who are similar to you will initially be easy because you understand each other. However, it has limitations because you are not encouraged to think or work differently. On the other hand, working with people who are different from you can be difficult, especially at the start and when you are under pressure. They may seem too slow or too fast, too interested in detail or not enough. However, they have skills that come naturally to them and these can complement yours. To first recruit and then get the best out of a diverse team, you need to know yourself and your colleagues well. This understanding will help you to reflect on some natural tendencies:

- to recruit people like yourself;
- to judge people who are different as difficult;
- to value your qualities more highly than the qualities of your colleagues.

There is no national cultural bias evident in the profiles currently held on the TMS database. In other words, for example, the proportion of introverts in Japan is not greater than in the United States. Personality type is independent of culture. However, once you are working in a group, the culture of the organization and of the team may also have a significant influence on your behaviour.

Connecting the individual and culture

Another tool that can help the international manager to understand his or her current level of competence in leading and working internationally is The International Profiler. This tool was developed by Worldwork Ltd, London, an organization that supports consultants and trainers who are working in the field of intercultural development. Throughout the book we focus on the following qualities, which are a mix of personality traits, qualities and skills:

Openness

This quality is fundamental to working internationally. It means we are curious about other ideas, other ways of doing things and other people and do not feel threatened by them. Showing interest in another person and their culture is often the starting point for a good relationship.

Flexibility

When we work internationally, we cannot expect just to do it our way. We need to adapt, change ourselves and adopt other ways of working. This can be challenging. If we come from a very time-oriented culture, how will we respond when we find our scheduled meeting is not just a little late but has been moved to the next day? We also need to be flexible in our thinking and, in particular, to suspend our judgement about other people. In our own culture, we have often acquired knowledge, experience and perhaps even wisdom that allow us to come to quick and frequently reliable conclusions about new situations and people we encounter. This is not likely to be the case in encounters in cultures unfamiliar to us. Wait and see is a good maxim when crossing cultures.

Personal autonomy

> I do not want my house to be walled in on all sides and my windows to be stuffed.
> I want the cultures of all the lands to be blown about my house as freely as possible.
> But I refuse to be blown off my feet by any.
>
> *Mahatma Gandhi*

Gandhi recognized how openness and curiosity are fundamental but also understood that you need to keep your feet on the ground and keep sight of where you are trying to get to. A number of things make up personal autonomy: goal-focus, persistence and the belief that you can influence events but also a set of strong personal values, which give you strength in difficult circumstances.

Emotional strength

This quality is critical when you are exposed to a foreign or international environment with countless cultural differences to handle. The successful expatriate, in particular, will require a certain amount of resilience and the ability to cope with stress as well as a sense of adventure to be effective in these circumstances. You can become very stressed by being outside your comfort-zone and will inevitably suffer setbacks, embarrassment and failure as a result of not handling the unfamiliar culture appropriately. Do you have the emotional strength to bounce back or does it take a while for you to recover? Or, on the other hand, do you find the challenge of the unfamiliar exciting and stimulating?

Perceptiveness

Your ability to be aware of yourself and how you come across to members of other cultures – a kind of emotional intelligence – is a crucial individual competence of mindful international managers. This quality, combined with the ability to take in and interpret the non-verbal signals of others, can help to overcome the obstacles in the intercultural communication channel.

Listening orientation

Another key, communication-oriented skill is your ability to understand fully the person you are talking to. You do this by testing your understanding of what the person says, exploring the meaning of the perceived message and in dialogue co-constructing the intended message. This is more reliable than simply assuming you have understood – something that managers under pressure to push things ahead may tend to do. It means using the language of active listening.

The language of active listening

Showing you are listening
Right
Ok
I see

Testing your own understanding
If I am not mistaken, you are saying ...
What I have understood is ...
Correct me if I'm wrong but what you're saying is ...

Testing the understanding of your interlocutor
Did I get that across ok?
Shall I repeat that?

Summarizing
Let me go over that again
Just to recap, ...

Repairing misunderstanding
There seems to have been a misunderstanding.
I think we may be getting something wrong.

Transparency

To complement your listening, you also need to speak clearly and on a level that the other party can understand in order to make sure your message gets through. This is something that native speakers of English as the lingua franca of international business may tend to neglect. Speaking too quickly and unclearly, using complex words and idioms as well as failing to place your message in a clear context will reduce *transparency* and understanding. We go into this in greater detail in Chapter 7.

Cultural knowledge

In the last chapter we explored the importance of understanding your own culture and then building your knowledge and insights into other cultures.

Influencing

Another important competence, especially today in a flatter, more virtual world, is the ability to convince and persuade others to do what you want and gain their cooperation. The skills that make up this competence, which is in many ways also a leadership competence, may differ from the skills in your repertoire but may be absolutely essential when you are trying to influence members of cultures different from your own. We describe these competencies in Chapters 6 and 7.

Synergy

Finally, getting the most out of culturally diverse groups means encouraging and valuing the contributions from all members of the group rather than suppressing them in the search for a simple solution reached without controversy. Handling a variety of culturally influenced perspectives needs to be seen as a way of using the potential and creativity of cultural diversity.

Nobody can possess all these qualities to a high degree. According to our personality and our analysis of what is needed in a particular situation, we choose to emphasize some more than others. However, the 'pushers' who score highly on '*personal autonomy*' and '*transparency*' need to develop their pull qualities such as 'listening' and 'flexibility' and vice versa.

Personality and your international profile combined

Your particular personality characteristics and personal qualities combined with your particular profile of international competencies will shape how you handle a number of the key functions of a manager working across cultures: managing relationships, handling information, making decisions and organizing.

Managing relationships

Extroverts look for opportunities to meet new people. Work is a chance to network, to promote oneself and to stand out from the crowd. More *introverted* types get their energy from within themselves and are more self-motivated to achieve their tasks. They are more likely to build close relationships with a smaller number of people.

As a mindful international manager, whether you are an introvert or extrovert, you need to develop and use interpersonal openness and to focus on building relationships, not least because some cultures are more relationship-oriented than task-oriented. In these cultures, relationships are the key. People will do something for you (for example, deliver on time, sign a contract, make you their preferred supplier) because they like you, they feel loyalty towards you or they feel they can trust you. You cannot just rely on the quality of your products or services.

How far do you identify with these competing values?

What is the preference of your *national or ethnic* culture?							
More task-oriented	3	2	1	0	1	2	3	Less relationship-oriented

What is your *personal preference* here? Is it different from that of your *national or ethnic* culture?							
More task-oriented	3	2	1	0	1	2	3	Less relationship-oriented

Being open enough to build relationships with members of other cultures – maybe in contrast to your personal preferences – is another key competence of the effective international manager.

Key competence: Openness through welcoming strangers

Effective international managers tend to be open to new people and to building relationships with them. They find it interesting to get to know people who are different from themselves – people with different experiences and values from their own. They are proactive in establishing relationships with others and often have a wide network of contacts.

Handling information

Some people are very *practical* in the way they work. They like tasks to be clear and planned. They want to know exactly what they need to do and are prepared to repeat tasks to a high level of quality. On the other hand, those who are more *creative* tend to get bored quickly, may not be so interested in detail and complexity and are prepared to work when things are not clear, or even when they are ambiguous.

In an international work context, *transparency* (see Chapter 7) – for example clearly defining tasks and embedding them in a clear context – is very important because there is a much greater chance of misunderstanding as a result of language problems, differences in culture and geographical distance. However, effective international management often means not understanding everything at once. Managers need to be able to tolerate this kind of ambiguity and deal with the resulting complexity.

Making decisions

Analytical types pride themselves on their objectivity – their ability to analyse problems and situations and work out the best decision. More *belief-oriented* people make their decisions on a more subjective and personal basis. Beliefs and principles have a greater influence on their decisions. They may well possess a high degree of *personal autonomy*, especially in having a set of strongly held values to support them.

Analytical types will probably be more at home in cultures in which communication tends to be direct and explicit and in which people spell out the factors for decision-making. Clearer boundaries and written guidelines may well be in place. On the other hand, more *belief-oriented* people may feel more at ease in cultures in which communication tends to be indirect and implicit and in which people avoid confrontation and maintain harmony, if at all possible.

Organizing

If you are *structured* in your work preferences, then you are probably focused on finishing tasks, keeping to deadlines, and getting on with things. A more *flexible* orientation means that you are probably less of a planner, curious and open to change, and sometimes find it difficult to finish a task which has been set.

To be an effective international manager, you need to be curious and open to diversity. But you also need to push ahead often in the face of difficulties and distractions to achieve your objectives. Adapting to the pace at which different cultures work may be hard if you have very *structured* preferences. You may easily become impatient in cultures where decisions take longer. For more *flexible* types, there is perhaps a chance of 'when in Rome, do as the Romans do' or even 'going native' – being very open to another culture but losing sight of what you are meant to achieve.

Best practice: Get to know your colleagues

Effective international managers may need to invest more time in building relationships with the people they work with. They cannot always or mainly rely only on hierarchy and positional power to exert influence or on the compelling logic of the task to get things done.

> ## Key competence: Influencing through rapport
>
> One aspect of influencing that is important for effective international managers consists of the ability to express warmth and attentiveness when building relationships. They make the other person feel comfortable and at ease. They are able to build personal as well as professional connections with the people they work with. This helps them to empathize with their interlocutors and to understand their perspective better. With time, they are thus better able to enlist the cooperation and support of their colleagues in achieving their professional goals.

Investing time in relationships may also help you enjoy your job more.

> Social relationships are vital to reach a result. So if you have everything but not the relationships, you will not obtain results. You are not in the army where you have to do it, full stop. So bad relationships can compromise a good technical job. You have to have it.
>
> *Camillo Mazola (Italy), Henkel, Italy*

When you start an international project, the kick-off phase is vital. You need to allow time for the team members to get to know each other. Formal introductions are a starting point but informal socializing will be much more important in some cultures and for some individuals.

> I think we are more oriented to relationships with people, no? Sometimes you have a very big problem, you go to take a coffee, you take a dinner, and you talk about everything – family, sport, and things like that.
>
> *Alejandro Pena (Mexico), Henkel, Germany, talking about working in Mexico*

For people from cultures which are less relationship-oriented and more task-oriented, this phase of getting to know the team may seem a waste of time. However, if you get this step right and build on it, you will save a lot of time and misunderstandings later.

> The second (important thing) would be relationships. Show a caring attitude, be genuinely interested in finding out about people and what they do, learn the language, eat the food. It's very important to share food with people to show respect.
>
> *Brian Cracknell (UK), Language Works, Malaysia*

When you work in a domestic team, you can assume a common background and may quickly get to know and understand the personalities of the different people in the group. When you work internationally, you have to deal with the additional potential barriers of language and cultures. So you should not assume so much. If you do not restrict your assumptions, you may make some poor initial judgements of people because you cannot separate the effects of culture on behaviour from the effects of personality.

The only route to success is to invest more time in the people and be more mindful of their culturally based values and behaviours and of their individual personalities.

Best practice: The role of leadership

The behaviour of the leader of a team, a group or a company and its declared values are the most influential factors in shaping culture.

Mindful managers in international leadership roles firstly need to know themselves. When interacting with others, they need to be mindful of their own personality, their own cultures and their leadership styles. In particular, they need to consider the leadership style which will work best in an international context. We elaborate on this in Chapter 13.

> In Sweden, if we have something to talk about in management we put people around the conference table with a cup of coffee. Then we talk about it. It doesn't work like that over there [the Baltic States]. You have to find another way in line with the authoritative model which the management is using.
>
> *Erik Hallberg, (Sweden), TeliaSonera, Sweden*

In a new venture, the leadership style is reinforced or rejected by success or failure. If the business or project is successful, people may assume that the leadership style was appropriate. However, it may not be the right leadership style to sustain success and maintain motivation. Expatriate managers coming into a new culture often make the mistake of believing they are in a start-up situation where they must make an impact. In fact, they are often in a 'sustain and maintain' situation, which means identifying existing success factors and reinforcing them.

You can use a SWOT analysis to understand better the existing success factors. It will give you a profile of the personality and competences of your team. It will also give you an opportunity to observe your new team.

SWOT analysis chart

	Helpful	Harmful
Internal (features of the team)	Strengths	Weaknesses
External (features of the environment)	Opportunities	Threats

Follow this procedure:

- brainstorm the strengths of the team or group: what are we good at doing?
- brainstorm the weaknesses of the team or group: what are we bad at doing?
- discuss the opportunities for success which the team can take advantage of: what can we achieve together?
- discuss the obstacles and threats to success: what has stopped us or is going to stop us from succeeding?

Once you have completed this, identify some key actions, for example:

- Training to develop competence.
- Focusing on specific objectives.
- Removing an obstacle.

A SWOT analysis can be a key step in getting to know your team, and also in helping you to decide on an appropriate leadership style.

Projects can be slow and frustrating but they are always interesting as new ways of working together emerge and we create better personal relationships which you kind of take for granted on single country projects.

MENA planning director (Britain), DriveDentsu, Japan

CASE STUDY 2   Laurence Berger

Read the case and then consider the questions below.

The individual

Laurence Berger is 30 years old. She is French but is now based in Frankfurt. She works in finance for a large multinational. Her job is to monitor the financing of large capital investment projects, such as the construction of a new factory. She has been promoted rapidly and is now in charge of a remote team which supports this work. She is a very hard-working and conscientious person. She likes to feel that she gets on well with everybody and finds it difficult when she can't build positive relationships with the people she works with.

The team

Laurence works with a small team based in the United Kingdom. The members of the team are all experts in their fields and extremely competent in costing major capital projects, and also in planning and monitoring spending. They are all British and have worked closely together for some years. All of them expected one of their fellow team members, Barry Venables, to get the job which Laurence now does. They don't dislike Laurence but have yet to be convinced that she can lead them.

The organization

The company has a policy of maintaining centres of excellence and the United Kingdom certainly has one in major project planning and financing. However, top management has felt that the UK team was not well integrated into the main corporate finance team in Frankfurt. Laurence seemed like a good choice to lead the team as she is not German or British and is not well known in the organization. The people who appointed her to the job believed that everybody liked Laurence; that the UK team would be sure to like her too; and that this would help with the team's integration into the finance team.

The incident

Laurence has been to the UK site three times in order to establish her position in the team and to get to know the other team members. These meetings have worked well on an operational level and she has been impressed by the efficiency of the team. However, she feels that she is being treated as an outsider. She dines alone when she visits and finds the team members, especially Barry, rather cold and unwelcoming. When she gets back to Frankfurt, she has to work really hard to keep the channels open with the UK office. Certainly they are no more integrated than before. If anything, they are more distant.

Reflections

Her boss says: 'Just be patient. It will take time.'

She thinks: 'These guys are never going to make me one of the team. And the remote location and the culture over there make it all the more difficult.'

Barry thinks: 'I guess she thinks she's really international, speaking all those languages. Well, she doesn't understand us.'

The rest of the team thinks: 'She seems very nice. Clever, and really trying to make it work. It's going to take time. Maybe we should come to Frankfurt next time.'

Questions to consider

1 What is stopping Laurence from building a team?

2 What can she do to integrate the UK team more into the core finance team in Frankfurt?

Suggested answers can be found at the back of the book.

Situations

04

This chapter focuses on:

- How international managers need to understand the influence of culture, personality and situations on our decision-making.
- How we can develop decision-making skills to cope with the many difficult situations international managers face.

Situations

In a particular situation, our actions are not only influenced by our personality, individual qualities, and cultural preferences but always also at least partly by the special nature of the situation we are in. Every day managers face both familiar and new situations. For example, a familiar situation could be a customer who has not paid on time; a new situation could be a bank withdrawing credit from the company. A key skill is knowing how to deal with these situations. International managers face similar situations but they are made more complex because of the international context.

Situational judgement

Situational judgement is the skill we need to make difficult decisions. It is usually assessed through tests that give candidates decision-making choices. For example:

You work in the credit-control department of a medium-sized company. Your job is to monitor customer payments and take action when payments are not made on time. You notice that there is one customer who has a very bad credit record with a long history of missed payments. You can't understand why your company is still supplying goods to this customer and continuing to build up debt. You ask a colleague who tells you this customer is a small firm owned by the daughter of the CEO of your company. Your colleague has the impression that different rules apply to her.

Do you...

    a Write an email to your boss, the Head of Credit Control, asking why this customer has been treated differently?

    b Telephone the customer and request immediate payment of the outstanding debt?

    c Telephone the customer and negotiate new payment conditions?

    d Do nothing, accepting that this is the way of the world?

    e Look for a new job, thinking I don't want to work for this sort of company?
    or: _____

In classic situational judgement tests, there is a right and wrong answer. Employers usually develop the test to assess both skills (communication, decision-making, problem-solving) and also shared values. The answers provoke the candidate to think about their values – what they consider right and wrong – but also what is the most appropriate thing to do in this situation.

Culture, personality and situation

As we saw in the last chapter, we need to consider three factors which could affect our judgement:

Culture

We have seen in Chapter 2 how the groups to which we belong influence our behaviour.

Personality

The international manager needs to guard against cultural stereotyping and understand, as we saw in Chapter 3, that behaviour may equally be influenced by personality, individual qualities and personally held principles and values.

Situation

The particular nature of the situation we are in may influence our action more than cultural and individual preferences. We need to use our analytical abilities as well as our experience of different situations to decide on the best action or way to behave. Our understanding of these three influences leads to the development of skills – more appropriate communication, more appropriate decision-making, more effective relationship-building and more effectiveness generally when working internationally.

Shared values and decision-making skills

In all cultures, the so-called golden rule of ethical behaviour is understood: 'Do unto others as you would have them do unto you' or treat people as **you** would like to be treated yourself. This may be considerate and appropriate in our own cultures but could disregard the fact that people from other cultures may have different but equally legitimate preferences as to how they want to be treated. The golden rule could also be regarded as ethnocentric in nature. 'My way is the right and better way' is a possible implicit belief underlying the golden rule.

Mindful international managers should consider whether they need to apply what is known as the platinum rule: 'Treat others as you think **they** would want to be treated'. In other words, think about how they think and behave, rather than how you do; take their perspective. This approach encourages you to be tolerant and to accept other behaviours and values. But it may also confront you with a conflict between your values and those of the culture you are working with. This can occur when your behaviour as a manager is governed by the *universalist*, code-oriented values (see Chapter 11) of good international corporate governance. This can mean, for example, that hospitality and gifts that are a normal part of relationship-building and not a bribe in one culture are regarded as corrupt in another. Here the platinum rule 'collides' with the golden rule.

In the last chapter, we saw how the international manager needs to show sensitivity and understanding of others with their individual and culturally influenced preferences. This needs to be supported by the confidence to do what he or she thinks is appropriate in a certain situation – a balance between collective judgement based on shared values and autonomous in-dividual judgement based on your analytical skills, theoretical knowledge and experience of life.

Scenarios

There are five more scenarios below for you to decide on the best action. There is never a clear right or wrong answer, although certainly some decisions are better than others. You could approach some of the scenarios by using the insights into managing conflicts we present in Chapter 11. At the back of the book there is a commentary on each scenario.

1 Poor performance

You have recently been promoted to team leader. You have five colleagues reporting to you. Four have welcomed you and so far continued to perform at a high level. The fifth colleague, Douglas, has been problematic from the start. He does the minimum in his job and has not implemented the new IT system, as everybody else in the company has done. He is an intelligent man but he seems bitter and uninvolved. You find yourself taking on some of his tasks and you notice that the other team members consider it very unfair that he gets away with doing very little work. You have spoken to your predecessor who never confronted the issue saying: 'Doug is untouchable – he is disabled and he also sits on the works council. You will just have to live with him.'

Do you ...

    a Meet him individually and set him some clear targets for improved performance and then, if he does not achieve them, give him a formal warning of proposed dismissal?

    b Organize a team meeting in which the whole team commits to annual objectives and tasks, including Doug and then wait to see if he fulfils his tasks?

    c Talk to your boss about Doug and agree on a joint strategy for dealing with his poor performance?

    d Follow the advice of your predecessor and do nothing?

    e Talk to your HR department about the legal requirements for dealing with poor performance and then follow them strictly?

2 A rude boss

You have been sent on a two-year foreign assignment to your company's subsidiary in China. You have been assigned to the production department where the manager is an experienced local called Liu Song. Your job is to advise on the implementation of new processes in the Chinese plant. After a month, you are feeling more and more uncomfortable. Liu seems to treat his staff very roughly – shouting at them and criticizing them. You are not sure if he does this just in front of you to impress you. In fact, you feel the whole department is in fear of him. The results are very good and he takes all your advice on the new processes. However, you feel his leadership style is a very long way from the expected behaviour of other bosses in the company.

Do you ...

    a Wait some more weeks to observe and reflect on how he is working?

    b Talk to other colleagues in the department to see what they think. This will be difficult as they are all Chinese and only a few speak English.

c Talk to your boss back in the head office about the behaviour and ask for his advice?

d Talk to Liu and ask him why he seems so upset with his workers?

e Accept the behaviour as different and the way things are done locally?

3 Corruption

You are working in the sales department of an international company. You look after customers in Eastern Europe and Russia. Business is very tough in the well-established markets in Western Europe but is growing rapidly in your area and you have just been given a big bonus for exceeding your sales targets. You inherited one big key account from your predecessor – a retail chain that operates across the region. This is your reference customer and has certainly led to you getting a lot of new business. The purchasing manager, Igor, who you deal with, is normally very friendly but the last time you met him seemed a bit cold.

You asked a colleague about this and he said that your predecessor used to invite Igor and his family to join them on a winter skiing holiday. It was never very clear who paid but your colleague suspects your predecessor used to finance much of it through expenses. This type of hospitality is against the code of ethics of your company but there is usually some flexibility in the interpretation of the code.

Do you...

a Explain to Igor that there are strict ethical guidelines and so you can no longer invite him and his family?

b Ask Igor to join your company's annual skiing trip for employees but make it clear he will have to pay?

c Take Igor out to lunch and offer him better price incentives but don't mention the skiing holiday?

d Talk to the director in charge of sales and ask for his advice on how to deal with this situation?

e Do nothing but continue to provide good products at good prices?

4 Divided loyalties

You're the key-account manager in an international cosmetics company. You look after a major customer which has branches across the EMEA (Europe, Middle East, Africa) region. You have had a long, professional relationship with the cosmetics buyer in this company, Helga Ebke. Your range of products has been doing very well in the Middle East, in particular in their Dubai store. On a recent trip, you met with the store manager, Ahmed Malami. He confided in you that he was about to leave the group and become a director of the region's largest luxury goods chain. He offered you an exclusive deal whereby they become the sole promoters and sellers of your cosmetic range across the region.

Do you ...

    a Inform Helga of the approach you have had from Ahmed?

    b Inform Helga of the threat posed to both your businesses by this regional luxury-goods chain, without telling her about the plans Ahmed has?

    c Continue to focus on your business and relationship with Helga without mentioning any developments in Dubai?

    d Hint that Helga needs to talk to Ahmed about his future plans?

    e Call Ahmed and tell him to tell Helga about his plans before you do?

5 Close relationships

You are a man and have been sent to work on a project in Central America. You will be based in Mexico for about a year. Your objective is to establish a new SAP-based database system in all the sales offices of the region. Your team is international but you have two local project members: one of them, Martine, is Mexican and a very successful brand manager. You respect her work but find that she is very personal in the way she relates to you. She tends to share her personal problems as much as the professional, telling you about difficulties she has at home as well as with one or two colleagues in the team. At first, you appreciated her emotional honesty but now you feel it is negatively influencing her judgement. She gets upset and even cried in your office recently when she was telling you about her mother's illness. You would like to get the relationship back on a more professional basis.

Do you ...

    a Ask her colleague, the other local project member, to talk to her and explain that she can't continue getting so emotionally upset at work?

    b Talk to Martine yourself and explain that she needs to separate her private and professional life in future?

    c Talk to the whole team about the need to focus on key deliverables and not be distracted over the next few months?

    d Accept that Martine is an emotional person and needs to have the opportunity to express herself sometimes?

    e Accept Martine's behaviour for this project but determine to never let yourself get so close to a colleague in future?

Direction

05

This chapter focuses on:

- How people from different cultures may differ in their need for direction.
- How people from different cultures may differ in the way they deal with uncertainty.
- How people in organizations can interpret vision statements differently across cultures.
- How managers can influence colleagues to commit to goals and objectives through rapport building and through using a range of communication styles.
- How managers need to take account of the importance of the past, present and future in different cultures.
- Applying the insights of this chapter to a case study.

The relationship between setting direction and uncertainty

Whatever cultures you belong to, you will certainly agree that a group, a team or an organization needs to know what direction it is going in. Managers need to set out and communicate the purpose and the objectives of their team to all team members. They need to make sure that all members of the team have their own objectives and that they know how these contribute to the team's goals. Choosing the right goals is a critical strategic skill for all leaders. In this chapter, we are going to explore how clear and detailed these plans need to be when managing across cultures and also how we communicate these goals and get commitment to them.

> Germans tend to like technically clear environments. They want to know what the goals of a project are, what resources they have and so on. They need a clear plan. There are people from other countries, perhaps the United Kingdom and the United States, who like to experiment. They have a framework concept and then they start and build up experience, so they work a little bit with uncertainty.
>
> *Peter Wollmann (Germany), Zurich Group, Germany*

Somebody setting the direction for a group or an organization removes uncertainty about desired future actions. Both organizational cultures and national and ethnic cultures reflect different attitudes towards uncertainty, an insight which Hofstede (1980, 2001) and Sully de Luque and Javidan *et al* (2004) brought to intercultural management. In common with researchers, German manager Peter Wollmann believes that the Germans feel a need to reduce and avoid uncertainty, for example, through making plans and defining procedures. They want to create certainty through having clear goals, and clear steps and processes to reach the goals.

> Chinese don't need rules to solve problems ... they use their personal wisdom.
>
> *Manager (China), car manufacturer, China*

A culture with less need for order and for avoiding uncertainty will not have the same expectations. The uncertainty of life is not viewed as a threat and therefore there is less need to plan in order to reduce and avoid uncertainty. Setting the direction can thus be less explicit.

How differences in uncertainty avoidance may express themselves in business and management

Higher uncertainty avoiding cultures	Lower uncertainty avoiding cultures
Feel uncertainty in life to be a threat	Accept uncertainty in life
Known risks are taken	Willingness to take unknown risks
Show stronger resistance to change	Show less resistance to change
Rely on formalized procedures, rules, communication confirmed in writing	Rely on informal interactions and norms rather than formalized procedures and rules
Agreements documented in contracts	Word-of-mouth agreements
Results of meetings documented in minutes	Results of meetings often undocumented
Less willing to change employer	More willing to change employer
Belief in specialists and expertise	Belief in generalists and common-sense
Technological solutions are attractive	Technological solutions are less attractive

(Adapted from Hofstede, 2001, and Sully de Luque and Javidan, 2004)

How far do you identify with these competing values?

What is the preference of your organizational culture?							
Less uncertainty avoidance	3	2	1	0	1	2	3	More uncertainty avoidance
Processes, rules less important	3	2	1	0	1	2	3	Processes, rules more important

What is your personal preference here? Is it different from that of your organizational culture?

Less uncertainty avoidance	3	2	1	0	1	2	3	More uncertainty avoidance
Processes, rules less important	3	2	1	0	1	2	3	Processes, rules more important

Large organizations often try harder to avoid uncertainty as the size of the potential loss resulting from a mistake becomes higher. Smaller companies may work better with uncertainty, able to adapt to a changing environment quickly and flexibly. However, all companies want their people to know where they are going. They vary in how much direction they give and how much flexibility they permit as to how they will get there.

Direction and vision

Organizations use vision and mission statements to communicate direction. But communicating direction in this way is a culturally sensitive matter. The vision has to make sense to the organization's employees. People may receive vision and mission statements very sceptically if their management is not sensitive to a range of individual and cultural preferences among its employees.

Many employees will be sceptical if management oversimplifies the vision – for example, by saying that the company wants 'to make the planet a better place'. Employees may switch off if they think the mission is arrogant – for example if the mission is 'to be number one in the global market place'. How people react depends in part on deeply-held personal and cultural preferences. The vision must be one that is compatible with these values and aspirations.

This is particularly difficult to achieve across a wide range of different national and ethnic cultures represented in an international organization precisely because national culture influences these values and preferences.

It may be difficult for management to achieve buy-in to a corporate value statement if it is not compatible with a very wide range of different, locally held values.

In the same way, culture also determines the meanings given to apparently universally acceptable vision statements. 'To be commercially successful' may mean increasing a company's profits, its share price, its dividend and its value to a shareholder-oriented corporation in a country such as the United States or the United Kingdom. To a small or medium-sized, family-owned and family-run company in other countries of the world, commercial success may mean being able to generate a reasonable income over the years and passing the company on to the next generation of the family.

Results and relationships

Setting the direction is a result-oriented process. Do we need to build relationships in order to set the direction? The answer is probably not if we limit ourselves to just setting the direction. But what is more important than setting direction is whether your team align themselves and commit to this direction. The manager needs to reflect on how best to do this. Some team members may commit because they are told to and/or because they understand the logic and sense of the objectives.

But many will only feel involved if you are involved with them – in other words, if you have shown an interest in and a desire to support them. This may mean that they trust you to act in their interests as well as the organization's. This is particularly important for managers who have no direct reports but must influence colleagues to do things without having the power to tell them to do it.

As we saw in Chapter 3, building rapport with your colleagues or partners means showing warmth and attentiveness in your relationships with them. It also involves showing that you are interested in them and care about them and demonstrating that you are interested in the 'we' rather than 'you' and 'I'.

How do we build rapport with our colleagues? It is far easier when we work in the same physical location because we can spend time round the coffee-machine or over lunch getting to know each other. We can inquire about them and their lives and build a relationship which is not just about delivering performance. It is more difficult from a distance when relationships tend to be much more task-oriented. However, there are opportunities to do this in most of the moments when we communicate. We just need to take them – aware, though, that members of task-oriented cultures may find the relationship-building puzzling, unnecessary and a waste of time.

Here are some simple ways of building rapport:

- Emails and other written messages: We can wrap these messages up with opening and closing remarks which express interest in the people we are contacting. We can send text messages which are not about business.

- Telephone calls: We can sometimes call without a specific results-orientation but simply to see how they are and how life is going.

Communication styles

Managers operating locally in their home environment will probably discover their preferred way of leading and communicating direction. This may be a very informal, 'chummy' style where all colleagues are treated as friends or it may be a very charismatic style based on strong personality and conviction. The more international the scope of work, the more leadership and communication styles the manager will observe.

Communicating direction: Big picture or detail? Push or pull?

Communicating a message about the future to a diverse group is a challenge. Some members of a team or organization will be inspired by the ambition and vision of the big picture; others – the more pragmatic and down-to-earth types – will want to know the detail.

Big picture or detail

How do you see yourself? Are you a big picture person or a detail person?

- Do you skim the headlines in a newspaper getting a quick overview of the news?

- Do you find an article and report and read it all the way through?

- Do you get bored quickly if you have to repeat a task more than a few times?

- Do you get satisfaction from repeating tasks to a high standard?

- Do you like talking about ideas and concepts?

- Do you like talking about processes and how things work?

If you are communicating direction to diverse functional groups – each with its own culture, eg finance, marketing, R&D, HR and production – you need to be mindful of the process. How are you going to make sense of it for such an audience? This may involve choosing between the big picture approach or the detail approach. It may involve other choices of stylistic features such as those listed below.

Communication style

Profile your own preferred style of communicating by locating yourself on the scales below. Then use a different colour pen to do the same for your audience.

big picture	3	2	1	0	1	2	3	detail
formal	3	2	1	0	1	2	3	informal
distanced	3	2	1	0	1	2	3	close
conceptual	3	2	1	0	1	2	3	pragmatic
neutral	3	2	1	0	1	2	3	emotional
expansive	3	2	1	0	1	2	3	concise
optimistic	3	2	1	0	1	2	3	realistic
statements	3	2	1	0	1	2	3	questions
silent listener	3	2	1	0	1	2	3	active listener
soft arguments	3	2	1	0	1	2	3	hard facts

Pushing

This approach to communicating direction means that you communicate your message forcefully and with conviction. In a hierarchical or uncertainty-avoiding culture where expertise may be thought to be in the heads of individuals with power and/or expert knowledge, this might be the preferred style. You need to be well-prepared and demonstrate a belief in your message.

Pulling

This means that you start by understanding the position of the people you are talking to. You may ask questions to align your message with their expectations. You allow them to interrupt and ask you questions. The communication is seen as a dialogue in which both parties find a solution together. This approach will work well in a flatter organizational culture where there may be less belief in the power of the expert.

In both approaches, you need to be clear about your objective. The difference is how you achieve it – push or pull.

Mindful international managers realise that there isn't a single style of communicating and influencing which is appropriate and effective for all individuals and all cultures. What is more, they are able to select an approach from a range of styles which best suits the people and cultures in question. The style they choose may be more similar to that of their audience or the person they are talking to and different from their own preferred 'default' style.

Key competence:
Influencing by using a range of communication styles

One aspect of influencing which is important for effective international managers is the ability to select from a range of styles an approach which best suits the situation, the people and the cultures in question. They are able to analyse their interlocutors' preferred communication style and tune into their wavelengths. They can thus use a style which their interlocutor feels comfortable with. They have a broad repertoire of communication styles with the result that they can communicate effectively and appropriately with people from different cultures and backgrounds.

Long- and short-term orientation

In communicating direction, is it more appropriate to emphasize the long-term or the short term? The Chinese Culture Connection first brought this concept of long-term orientation as opposed to short-term orientation to international management thinking in 1987, a concept that Hofstede (1994, 2001) also reported on. It is a common belief that US companies tend to focus on short-term profit – bottom-line results – and that Japanese companies may focus more on long-term return on investment in order to achieve market position. Regardless of whether this stereotype is accurate or not, it identifies an important cultural preference, which you may need to consider when communicating direction in international business.

> The profound person understands what is moral. The small person understands what is profitable.
>
> *Confucius*

Confucius felt that *li* (profit, gain, advantage) was not a proper motive for actions affecting others. A different attitude towards virtue distinguishes long- from short-term orientation. In long-term oriented cultures, the virtues which are valued and promoted are those which are geared towards future rewards, especially the value of trying hard to achieve goals, even in the face of difficulty; and the value of being thrifty.

In cultures with a shorter-term orientation, virtues are promoted which relate more to the present. Money is not saved but spent. Concrete results are looked for quickly. Investors expect a quick return on their investment. In a longer-term culture, people are willing to wait longer for good results and investors are less impatient to gain from their investment.

The long view and the short view

How do you see your culture at work? Choose the statement which more closely corresponds to your view.

a We value colleagues who are persistent and patient. (0)
b We value colleagues who are dynamic and focused on results. (1)

a We value people who have acquired their status and reputation over a long period of time. (0)
b We value people who have risen quickly and reached their position at a young age. (1)

a We value personal time for life outside work. (1)
b We do not value personal time. (0)

a We tend to save and be thrifty. (0)
b We tend to spend and acquire goods. (1)

a We tend to make long-term investments (eg in property). (0)
b We tend to make short-term investments (eg in money or on stock markets). (1)

a We focus on market position for long-term returns. (0)
b We focus on short-term results. (1)

a We believe that we can identify clearly what is right and wrong. (1)
b We believe that right and wrong are rarely black and white. (0)

Scoring: the higher your score, the more you see your culture at work as short-term oriented.

Past, present and future

When it comes to communicating direction and where the future for the team or organization lies, the mindful international manager also needs to be aware that cultures may differ in the value they attach to the past, the present and the future. This is an insight developed by the anthropologists Kluckhohn and Strodtbeck (1961) and was made famous in the international management world by Trompenaars and Hamden-Turner (1997). This different emphasis may have effects on how managers give direction and how a multicultural team or workforce regard direction once it has been given.

Past orientation

In some cultures, people believe everything can be found in the past. Life repeats itself so we can learn from the past how to deal with the present and the future. This means we need to see the direction that other people took in the past and learn from them. Cultures which stay close to their traditions and rituals attach high importance to knowing and understanding the past. In addition, older people are highly respected because they know more about the past than the young. As a result, when international managers communicate direction, they need to place the future plan very much in the context of the past and show that they understand and respect the past.

Present orientation

Some cultures and groups, for example many sports teams, are much more present-oriented. They believe that success comes from focusing on the moment, not dwelling on past successes or failures or dreaming about future achievements. Countries suffering on-going difficulties, such as war or deprivation, can also be more present-oriented than more fortunate countries. They may believe that it is not worth spending too long planning and predicting, as the key to survival is in the present. So this means that, when communicating direction, immediate benefits need to be stated clearly. If the plan only promises change in three years, your colleagues may not believe in it.

Future orientation

Future-oriented cultures do not believe in dwelling too much on the past. A culture which focuses on the future needs to be optimistic. There is a belief that anything is possible with the right planning and resources. People believe you need to have a vision and sense of purpose to get the best out of your future. In these cultures, international managers need to be very positive about the future and the opportunities it will bring. Here especially, the manager needs to communicate conviction.

Then, now, next

How would you represent your national or ethnic culture?

Using a variation of the Cottle Circles Test, published in Cottle (1967) and made famous by Trompenaars (1993), draw three circles on a piece of paper as an illustration of your culture's time orientation, each representing either the past, the present or the future. Use different sized circles to represent their relative importance. Arrange these circles in the way that best shows how your culture tends to feel about the relationship of the past, present and the future. If the circles you draw intersect, you see a connection between the various periods. If they are separate, you see no connection.

The three circles below would indicate that the past is very important in comparison with the present and that the future is relatively speaking less important. All three periods are unconnected with each other.

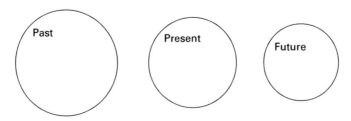

The next three circles show how the three periods are regarded as equally significant and how the present is influenced equally by the past and the future.

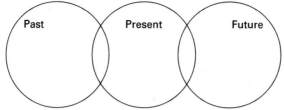

Best practice: Top-down or bottom-up or something else?

How involved do you want your team to be in setting the direction? Is strategy the preserve of senior management or can others contribute to defining the direction and the objectives?

Top-down communication

In Chapter 2 we saw how some cultures are more hierarchical than others. In these more hierarchical organizational cultures, there is often an expectation that top management should set the direction. Seniority gives leaders authority and encourages a willingness to obey and follow.

> The Malays still have almost a feudal attitude to power. The man who is at the top gets our support because he is at the top. Whether he's wrong doesn't come into it. We must follow him.
>
> *Brian Cracknell (UK), Language Works, Malaysia*

Bottom-up communication

In less hierarchical national and organizational cultures, you need to make sure that you don't 'talk down' to your colleagues, especially if you are their boss. In these cultures, the process of consultation and gaining consensus is vital for getting commitment – achieving buy-in – to a common goal.

> In Scandinavian countries it is no problem that a direct report of the CEO becomes his project leader, whereas in African countries where I have been working recently, this is impossible.
>
> *Thorsten Weber (Germany), HLP, Germany*

It is not always a question of hierarchy. In very structured and formal organizations or in cultures with a strong need to avoid uncertainty, everybody has a role and contributes only within their specific field of expertise.

The feeling here is that you are responsible for bringing in your piece. It must be done. You should answer the questions you have to answer. But it's not the kind of cooperative working and learning we have more in the US.

Timothy Taylor (United States), Henkel, Germany

Communicating direction to a team or more informal work group is vital. International managers need to get their international teams all moving in the same direction but, from the intercultural perspective, the mindful manager needs to be flexible about how to do this.

Techniques	Communicating direction Advantages	Disadvantages
Top-down		
The leader decides and then communicates direction	Can be inspiring if you have a broad enough range of influencing skill	Less suitable for less hierarchical cultures
Bottom-up		
The leader listens to the ideas and anxieties of the team's members before s/he and the team reach consensus about direction	Can create new alternatives and synergies	May become a talking shop if you don't drive things forward. Less suitable for more hierarchical cultures
Talk to individuals		
Giving direction on a one-to-one basis	Each team member gets understanding of direction and may buy in to it. May be a useful addition in individualistic cultures	Does not develop team spirit
Talk to team		
Giving direction to the whole group	Can be inspiring if you have a broad enough range of influencing skills	May fail to gain buy-in from some individuals who the manager does not notice

| Communicating direction | | |
Techniques	Advantages	Disadvantages
Big picture		
The leader stresses major goals and opportunities	May achieve a broad commitment. May be more suitable in cultures tolerant of uncertainty	May fail to convince pragmatic team members, who may dismiss it as a public relations exercise and not take it seriously
Details		
The leader presents goals and perhaps also methods in detail	Will appeal to the practical team members. May be more suitable in cultures with a high need for certainty	Leads to reflection about specific individual roles and not enough about the team as a whole

In many cases, the answer is to balance a top-down with a bottom-up approach. Effective international managers need to have clear sense of where they want to go. But then they need to involve their teams in implementing this direction and adapting it to the particular needs of the situation. In this way, they may not only be creating something new in the culture of their organization or part of the organization. They will also be building on the cultural diversity of the group.

> I usually started by saying that this is our goal, now let's sit together and see how we can adapt it to fit you and your country in your company. So it was a common process as much as possible.
>
> *Birgitta Gregor (Germany), HLP, Germany*

CASE STUDY 3   Phil Carey

Read the case and then consider the questions below.

The individual

Phil Carey is an IT manager in the United States. He works for WFC, an international food company with its HQ in Brussels. He used to work for Matty's, a household name in the States producing ready-to-bake meals. Matty's was taken over by WFC 18 months ago and a key role for Phil is to integrate Matty's Customer Relationship Management (CRM) System into WFC's global SAP-based IT system. Phil is very proud of having developed Matty's IT infrastructure and support. He is a competent CRM specialist but has no international experience. He is a family man, and people in the United States regard him as easy-going and friendly.

The team

Phil is part of a global IT team. He reports to Max Stellter, a Swiss citizen who is head of IT in Brussels. Max has been with WFC for 10 years working in Switzerland, Singapore and now Belgium. He speaks French, German and very good English. Max is ambitious and very results-focused. He is always courteous but keeps his distance from his team members. Max has set up a team of six to support sales with an integrated CRM system. Two other members of the team come from the main sales unit in Brussels – Susan Key, an Australian, and Kika Malouda, a Moroccan. The other two are based in Brazil and Thailand.

The organization

WFC was founded in 1978 as a result of a merger between Amor, a French dairy product company and Pellinero, a Spanish frozen-food company. These two divisions still represent over 40 per cent of the business. However, the head office moved to Brussels 15 years ago and there a multinational group supports a global business. The current CEO is a Mexican – Juan Reales. The culture of the head office is 'technocratic' while local offices around the world have stayed close to their roots. IT is a challenging area for head office as it is trying to leverage size and best practice across the group. Not surprisingly there is resistance to both the centralization of information (in particular monitoring of key performance indicators) and also what is seen as the bureaucratization of work – more and more online forms and reporting.

The incident

The CRM team has a regular weekly web-meeting. One of the items on the agenda is knowledge transfer – a chance for individuals to present insights and learning from their own experience. During the last meeting, it was Phil's turn to share experiences and he presented his development and implementation of the Matty CRM system: he really enthused about his 'baby'. He thought that this was a great chance to sell the competence of his IT team and therefore their contribution to this global project. After about five minutes, he stopped talking and invited questions. Nobody asked anything. Max thanked him for his contribution and moved on to the next item. All the rest of the team became engaged as they discussed the pilot roll-out in Brazil. Phil felt totally deflated and wondered what he had done wrong?

Reflections

The following remarks were made to Max after the meeting:

'What was he talking about? His accent is so strong I couldn't understand a word.'

'Why should we want to hear about Matty's CRM system? We have our own to roll out.'

'The Americans are always like that. Boasting about their successes.'

'I wanted to interrupt but I didn't get a chance.'

'Phil seems like a nice guy. He needs to find out more about what's going on here in Brussels.'

Questions to consider

1 What does Phil need to understand about his personality and culture and the differences between him and others in the team?

2 What skills does Phil need to develop?

Suggested answers can be found at the back of the book.

06 **Organization and change**

This chapter focuses on:

- What values and attitudes may hinder or support the management of change in international business.
- Cultural success factors in mergers and acquisitions.
- Working in international projects as a driver of organizational change.
- How people working internationally must sometimes adapt to working without a leader.
- How communication is of critical importance to managing change successfully.
- Applying the insights of this chapter to a case study.

Attitudes towards change

International management operates in a constantly changing environment, which makes it imperative for international organizations to be able to change quickly too. Managing such change is a frequent task of international managers. The mindful international manager must therefore understand what are the drivers of change in cultures and in people, and what are the blockers of change.

A framework of values developed by Schwartz (1992, 1994, 1999) contains a key set of values called 'conservation' (see also Schwartz and Bardi (2001) for examples). People who think these values are important may find it difficult to accept change.

Possible blockers of change: conservation values

How far is the person described like you?

Conformity							
Does what he/she is told, follows the rules, behaves properly, shows respect to his/her elders, is obedient, is polite, does not disturb others							
very little	3	2	1	0	1	2	3 very much

Security							
Avoids danger, is organized and tidy, finds social stability important							
very little	3	2	1	0	1	2	3 very much

Tradition							
Is satisfied with what he/she has, finds religion and customs important, does things the traditional way, is modest							
very little	3	2	1	0	1	2	3 very much

(Adapted from the Portrait Values Questionnaire developed by Schwartz et al, 2001. An earlier version of the questionnaire is reported on in Schwartz, Lehmann and Roccas, 1999. These questionnaires are reproduced in part or in full in various internet and print publications. See for example Burgess and Steenkamp, 1999), Schwartz et al, 2001) and Davidov, 2008)

People who think that these conservation values are important want to know where they stand. They tend to prefer the established order. To get buy-in for change from people with these values, the effective international manager needs to communicate about changes in the organization very clearly and convincingly:

- *Organization and roles.* You need to state clearly who will report to whom and what they will be responsible for.
- *Processes and systems.* You need to state clearly and step by step how new processes will work.

You have to adapt to people who need to refer to what has been said and what has been agreed and planned. If some are very creative and loose, then you can do it in another way, more relaxed and informal.

Lorenzo Pestalozzi (Switzerland), CRPM, Switzerland

On the other hand, the international manager could be working with people for whom a different value set in the Schwartz framework is more important. This set is called 'openness to change'.

Possible drivers of change: openness to change values

How far is the person described like you?

Hedonism							
Seeks fun and pleasure, wants to enjoy life							
very little	3	2	1	0	1	2	3	very much

Stimulation							
Does lots of different things, seeks new activities, likes surprises and excitement							
very little	3	2	1	0	1	2	3	very much

Self-direction							
Is creative and imaginative, likes freedom to decide, plans and chooses, is curious, wants to understand many things, likes to be independent and self-reliant							
very little	3	2	1	0	1	2	3	very much

(Adapted from the Portrait Values Questionnaire developed by Schwartz *et al*, 2001)

People who score high on this scale are more likely to be open to change than people who score high on the conservation set of values. In fact, they may well get bored without some change. The mindful international manager needs to keep them involved by giving them opportunities to do new and different things and to give them freedom in their work so that they can enjoy themselves.

Key competence: Spirit of adventure

Effective international managers are emotionally strong and have a sense of adventure. They look for variety, change and stimulation in life and avoid what is safe and predictable. They put themselves into uncomfortable, ambiguous and therefore demanding situations.
But they know they can learn from the experience.

Making change happen

To what extent is it actually possible to influence events in private life or at work and thus, for example, bring about organizational change? To what extent do people feel they have some control over what happens to them and their colleagues? To what extent do they feel they are at the mercy of external factors? International managers charged with implementing change need to know that not only individuals but also cultures differ in their answers to these questions.

According to Rotter (1954), people with a high *internal locus of control* believe that they can shape their future and that of their colleagues, whereas people with a high *external locus of control* feel that their lives are shaped by external forces, over which they have no control.

Research (for example, by Flytzani and Nijkamp, 2008) shows that most managers have a high internal locus of control. They believe that they can influence their lives and careers and those of others. However, many of the people they manage have a lower internal locus of control; indeed they may well have a high external locus of control.

The causes of this are partly cultural (for example strong religious beliefs may encourage people to believe fate has a large role to play in their future), partly personality (for example, you have inherited a strong drive from your parents) and above all situational. If you have never had opportunities to influence your career or success in life, it is not surprising if you come to the conclusion that they are outside your control.

Managers with a high internal locus of control need to be careful not to assume that their own motivation and their belief in their power to achieve are shared by everybody. This can translate into arrogance and a lack of sensitivity to the feelings and motivations of others.

The mindful international manager may believe in the need for change but many members of an organization may be anxious about, even fearful of, the change. Clear, top-down messages (see Chapter 5) will not necessarily reassure employees who feel they are victims of yet another round of change.

Changing organizational structure

To remain agile in a fast-moving business environment and also to reduce costs, many organizations have reduced the number of hierarchical layers that they have. This is not only a structural change. It needs to be supported by cultural change. Both types of change demand flexibility from the mindful international manager. Mindful international managers need to be aware of the possible deep-seated blockers to this kind of change in themselves and in their staff and their colleagues.

The cultural iceberg for a many-layered organization could look like this:

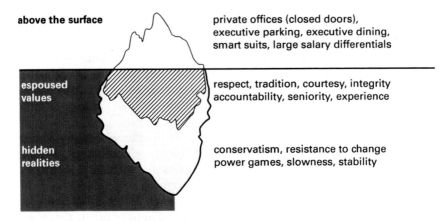

above the surface

private offices (closed doors),
executive parking, executive dining,
smart suits, large salary differentials

espoused values

respect, tradition, courtesy, integrity
accountability, seniority, experience

hidden realities

conservatism, resistance to change
power games, slowness, stability

> For Germans, if there is a hierarchy, there is a push to work in that team because authority has more influence in German guys. In Latin guys, hierarchical pressure is less important so you must have more and more charismatic leadership because the hierarchy is not enough. In Germany I saw teams producing good results even if there was a very bad feeling among the team members. People execute orders even if they are not happy.
>
> *Camillo Mazzola (Italy), Henkel, Germany*

The cultural iceberg for a flat organization could look like this:

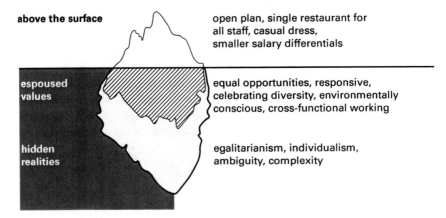

above the surface

open plan, single restaurant for
all staff, casual dress,
smaller salary differentials

espoused values

equal opportunities, responsive,
celebrating diversity, environmentally
conscious, cross-functional working

hidden realities

egalitarianism, individualism,
ambiguity, complexity

Making the cultural transition to an organization with fewer layers takes time. In particular, managers need to address the issue of motivation in a way that is sensitive to the values of their people. For example, in a delayered organization there are fewer promotion opportunities: there are fewer rungs on the career ladder so you may have to wait longer to move up. So it may be necessary for managers to try to create other opportunities for the development of their people, which are clear and well supported. If they do not, staff turnover may well increase.

Change and cross-cultural mergers and acquisitions

Organizational and cultural change often occurs because of a take-over, merger or joint-venture. As these mergers and acquisitions often affect organizations from different national (as well as organizational) cultures, the international manager may well be caught up in such a change process and needs to be mindful of the factors affecting it.

Failure rates in mergers and acquisitions are notoriously high – as much as 60 per cent by some accounts – and the risk attached to cross-cultural M&A's is understandably thought to be even greater. To try to reduce the risk of failure, the suitability of the two organizations to be merged – what is known as the fit – is investigated as a basis for deciding whether to go ahead with the deal or not. In this due diligence process, merging or acquiring organizations look at the financial fit, the market fit and the legal fit (anti-trust/monopoly issues) but very rarely the cultural fit. If cultural due diligence takes place at all, it is often after the purchasing decision has been made and is seen as part of the post-merger integration process.

Finding out whether middle management will support the new organizational structure resulting from an M&A is critical. There is often a large gap between the strategic view of senior management and the middle managers who have to implement the strategy. Cultural due diligence aims to find out where these gaps are, ie whether there is a cultural fit or a clash:

- *Leadership styles.* For example, does your national and organizational culture expect and encourage delegation and autonomy (smaller power distance) or is close supervision expected (larger power distance)?
- *Communication.* Do you communicate mainly by phone and face-to-face (higher-context communication) or do you rely on email (lower-context communication)?
- *Vision and objectives.* Does your organization focus on customer service and satisfaction, stock levels, bottom-line profits, or employee retention?
- *Business drivers.* What are the critical drivers: price, quality, market share?
- *Structure and processes.* Do you have SAP-driven business processes and measures (higher uncertainty avoidance) or do you rely on more personal reporting (lower uncertainty avoidance)?
- *Physical.* Are you used to working in an open-plan office or behind closed doors? Do you dress formally or casually?
- *Working time.* Do you keep strictly to contracted working hours or is there a culture of working long hours?

(Adapted from Stachowicz-Stanusch, 2009)

These are some of the questions that an international manager needs to be mindful of when involved in a cross-cultural M&A and which can form part of a cultural audit. The gaps may be too great and mean years will pass before the two organizations can get the best out of each other. Companies experienced in this process may decide to leave their new acquisition alone – to maintain its cultural identity, or it may decide to integrate quickly. If the latter, international managers will be exposed to dual acculturative stress – the pressure to adapt, on the one hand, to a new corporate culture and, on the other, to the dominant national culture of the acquiring company. This is the kind of situation that tests some of the international manager's key competencies which we draw attention to in Chapter 3 and elsewhere in the book: emotional strength, flexibility and personal autonomy.

Working in international projects

Projects are one of the main instruments of implementing and managing change in organizations. Ideally project leaders need to select project members who are both open to and positive about change. Each project member has to be a spokesperson for the project and needs to speak with conviction. Project leaders are often not the hierarchical boss of their project team members. Each project member will usually have a line manager to whom they report.

This 'transversal' context is more complex when working internationally. Project members may be working in a quite different national or ethnic environment in their line functions. Often they will also come from different professional or functional cultures and maybe even from different organizational cultures. Notice how the innovation project team below, which is the subject of a case study in Chapter 12, brings together different hierarchical levels, functions and countries.

Innovation project

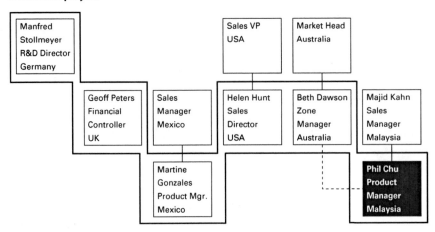

DPI Story © York Associates 2007

Phil Chu, product manager from Malaysia describes his situation like this:

> I am a product manager working in the main office in Kuala Lumpur, I report to Majid Khan, sales manager for pet food category. He's fair but a very demanding boss. This business is growing rapidly and I am responsible for a key category – premium dog food. We have very ambitious targets and my own remuneration package is linked to achieving these targets. I'm really pleased to be working on this international project but it is going to be difficult to find the time. I already notice that the other people in the project are quite direct and also demanding!

Effective project leaders need to make sure all project members appreciate what each of them have to do locally. It is important you spend time exploring the organizational and cultural background of each project member:

- Organization: eg reporting structure, main performance measures, leadership style;
- Culture: eg key dimensions such as power, time, communication, uncertainty avoidance, performance orientation.

A common cause of tension in international projects is the fact that they are usually initiated and driven by head office and often resisted locally because people don't like the idea of 'head office imperialism'! Mindful international project managers have to work even harder to show that they understand local cultures and also to explain their own cultural context and expectations.

> It was partly due to the business environment of a German company having acquired a US company. Maybe if it had been the other way around, the situation would have been totally different. And in the finance team we had more challenges than other teams, maybe because of the functional culture – we had more rules than others which we had to follow and implement.
>
> *Wibke Kuhnert (Germany), Henkel, Germany, about an international project*

Working without a leader

One result of working in international projects, and also virtually, is that your project leader is often not present. For individual team members this may in itself be a change and therefore needs the careful attention of both the project leader and the individual team members. The project leader has to build a strong organization and project culture which does not need micro-managing. The two keys to this are transparency, and autonomy and support.

Transparency

The team leader needs to organize and explain clearly scheduling, task allocation, reporting and communication within the project group. For example, some people may feel frustrated when a team member does not respond to an email within 24 hours or whatever period has been agreed. People can feel pressurized by unexpected demands (for example, a change of deadline without any discussion or warning). Expected behaviours and guidelines – in short, a project culture – need to be generated and agreed during the kick-off.

> Then, in the kick off, to give a short background, objectives, why this team and not another team, critical issues, responsibilities, reporting, allocation of tasks, who does what ... and, especially, next steps.
>
> *Camillo Mazzola (Italy), Henkel, Germany*

Autonomy and support

Project members need to be self-motivated as they may not get much support day to day. They need to be able to work on their own and keep to deadlines without being chased. This means that choosing team members who also have the right set of intercultural competencies, for example personal autonomy (see Chapter 3), is critical – but not always practicable because team members may be chosen for their technical or functional expertise or because the most qualified people are not available:

> For an important team, you have to spend a lot of time choosing the right guys. Sometimes this decision is taken very rapidly without consideration of the impact on the future. And because we sometimes don't have the time available, it happens that the best guys are not always chosen but the guys who have more time available.
>
> *Camillo Mazzola (Italy), Henkel, Germany*

The effective team leader needs to think about how team members are going to be supported during the life of the project. Sometimes the answer is to set up some peer or external coaching or mentoring or both (see Chapter 8).

> Q: How open are organizations to using coaching as a form of support?
> A: What we see is that it depends on the mindset whether the companies consider external help as weakness or as a professional strength for achieving a better performance.
>
> *Frank Kühn (Germany), HLP, Germany*

Certainly the project leader needs to keep in touch with all his team members and regularly check on their current thoughts and feelings about the project. When you are working face-to-face, it is sometimes clear from facial expressions and body language how people feel. If you are working virtually, you need to work much harder at understanding the mood of your team members.

Best practice: The four Ps

Effective international managers follow the four Ps to make sure their teams are well-organized.

Preparation

Because your colleagues work in different contexts, it is very important to prepare for your cooperation. Before a meeting, you need to define the timing, agenda, documentation and contributions you expect people to make during the meeting. Before a telephone call, send an email to agree the timing and purpose of the call.

People working in cultures that value certainty and try to avoid uncertainty (see Chapter 5) may well interpret signs of thorough preparation as an indication of good management. However, people working in cultures that place less importance on certainty may have a different view of this management style.

Purpose

Make sure that everybody understands the reason why you are doing something. Do not just assume they will understand it. For example, it may be that when working in your own culture, you always start a meeting with an update from all the participants. In other cultures, they may do this before in writing. You need to explain why you want to include this step at the beginning of the meeting.

When you start a telephone call, clearly state the purpose – what you hope to get out of the call: 'I'm calling about the shipment. I'd like to clarify the dates.' It may be necessary to make your needs and intentions clear to an extent that is not necessary in your own culture in order to help create trust. This ability is a key competence of the mindful international manager.

> Key competence:
> Transparency through exposing intentions
>
> Effective international managers make clear what their needs and intentions are – they say not only what they want but why and how. They make key messages explicit. They don't concentrate only on the foreground but fill in the background too. This helps to build up trust.

Process

Make sure that everybody understands how you want to work. Go through the steps, especially your expectations for actions and follow-up. Many meetings fail because it is not clear to the participants how to follow up. They may misunderstand the urgency or importance of a follow-up action.

But be open and flexible enough to accommodate the wishes and needs of your team members where possible. The mindful international manager recognizes these needs and is able to balance a focus on goals with openness and flexibility.

People

Always remember that organization means organizing people. They are not just material resources. They may be anxious about a new process or they may feel that they have not been involved. Get feedback from them and tune in to their feelings about the project or their part of it.

> Naturally being more Latin, I constantly use planning methods and tools to control my spontaneous and creative side. I let it roll free or imprison it a bit, depending on the activity. If it's for developing business in an unknown environment, finding new markets, then I let my creativity loose, and just fit loose guidelines. If the environment is more local or more basic management topics, then I plan and structure more what I do.
>
> *Lorenzo Pestalozzi (Switzerland), CRPM, Switzerland*

CASE STUDY 4   Pierre Menton

Read the case and then consider the questions below.

The individual

Pierre is 45 and worked for Dupont, a French engineering company for 15 years. Two years ago it was taken over by a much larger US technology company – TCE. Pierre is a process engineer, leading a group of 25 technicians. He is sociable and well-liked; he enjoyed working for Dupont; and he felt at ease and got on well with his colleagues. Pierre has found it difficult to adapt to the new owners. He now reports to a US boss, Fred Peters, at the European head office in London. He finds it hard talking English during the teleconference meetings. He accepts that this is a consequence of globalization but he's not happy.

The boss

Fred Peters, 47, has worked for TCE for 20 years. He has a background in engineering but he is now vice-president, operations, for TCE's European business. He is based in London. His wife and children have stayed back in the US so he lives alone in a company apartment. Nearly 20 managers report to Fred from across

Europe. His job is to streamline operations across the group: this means reducing excess capacity by closing down smaller plants and reducing the number of employees at most factories. Fred needs to do this in the old Dupont business and has decided that Pierre can support this process. He has decided to promote Pierre and use his influence to sell a new 'Empower the Team' initiative.

The meeting

Fred arranged a telco with Pierre. During the call Fred presented the new initiative. He also offered Pierre the new position and talked about the opportunity this would be for Pierre to make an impact in TCE Europe. At the end of the call they agreed that Pierre would think about the offer and get back to him.

Reflections

After the call:

Fred: 'He didn't say much. When I met him last time, he seemed like a friendly guy – someone we could work with. He's got to see this is an opportunity. If the French don't start to make these changes, we're going to have to close down the whole plant. Maybe he's not the guy for this job.'

Pierre: 'I think he offered me a new job. He said more money, but why me? What is this "Empower the Team"? What does he want me to do? I think he wants me to help him reorganize the plant. That means fewer jobs. But I heard they may close down this plant.'

Questions to consider

1 What does Fred know about the French plant? Do you think he can make this change initiative work?

2 What do you think Pierre should do? Should he take the job?

Suggested answers can be found at the back of the book.

Roles

This chapter focuses on:

- The range of possible roles for international managers.
- The clash that may result from a manager having both an international and a local role.
- The contrasting roles of the manager as expert and the manager as manager.
- The crucial role of the manager as an influencer, connector and facilitator.
- The skills needed to facilitate communication across cultures.
- Applying the insights of this chapter to a case study.

Management roles and styles

Managing across cultures is crucially influenced by the differing perceptions and beliefs about the roles a manager has to play – about what people expect a manager to be and do. A manager can wear many hats. Some hats are favoured more in some cultures than in others.

Many managers have a largely operational role, working without much administrative support: they may spend a lot of their time organizing and administering. Other managers have a 'hands-off' role, delegating most of the work, and working at a distance from their teams so that they themselves as managers can think and act more strategically. The manager as coach is a relatively new role. In this role, managers support and develop their staff.

> Ideally, when you are a leader and you give a clear direction, the team understands that this is the right direction. And that takes some time because you need the commitment and so on. Sometimes to save time you push the team before you have the commitment. Sometimes you can't do the perfect job. You have to do the job.
>
> *Camillo Mazzola (Italy), Henkel, Italy*

Supportive and directive styles

Hersey, Blanchard and Johnson (2001) in their situational leadership model describe leadership style in terms of the amount of direction and support that leaders give to their staff. Although this model doesn't refer explicitly to the work of international managers, its flexibility makes its especially suitable for dealing with the wide variety of subordinates and their culturally influenced expectations of a manager that the international manager is likely to encounter.

Directive behaviour relates first and foremost to the task to be done. Highly directive behaviour consists in the leader telling people what to do and how, and when and where to do it. The highly directive leader sets goals, organizes, directs and controls.

Supportive behaviour relates more to the relationship between leaders and the people reporting to them and to the nature of their interaction. Highly supportive behaviour consists in the leader engaging in two-way communication with their people, listening actively, and facilitating interaction. The highly supportive leader gives emotional support and provides feedback.

High	**Supporting leaders ...** > facilitate their people's efforts > encourage > participate > share responsibility for taking decisions *Appropriate for managing staff with moderate to high competence but who lack confidence or motivation*	**Coaching leaders ...** > explain > ask for suggestions and ideas > support progress > sell and persuade > take decisions with dialogue and explanation > direct and monitor closely *Appropriate for managing staff with some competence but less confidence and commitment*
Low	**Delegating leaders ...** > give responsibility for taking decisions and solving problems to their people > observe > monitor *Appropriate for managing staff with high competence and high commitment*	**Directing leaders ...** > tell > guide > monitor task accomplishment closely > take decisions and pass them on *Appropriate for managing staff with less competence but high commitment*

Supportive behaviour (vertical axis)

Low — Directive behaviour — High

Adapted from Blanchard, Zigarmi and Zigarmi (1986), Hersey (1985) and Hersey, Blanchard and Johnson (2001).

The grid on the previous page contrasts the supportive and directive styles of management. It defines four styles of management and describes the kind of staff each style is suited to.

Management Styles

Using the grid above, reflect on your own management style:

- Your own preferred style of management.
- The preferred management style of the organization you work in.
- The type of staff you are dealing with.

International roles and local roles

More and more managers have both a local and an international role. These roles may conflict with each other. The international manager may well have a demanding line manager locally who pushes for resources and results. At the same time, this international manager may have to take part in international projects that are important to the company's global success. These projects are usually initiated by head office and local companies may quite often resist them.

> For international projects, you often have problems coming up between headquarters and subsidiary.   *Birgitta Gregor (Germany), HLP, Germany*

Headquarters may see its task as exploiting the size of the organization, spreading best practice across the company and maximizing global results. The task of local subsidiaries is usually to maximize market share, sales and profitability in their market. Much research and experience have shown that headquarters-subsidiary relationships are typically often strained and the international manager is often caught up in this tension, which again demands emotional strength and flexibility to handle.

Mindful international managers, whether they work in head office or in a local subsidiary, need to understand both contexts and the causes of resentment and conflict that such conflicting tasks may mean for the individual manager working internationally.

> As the organization gets bigger, Head Office wants more and more control. In the beginning, we had a lot of freedom to act. Now, they are always asking for budgets, forecasts and updates. They don't understand how difficult the market is in Finland at the moment. I'm trying my best to get more customers but it's difficult. They just ask for more. It's very stressing.
>
> *Finnish sales manager talking about her relationship*
> *with her German head office.*

Once you have understood why there is resistance, you need to identify some common goals that will unite local and international teams. The obstacle to overcome is often that local staff do not buy into the international objectives: they are not an incentive or motivation for them. In this case, you can review roles, so that you understand better what is needed locally and what you can realistically expect internationally.

> Finding the fine line between having clear role definitions and fluidity and flexibility, this is the art of project and team management.
>
> *Torsten Weber (Germany), HLP, Germany*

The role of the expert and the role of the manager

In many cultures, managers are firstly experts in their chosen field – for example mechanical engineering, accountancy or law – and only secondly managers. Organizations recruit such managers because of their qualifications and experience in a specialized area. They then promote them because they have shown themselves to be very competent in this 'technical' field. They may, however, end up in a management position that allows them very little time to be an expert, because they are now fully occupied with managing people and operations.

This concept of the manager as an expert may also shape the expectation of a manager's staff. For example, do you agree with this statement?

> It is important for a manager to have at hand precise answers to most of the questions that subordinates may raise about their work.

This bar chart shows the percentage of managers asked who agreed with Laurent's famous question:

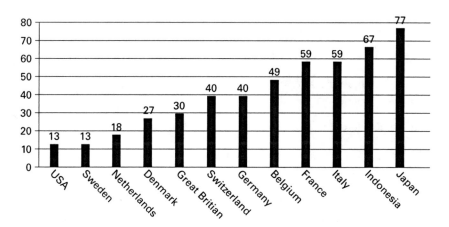

Adapted from Laurent 1986: 94

In some cultures, this belief in expert knowledge is very strong. It is connected with the culturally based preference for avoiding uncertainty and creating certainty that we saw in Chapter 6. Knowing a lot about something may allow some cultures to handle the uncertainty of the future better. People believe that their expert knowledge equips them to deal with a wider range of future possibilities.

Signs of this are visible to all. For example, the high status given to professional qualifications and titles indicating expert knowledge and competence rather than hierarchical position (see Chapter 2) shows that the culture values expertise highly. When working in such a culture, you may not be expected to contribute in an area outside your field.

> Some [people] very clearly were thinking 'Why are you saying this? This is not your territory.' The feeling here is that you are responsible for bringing in your piece, it must be done. You should answer the questions you have to answer.
>
> *Timothy Taylor (United States), Henkel, Germany*

In some cultures, there is a stronger generalist tradition in education. In these cultures, qualifications may have a smaller role to play and experience is valued instead. People may see a qualification in an arts subject – history or philosophy, for example – as a sign of a good general education that has developed sound analytical and presentational skills. They believe that training on the job will fill the gap in specialist knowledge.

The value attached in a particular culture to the subject of a qualification also varies across cultures. In many cultures, both in the developed and developing world, professions such as law and medicine are highly prized. In the United States, a law degree is a common qualification for the business world. There are said to be more lawyers per head of population in the US than anywhere else in the world. France and Germany have a long tradition of educating good engineers and qualifications in engineering have a high status. In the United Kingdom, engineers have lower status and are less well paid.

Expert knowledge in business and management

Profile your culture's attitudes towards expert knowledge by considering these questions:

- What types of qualification are most highly valued?

- Who tends to get to the top of companies – sales, financial, legal people...?

- How easy is it to move from one field of professional expertise to another – for example, to make a switch from a technical field into a commercial field?

- Is it important to put titles and letters before (eg Dr or Dipl Ing) or after your name (eg BA Hons) on your business card?

- Are business qualifications (for example MBAs) becoming a necessary qualification to progress up the management ladder?

The role of the influencer

Influencing people by convincing them and persuading them is a key activity of the successful international manager. Managers by themselves can achieve surprisingly little. They are dependent on others to support them. They need to get the support of their colleagues, their staff and their own managers and influence them so that they contribute to the goals that the organization has set.

This influence can be exerted in a number of ways and we have already described some of them in Chapter 5. In cultures with a strong need to avoid uncertainty (see above) managers can often use expert knowledge and objective facts and argument to convince people that a particular course of action is the right one. We now turn to other ways of enlisting support.

Influencing through networks

In other, perhaps more relationship-oriented cultures, international managers can use different networks of relationships to exert influence. This occurs on the basis of the rights and obligations that result from knowing somebody personally or being put in touch with somebody through the network.

Many companies have reduced the number of layers of organization with clear reporting lines, to create flatter and more networked organizations, which themselves are linked to other organizations by different sorts of networks. Such networks function not least through the relationships of managers with other managers.

However, these networks are created not merely by good relationships but sometimes build on existing networks of relationships. One of the very difficult things to understand when working in a new culture is the basis of the networks that tie people together.

Some networks may have a particularly high status in a culture. International managers need to be able to recognize high-status networks as they will have particular influence in a culture. The network may be based on different types of cultural grouping. For example:

- *Tribe.* In tribal cultures, as can be found in many parts of Africa, membership of a certain tribe is often crucial to success.

- *Education.* In some cultures, an 'old school network', based on having attended a certain school or university.
- *Age.* Both extremes can be found. In some cultures, older, more experienced people form the elite network; in others, youth is the important entry card.
- *Family.* In cultures where the extended family is the main social unit (for example, in many Asian and South American countries), key networks may well be based on these extended families.

Another type of network is described by the concept of *guanxi*. At the heart of Chinese society, *guanxi* is a network of friends and acquaintances who feel they have obligations to support one another. They will ask for favours from those with whom they have *guanxi*. In this way, a network of good contacts in China can help you achieve things which are otherwise impossible to achieve. Having good *guanxi* is a powerful instrument for getting things done, getting new business and also getting a new job.

The mindful international manager has to take care to understand how these networks work in each new culture.

> First of all, even after a few weeks here, I am still observing how people approach things, how they expect things from you.
>
> Luis Ortega (Spain), Henkel, Germany,
> talking about working in Turkey

Influencing through people with influence

Power plays an important part in all business. You need to understand who has power – who is the right person to influence.

> It's very challenging actually to identify who has influence in the room, who is advising the boss. It's not obvious. Everybody looks equal but they are not. In this group there are one or two who give the boss very strong advice and you can be sure he listens to them.
>
> Thomas Ruckdäschel (Germany), T-Systems, Germany,
> about working in the Middle East

Mindful international managers are aware that influence in an organization cannot only be achieved by doing a good job and hoping this will bring the influence they want. They are sensitive to where 'political' power lies – especially in relationship-oriented and in hierarchical cultures. They learn how to identify the key influencers in an organization and are willing to try to influence these key figures, who in turn can influence others and the organization in the intended way.

The person with influence and the power to decide is often protected by informal 'gate-keepers' – personal assistants and other staff who do not themselves have the power to decide. However, a key way to reach the person with power is to build relationships with these staff. They may open doors for you if they like and respect you. If you are used to working in a very task-oriented culture, this may be difficult to adapt to. Maybe you feel you should be able to talk to the person who can get things done. However, in cultures which place greater emphasis on relationships, you may only be listened to if you are liked or trusted.

> Key competence:
> Influencing through sensitivity to context
>
> Effective international managers understand where 'political' power lies in companies. They give time and energy to identifying who holds this power and how to get access to them. They understand the contexts in which decisions are made and how to influence decision-makers in order to exert the influence they are aiming at.

The role of the connector

Bringing people together across all kinds of cultures – acting as a connector – is a key role of international managers. In this role, they can help to break down the silo mentality.

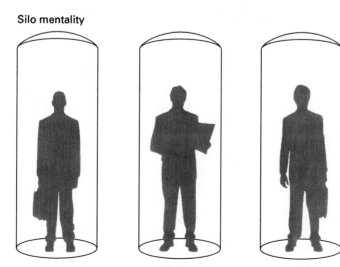

Silo mentality

In organizational cultures, the silo mentality grows as a result of over-structuring the organization, which may result in putting people into silos or boxes, or in people retreating into silos themselves. These silos, or departments, can become highly effective centres of expertise. But they may equally well turn into little kingdoms which their heads jealously guard and which are insulated from positive outside influences.

In national cultures, this mentality can be seen when we compare majority and minority cultures. A majority culture is one which has a dominant position of some kind, for example, through its political or economic influence within an existing society cultural group, or indeed globally. The United States has been the world's main majority culture for the last 60 years but economically speaking, at least, is being challenged by China. In the 19th century, Britain and France with their extensive empires were globally speaking majority cultures. A majority culture tends to look inwards and to find many of the answers it needs within its own culture. It may assume that the outside world wants to imitate its own culture.

In Europe, a Scandinavian country such as Norway is a good example of a minority culture. People living in minority cultures tend to look outwards for trade, jobs, education and business opportunities. As a result, the culture may be more open to the influence of other external cultures.

International managers need to build a strong working culture with shared values and expectations. However, they need to make sure at the same time that this culture is open and curious about other cultures. This can start with international managers themselves being open to new ideas, behaviours and people from different cultures.

Key competence: Openness through new thinking

Being receptive to ideas which are different from those common in their own culture is a quality of effective international managers. They are curious and try to extend their understanding of different professional areas, different organizations and different cultures. They put themselves in the position of people who are very different from themselves and they try to see things from other people's standpoints.

From a functional point of view, this aim of creating openness can mean building cross-functional teams and networks. The manager needs to take on the role of the connector. Managers need to take every opportunity to bring functions together. For example, training courses can provide a chance for people from technical fields to develop more understanding of their colleagues in the commercial area, and vice versa.

Knowledge transfer sessions can be built into weekly or monthly team meetings so that expertise in a particular area does not remain just in the heads of certain individuals. Other communication channels can be used such as annual workshops, newsletters and video-conferences to build stronger cross-functional networks. Connecting can go even further. Cultures that value expert knowledge less may enable people to move across functions in their career – for example from production into marketing.

The role of the facilitator

As a connector, you also need to be a good facilitator – literally making the connections work more easily. Meetings, whether they are face-to-face or virtual, provide the main opportunity for teams and network to understand and influence each other better.

Before the meeting

It is common good practice to prepare for meetings by drawing up agendas, issuing project and business updates, and sending out invitations to attend. However, the international manager will soon discover that participants from some cultures are much more likely to prepare than others. Therefore sending out an email with the meeting's agenda etc may well not be enough. It may be more effective to call any member whose active participation is going to be critical in order to make sure they are ready to contribute.

During the meeting

You need to build some repetition into an international meeting, as not everybody will have read the agenda and any notes before the meeting. Start by reinforcing the purpose of the meeting. There is enormous room for misunderstanding this. Some may feel they are there to discuss and get to know each other; others may feel they are there simply to 'rubber stamp' a written proposal that has already been read. Tell the participants what the objectives of the meeting are and what specific outcomes are expected.

Attitudes towards time in international meetings (see Chapter 2) can lead to big frustrations. Depending on the national and corporate cultures of the setting and the participants, starting and finishing times can be absolutely strict or very flexible or somewhere in-between. The monochronic facilitator will feel the need to agree timing beforehand and then repeat the agreement at the start of the meeting; the polychronic participant in the meeting may see this differently. Most importantly, what should be done if you as the facilitator have not achieved your objectives by the planned end of the meeting? Should you continue or arrange another meeting? Here, culturally influenced values and norms of the participants will influence preferred solutions.

At the start of the meeting the facilitator also needs to agree with the participants on the process of communication (see Chapter 6: Best Practice). The communication in many international meetings can be very stilted – in other words, formal and unnatural, as participants struggle with English as a common language. The job of the facilitator is to propose a structure to the communication in terms of who speaks when and then to encourage comments and questions. Initially, the facilitator can demonstrate this good practice him- or herself by politely interrupting a speaker in order to clarify a statement, asking questions and summarizing. Ideally, the participants will imitate this behaviour. If they do not, then the facilitator must continue to be very active in facilitating the communication.

A very critical facilitation skill is dealing with the different levels of competence in the language of the meeting that participants may have. They can range from native-speaker competence to beginner level. Getting messages across in a meeting taking place in a language everybody speaks as their mother tongue is difficult enough. Even here, it is rare for everybody to understand the same thing. In an international meeting taking place in a lingua franca (often English), which only some or none speak as their first language, 'full' understanding is rarer. People who nod their heads may seem to understand but they may be doing so more because they want to be polite than because they understand.

Research shows that non-native speakers of English working with native speakers often feel confused and frustrated by the sophisticated language their native-speaker colleagues may use. They may also be annoyed by the inability or unwillingness of native speakers to simplify the language they use to help their non-native colleagues understand more easily.

> The English aren't always sympathetic to Germans when they speak English. To begin with, the English speak slowly, but then fall back into speaking the same speed and slang as if the listener is a native.
>
> *HR manager (Germany),*
> *power generation, Germany*

Non-native speakers sometimes see this inability of native speakers to adapt their language as a deliberate and unfair tactic to push through some course of action.

International facilitators thus need to be mindful of the very complex communication situation they are in and to adjust their language accordingly (see Spencer-Oatey and Franklin (2009) for examples). If they are native speakers of English or if they are more advanced speakers of English as a second language than the person they are talking to, they may need to create clarity for the other party, in particular by simplifying their language.

Clarity skills for native or advanced speakers

- speak more clearly and slowly than usual;
- emphasize and clarify key words;
- pause after key statements;
- increase redundancy, ie repeat and paraphrase, to give the listener a second and third chance to understand;
- avoid unnecessarily technical words, slang, idioms;
- restrict the range of vocabulary;
- use short sentences;
- use transparent sentence structure, eg 'He asked if he could leave', not 'He asked to leave';
- avoid contractions, eg 'I'll', 'shouldn't've';
- use labelling language, eg 'I'd like to make a suggestion', 'there are three possible actions: firstly,... ; secondly,... ; thirdly,... ';
- use more yes/no questions;
- provide answers for the interlocutor to choose from eg 'We can set up the equipment in two ways: like this... and like that... Which do you prefer?'

If facilitators find that their English is not as advanced as some of the participants, they can also use special techniques to create clarity.

Clarity skills for less advanced, non-native speakers

- speak clearly and slowly;
- pause and emphasize key words;
- increase redundancy, ie repeat and paraphrase;
- do not translate word for word from their first language;
- use 'prefabs' (prefabricated expressions), ie phrases and sentences learnt by heart that can be used to gain thinking time;
- ask for repetitions and explanations;
- double-check the meaning of apparently key words;
- ask your interlocutor to speak more clearly, slowly and simply;
- ask your interlocutor to remember that you are using a foreign language.

The facilitator will often notice that the non-native speakers of English working together in English often find it easier to understand each other than native speakers. This is because non-native speakers may express themselves more simply, more slowly and with more pauses. Perhaps just as important, because they know how difficult it is to function in a foreign language, they focus more on adapting their language to the needs of the listeners – another example of where mindful international managers needs to be flexible in their behaviour.

Key competence:
Transparency through clarity of communication

Clarity in their communication is a central ability of effective international managers. They understand that in international situations the potential for misunderstanding is high and thus the need for clarity is especially great. Native speakers work to make their language transparent and easily understood by those less fluent in the language in question. They are able to do this without appearing to talk down to people. Non-native speakers speak clearly and slowly.

After the meeting

Facilitators need to continue to be active by following up after the meeting – not just by sending out the minutes and confirmation of the details of next meeting, but contacting those who have agreed to take action. Following up on the actions and commitments is crucial.

Best practice: Defining roles

Role definition and expectations are critical in any work group or team. In an international role, the manager will have to fulfil a wider range of roles than at home, as definitions of the role of the manager will vary from culture to culture. Depending on the cultures with which they are working and the tasks they are performing, they may well need to be able to reflect upon what role is most critical and flexibly adapt to the requirements of the situation.

In international project teams, you are not usually able to observe team members perform their work. You only see the results of their work. So everybody in the team needs a clear understanding of what is expected of him or her. This is also critical to how the team is seen from outside, especially by local management. Team members need to know what the role involves and why it is important. Otherwise, they will soon think it is not as important as their local work.

The roles, tasks and skills of the international manager		
Roles	**Tasks**	**Skills**
Leader (see Chapter 13)	Strategy, influencing, inspiration	Decision-making, analysis, communication
Manager	Resource management, schedules, supervision	Coordination, organization, control
Expert	Knowledge transfer, quality assurance, innovation, project management	Subject expertise, creativity
Influencer	Introduce change, run projects	Communication (persuasion), political awareness
Connector	Connections, knowledge-sharing, relationship-building	Social skills eg rapport building
Facilitator	Communication, opening channels and building understanding	Communication, process management
Coach (see Chapter 8)	Develop people	Training, communication, coaching skills

CASE STUDY 5   Sun Mei Ling

Read the case and then consider the questions below.

The individual

Sun Mei Ling is a 32-year-old microbiologist working in Beijing in an R&D centre belonging to a major German pharmaceutical company. Before getting this job she worked in a government laboratory. Her work involves testing new substances and her role is critical in many projects. She works on a day-to-day basis with Helga Schreiber, a German project manager with a similar scientific background. They are both part of a team of scientists, most of whom are Chinese nationals but also including about a third who are expatriates, mainly from Germany and other European countries. Sun Mei Ling is a quiet person who takes pride in the quality of her work. She took this new job because it is much better paid. However, she finds that it is not clear what is expected of her and she is becoming more and more frustrated although she does not show this.

The team

Helga Schreiber, aged 35, has been expatriated to China for a three- to four-year assignment. This is her first long-term international posting. Back in Germany in the main R&D centre, Helga quickly rose to become a senior project manager with responsibility for some major initiatives. China is critical to the company's future and the new R&D centre in Beijing has been set up to adapt products to the local market and also to innovate specifically for China. Helga has recruited Sun Mei Ling to take over responsibility for microbiological lab-testing. She wants to free herself up so that she can concentrate on building a network with Chinese labs and external partners. Six months later, she is finding it very difficult to get Sun Mei Ling to take the initiative and to run things on her own. She thinks she has explained in detail what needs to be done but finds that Sun Mei Ling does it just once and then waits to be told again the next time.

The organization

The R&D centre in Beijing is finding it difficult to maximize the potential of its Chinese staff. The centre is run by a German with international experience but not in China. Three years after setting up the centre, the results have been disappointing and head office in Hamburg is wondering whether this investment was worthwhile. It seems that the two groups – Chinese and expatriates – have not found a way to work together.

Reflections

Sun Mei Ling (speaking to her husband): 'Helga leaves me on my own. There is often nobody else in the lab. I don't like to complain but I don't have a good feeling.'

Helga to the head of the centre: 'This is not working. I want Sun Mei Ling to take the initiative. I want to feel confident I can leave her on her own and that she will get the job done. Every time I come back, I have to start again and explain it all over. She seems very clever but doesn't take responsibility.'

The head of centre: 'Our European scientists are used to getting on with their work. They don't like much supervision – in fact they resent it if you interfere. I don't really know how to motivate the Chinese staff. They keep themselves apart.'

Questions to consider

1 What could Sun Mei Ling do to improve her working situation?

2 What could Helga do to achieve her objectives?

Suggested answers can be found at the back of the book.

08 **Support**

This chapter focuses on:

- How international managers can support themselves when working internationally.
- How they can support their colleagues working internationally.
- How they can develop their colleagues through coaching, mentoring and training.
- Applying the insights of this chapter to a case study.

Why support is so important

We have already talked in the introduction about the VUCA challenges facing people working internationally. The volatility, uncertainty, complexity and ambiguity in the world means that most of us need to be supported – we cannot do it alone. Working internationally can be a lonely and alienating experience – far away from home and the security of the culture you know and the people who care for you. Even the most independent of us need to turn to someone who can listen to us and advise us.

International managers need to recognize the challenges and respond by being mindful about developing themselves and about supporting and developing their people.

Supporting and developing

To what extent do you develop yourself by...						
stepping back from situations, observing and reflecting	1 2 3 4 5 6 7					
setting behavioural targets for yourself	1 2 3 4 5 6 7					

To what extent do you support your team by...							
being accessible and available	1	2	3	4	5	6	7
being sympathetic and understanding	1	2	3	4	5	6	7
being appreciative and grateful	1	2	3	4	5	6	7
To what extent do you develop your team by...							
being able to give advice	1	2	3	4	5	6	7
being able to answer their work-related questions	1	2	3	4	5	6	7
being able to develop the skills and confidence of your people	1	2	3	4	5	6	7

Ways of developing yourself

Mindful international managers need to develop the ABC set of competencies to become as effective internationally as they are at home:

	Nature of the competencies	Need the development of ...
A competencies	**A**ffective	attitudes and emotions
B competencies	**B**ehavioural	skills
C competencies	**C**ognitive	knowledge

It helps to think about how you can develop yourself by taking action on these three levels:

1 Attitudes

- Examine your feelings and thoughts about your work, yourself and your colleagues.
- Are you judging the situation and people too quickly? Are you patient when you work with people who are different from you?

2 *Skills*

- Identify the gaps in your own skillset.
- Reflect after some interaction (a meeting, call, an email) on whether you could have behaved differently.
- Find time to reflect on the process of how you are working, not just the tasks and results. This is a central feature of mindfulness. Can you improve the process? For example, consider the pace you work at. Do you need to speed up or slow down?

3 *Knowledge*

- Prepare for working with different cultures by reading and talking to people with experience of the culture – both insiders and outsiders.
- Spend time when you first start working in a culture by observing the behaviour.

Ways of supporting your colleagues

In what are known as *neutral* cultures, there is very little acknowledgement of the need for emotional support. In these cultures, the workplace and personal lives are kept separate and it is considered unprofessional to show personal feelings.

This means there are not many obvious signs of great enjoyment or great sadness – there are no great celebrations of success and not much dwelling on personal upsets. Employees are expected to keep their personal feelings to themselves.

On the other hand, in more emotional cultures (or *affective* cultures, as they are technically known), people tend to show how they feel to a greater extent. While crying at work may not happen often, expressing emotion verbally and non-verbally is accepted as part of life. In these cultures, it is possible to see how people feel from their facial expression and body language.

If international managers have been brought up in a neutral culture and find themselves working in a more emotional culture, then they need to decide how much emotional support they are willing and able to give. In neutral and task-based cultures, very little time is given to listening to personal problems. In more emotional cultures, successful managers will find time to talk to their staff about their personal lives. Sharing stories about your family life will be a significant part of working relationships. And when things go wrong at home, then the manager is open to hearing about it.

International managers need to decide on their own attitudes towards the emotional side of life at work. Where are you going to draw the lines?

Feeling upset at work

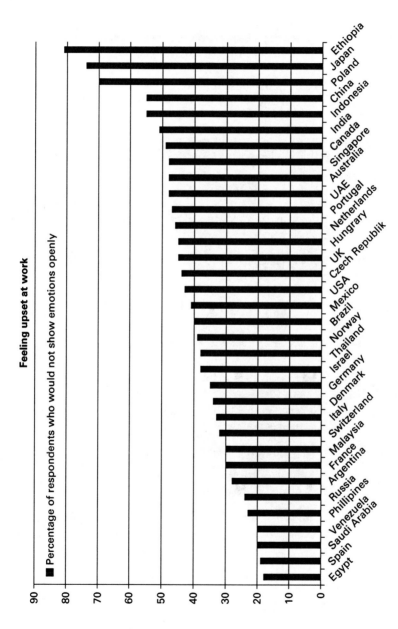

■ Percentage of respondents who would not show emotions openly

Adapted from Trompenaars and Hampden-Turner, 1997: 70

Ways of developing your team

Training

If you have special expertise in your work – for example, you may be a good presenter – you may want to pass this expertise on to your colleagues. As with all learning, it is important that the colleagues recognize the need and also respect the trainer/manager.

It is important for the manager in the role of the trainer to think carefully about how to run the training in another culture or cultures.

Typical trainer and trainee behaviours in various types of culture		
	More	**Less**
Power distance	Trainees are dependent on trainers and treat trainers with respect	Trainers and trainees treat each other as equals
	Training is trainer-centred	Training is trainee-centred
	Trainer is a guru	Trainer is an expert
Uncertainty avoidance	Structured learning situations and right answers are important	Open-ended learning situations and good discussions are important
	Trainer knows the answer	Trainer can say 'I don't know'
Individualism	Trainees speak up in the group and expect to be dealt with individually	Trainees don't speak up in the group and don't expect to be dealt with individually
	Face loss is not so serious	Trainees want to preserve face
	Individual initiatives are encouraged	Individual initiatives are discouraged
Masculinity	Brilliance in trainers is appreciated	Friendliness in trainers is appreciated
	Trainees' performance is important	Trainees' social interaction is important
	Failure is bad	Failure is less important
	Public praise to reward good trainees	Public praise to encourage weak trainees

(Adapted from Hofstede, 2001: 107, 169, 237 & 306)

In cultures with high power distance (see Chapter 2) there may be an expectation that the trainer speaks and the trainees listen. The trainees will have been educated in a teacher-centred culture, often in large classes, where the trainees may be used to sitting passively and absorbing knowledge. In lower power distance cultures, trainees will have been encouraged to challenge the trainer and expect to participate more actively in the training.

We need not only to be mindful about the cultural context but also about the personalities of our trainees. Kolb (1984) developed a model based on four learning styles, which Honey and Mumford (1992) later adapted to generate four learning types who have certain learning preferences: the Activist, the Reflector, the Theorist and the Pragmatist:

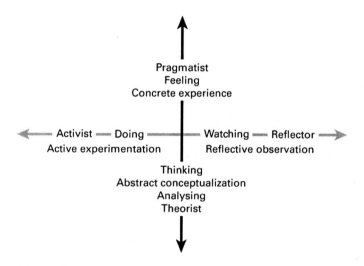

Adapted from Honey and Mumford (1994)

Business attracts a lot of Activists – people who like learning by doing things, so trainers need to make sure these types of learners are busy; otherwise they will lose interest. Pragmatists are also common – people who are willing to learn as long as they can see the point of it. They ask themselves: what can I do with this? Theorists and Reflectors are rarer in business, although there will always be some people who want to understand the concepts behind a recommended behaviour (Theorists) or want to have time to analyse and think about what they are going to do (Reflectors), before they do it.

Coming back to your objective to train people how to present better, there are many questions to ask yourself before you start. It helps to think about training as consisting of two stages:

1. *Input generated by the trainer:* theories, concepts, models, examples, explanations, demonstrations.

2. *Output generated by the trainees:* practice, transfer, accepting feedback, repetition.

You can then decide how to balance these two stages – whether to do more or less input or output will depend, for example, on the learning preferences of the trainees and the nature of what is being trained.

Coaching

Another way to develop your people is to coach them. The starting point, as with training, needs to be the recognition of a gap in skill, performance or confidence which, once bridged, will lead to greater performance and self-satisfaction. However, coaching is non-directive and involves developing an individual through one-to-one sessions in which the coachee takes a lot of the responsibility for his or her development. Coaching requires a trusting relationship between manager and coachee. They both need to share the intention to develop and improve the performance of the coachee. The coachee needs to recognize this need and to trust the manager to be the right person to coach him or her. Ideally coaching takes place face-to-face but you can also do it over the phone or in an audio-conference or video-conference.

International managers may find it difficult to take on the role of the coach because it requires time in an already busy schedule. More difficult perhaps is the need for the manager to play a less classically 'managerial', active and directive role and to become more the listener and supporter of personal change while a team member is given the chance to talk and develop.

Possible difficulties of the manager as coach across cultures

There may be barriers to coaching located in the manager's organizational culture. In our work we have found many 'traditional' managers who feel coaching is a luxury and not one which they ever had when they were younger. Successful companies often have a 'sink or swim' attitude towards performance and development – for example, sending the expatriate engineer to work on a project in a very different culture without any preparation, training or coaching. These companies could be even more successful if they invested time in coaching their people. Coaching is a way to unlock the knowledge and potential that is held in employees.

> What we see is that it depends on the mindset whether the companies consider external help as weakness or as a professional strength for achieving a better performance. There are even individual differences. They say, 'If I solve the problem myself, then I'm a strong personality'. Or 'Am I strong when recognising that there are some bottlenecks and weaknesses and then finding a good way... to find a way forward?
>
> Frank Kühn, Consultant, HLP Frankfurt

Coaching across national cultures can also be difficult because of the need to recognize and discuss weaknesses. In a culture where 'face' must be protected, this does not come naturally as feedback can be a threat to face. The skill of the international manager acting as a coach is to encourage the colleague to open up about the challenges and difficulties he or she faces. These difficulties are often not admitted to and only become visible when something goes wrong.

The stages of coaching

The Corporate Coach U programme provides an approach to developing people which can easily be followed by international managers coaching their people.

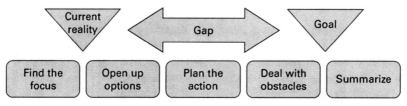

Adapted from: Corporate Coach U programme: The Coaching Clinic http://www.coachinc.com

Finding the focus: The first step is to focus on the issue and make sure both coach and coachee understand the precise nature of the issue. The manager needs to give the coachee the confidence to put the real issue on the table. Allow time to explore it and fully understand it.

Opening up actions: The second step is to explore what can be done. What are the options? The manager needs to encourage the coachee to think of the options. It is difficult to resist the urge to tell your coachee what to do, especially if you feel you know the best solution. The reason why you must resist is that you should be trying to encourage your coachee to take responsibility for finding and 'owning' his or her own solutions. This is especially important if you are managing people from a distance – you cannot be there to solve their problems.

Planning the action: When the coachee has found an option he or she thinks is realistic, you can move on to the third stage which is to plan the action. Again the coachee needs to commit to the timeline for taking the next steps. Your job is to help monitor these steps and support.

Dealing with obstacles: This fourth step is very critical. Very often when working across cultures, you do not see the obstacles although they are there and they stop people from doing things. In high-context cultures (see Chapter 2), for example, where 'no' is very rarely said, your coachee will not easily tell you about the obstacles – this could be an unsupportive local manager, an unspoken rule that discourages improvement (for example, in low performance orientation cultures) or a suspicion of change and new approaches (for example, in high uncertainty-avoidance cultures). Your job is to see or feel whether the action agreed at the last stage is really going to happen. As you get more experienced, you get better at reading the signs.

Summarizing: Finally, the coachee needs to summarize the action and commit again to the action planned.

This is a very simple five-step process designed to close a gap in performance by developing a skill or increasing confidence. Underlying the process are the techniques of being a good active listener: actively asking questions, exploring and checking understanding, and summarizing but also just listening and showing that you are listening. As the coach, you should aim for 80 per cent listening and just 20 per cent speaking.

Key competence: Active listening

Effective international managers not only listen carefully but also show they are doing so, for example by maintaining eye contact, nodding or taking notes. They clarify by summarizing and paraphrasing not only what they have said but what they understand others have said. When they see a misunderstanding has occurred, they pro-actively negotiate meaning with their interlocutor to create understanding.

The language of active listening

Showing you are listening
Right
OK
I see

Testing your own understanding
If I am not mistaken, you are saying ...
What I have understood is ...
Correct me if I'm wrong but what you're saying is ...

Testing the understanding of your interlocutor
Did I get that across OK?
Shall I repeat that?

Summarizing
Let me go over that again
Just to recap, ...

Repairing misunderstanding
There seems to have been a misunderstanding.
I think we may be getting something wrong.

Training can build a little bit of sensitivity but the next step is to train people on the job, to give them feedback on when they behaved well or not. So it is intensive coaching which is cut to the specific person.

Peter Wollmann, Zurich Financial Services

Mentoring

Another supporting role for the international manager is as a mentor. A mentor advises less experienced colleagues on career development issues, personal problems and organizational issues such as clashes between departments.

Usually the mentor is not the line-manager of the mentee and therefore has some distance from his or her day-to-day work. In some cultures, the wisdom of the older, more experienced person is well understood and appreciated. In the Western world, mentoring is often a more informal process of the older manager keeping an eye on younger colleagues who need someone to guide or advise them.

A very key role for the international manager is to mentor colleagues who are going to start working in or with new cultures. The more experienced you become, the more able you are to reflect on differences between your culture and others and also to focus on the challenges in the work situation. It is vital that organizations that want to become internationally competent capture the experience of their employees and share it. Some organizations have formal or informal knowledge management systems that allow such knowledge to be harnessed and made accessible to others. Although there are many books and websites that offer briefings and profiles of countries, these are often over-simplified descriptions. The international manager can describe life and work with greater credibility, including insights into behaviour, feelings and attitudes.

CASE STUDY 6   Nguyen Binh

Read the case and then consider the questions below.

The individual

Nguyen, 32, works for a German machine tool company – Biehler AG. He has just been appointed as technical sales representative in Ho Chi Minh City, Vietnam. He reports to Zhang Wei who is the regional manager for South-East Asia based in Singapore. Nguyen is a confident person who believes he can achieve his sales targets and support his customers in Vietnam. He is very proud to have got a job for a German company with a very good brand image. Previously he worked as a sales engineer for a Chinese company selling air-conditioning systems. Nguyen is ambitious and has taken the job mainly because of the salary and promotion prospects in the company. He would like to work in Europe for his next assignment.

His boss

Zhang Wei has been working for Biehler for 10 years. He has built up the business so that he now has a team of six sales-representatives working in the markets and back-office team of a further six sales support staff. Vietnam is the latest market where he has set up a local office with Nguyen in charge. He appointed Nguyen because he is keen, bright and knows the region well. Nguyen is young and will need support. Zhang especially wants to develop his organizational skills. He needs Nguyen to report back to Singapore systematically so that he can track progress in a new market.

The challenge

When he interviewed Nguyen for the job, they agreed that he would need further support to manage the business well. It is now six months later and the reports coming out of Vietnam are not at all clear. The business seems to be going well as Zhang can see the orders coming in but he has no information on the customer-profiles and therefore on their solvency. Zhang tried to set up a coaching-process with one face-to-face session every two months and then weekly telephone calls. So far, they have only had one face-to-face session at which Nguyen did not seem to understand the need for the coaching. The telephone calls have always been interrupted by customer calls and other business. Zhang does not have time to make more frequent visits to Vietnam.

The telephone call

Zhang decides to call Nguyen to complain about the quality of the sales-reports and insist on better and more reliable reports. Nguyen listens but does not seem to understand the importance of the reports. At the end of the call both of them are dissatisfied.

Reflections

Zhang: 'I have to do something about this. He seems to be a good salesman judging by the orders but I am worried that there may be problems I just don't know about. I thought he understood that he would need support for the first year and I was willing to do this. But he seems to think he's doing a great job and can't see the point of the reports. I haven't got time to go over there. Maybe I should put him in touch with Malik in KL who has been in the job for a lot longer and get him to talk to him.'

Nguyen: 'I don't see why Zhang is always calling me. Doesn't he trust me? I am getting the results and my customers are really happy. He keeps on talking about the weekly sales report. There's a lot of detail which I don't have time for. He wants me to find out every last detail about the customers. Surely the important thing is that I am winning new customers.'

Question to consider

What do you think Zhang should do to help Nguyen to change his behaviour?

Suggested answers can be found at the back of the book.

09

Feedback

This chapter focuses on:

- How feedback given in the right way can motivate and develop people.
- How culture and personality affect attitudes towards feedback and the way people give and receive it.
- How the international manager can achieve higher performance through mindful feedback.
- How the international manager can help to build a culture of feedback.
- Applying the insights of the chapter to a case study.

Formal and informal feedback

Feedback is a process of observing and then commenting on people's behaviours and skills in order to maintain or improve their performance. It is also used by organizations to understand how customers and other stakeholders feel about an organization's products and services (for example, in customer satisfaction surveys). We are going to focus on the internal and behavioural type of feedback. This can be managed in two ways:

Formally

Many organizations have a formal process of performance review or appraisal. This often takes place on a regular basis (for example, annually). It involves looking at past performance and then setting targets for future performance. It often relates to business objectives but, when well done, can also pay attention to personal preferences and attitudes. Some companies widen the scope of appraisal by introducing a 360° feedback process, in which managers, colleagues, reports and maybe others all give feedback (often anonymously in writing).

The benefit of these formal sessions is that they are fixed in the agenda and therefore usually actually take place. When done well, they can be a valuable opportunity to mark the end of one phase and the beginning of another. However, many managers and their reports complain that such formal feedback is just 'ticking the boxes'. In other words, it is a process they have to follow but do not believe in.

Informally

In this case, people give feedback when they note good or poor performance. For example, you hear a colleague give a good presentation and you comment on this afterwards. Or, you notice a member of your staff has been making mistakes in his work and you ask him what is wrong.

This type of feedback can be much more important for the receiver of the feedback than formal feedback. It is more immediate because it happens soon after the performance that the manager is commenting on. And it shows that managers notice the performance, behaviours, skills and moods of their team members. Feedback given immediately after the action assessed may more often lead to changes in behaviour and an improvement in performance.

> I like – with people I work with – to be able to reflect on ourselves once in a while, not very often but sometimes. And this is an important quality of a team. If you can look at yourself, see what you've done, clarify things and then go back to work. This helps me a lot and makes me feel good in a team. So I need open feedback processes. That's part of my team style.
>
> *Torsten Weber (Germany), HLP, Germany*

Although national and organizational cultures greatly influence the giving and receiving of feedback, managers should recognize that everybody can profit from feedback of some kind or another given in the appropriate way. Everyone needs feedback to do better.

Culture and feedback

Performance management and the role that feedback has to play in this are a cultural minefield. There are several key cultural dimensions which can affect how people give feedback and how people receive it:

Task orientation and relationship orientation

Giving feedback may be easier in environments in which organizations are seen as *instruments for managing tasks* rather than as *systems of social relationships*. Some organizational and national or ethnic cultures encourage very task-oriented behaviour. This means that people are expected to be very focused and specific about what they are doing. They need to know the what, where, why and how. Managers expect employees to perform tasks to a high standard as long as they clearly understand what they have to do.

In these types of culture, people often give feedback only when something goes wrong. Everything going right is the norm, so there is no need to comment positively on it.

> There's very little feedback. Very little of a look-back. 'What we did was right.' It's more facts and that kind of thing. In America, there'd be more of a validation, 'You did a good job', patting on the back a little bit. Here there's no need to talk about something which is not in question. Why mention it?
>
> Timothy Taylor (United States), Henkel, Germany

On the other hand, people in organizational cultures that are less task-oriented but more focused on relationships tend to do things for other reasons as well: because they want to be cooperative, or to show integrity, or because they are friends with their colleagues or feel loyal to their organization. Of course, they need to understand the specifics of the task too. They will do it well if they want to and these more personal, relationship-related factors are very important.

In these types of culture, there is often a need for supportive or encouraging feedback and you have to be careful about giving critical feedback as it may easily offend people.

Performance orientation

Cultures with a high performance orientation (see Chapter 2) encourage and reward performance improvement and so in such cultures people are likely to view negative feedback as necessary for improvement. As Javidan reports (2004: 45), in cultures with a lower performance orientation, negative feedback may well be viewed as judgemental and discomforting.

Uncertainty avoidance

Cultures with a high need to avoid uncertainty (see Chapter 5) are also likely to be those in which feedback is welcomed and actively sought (Earley, 1997; Sully de Luque and Sommer, 2000) because the feedback given can reduce the uncertainty that is felt and needs to be avoided.

Communication orientation

In cultures that prefer direct, low-context communication (see Chapter 2), people tend to be more prepared to give and receive feedback. They may be happy to receive positive feedback in a group or in front of their colleagues. They may be more willing to receive critical feedback on a one-to-one basis.

In cultures where people communicate less directly and face (see below) is an important consideration, it can be more difficult to give or receive direct feedback. It may be necessary to speak to people on a one to-one basis to find out what they are thinking. Even this will not be a transparent process without trust and understanding between you.

If you travel to North America, they may give much more direct feedback than anywhere else in the world. If you are not used to it, then you could sense it as rather hostile or aggressive. In Asia you have the complete opposite.

Ulrich Hansen (Germany), Henkel, Germany

Power orientation

The giving and receiving of feedback – especially 360° feedback – may depend on a relationship between the giver and receiver that allows dialogue to take place on more or less equal terms. The power difference between the two parties may need to be relatively small.

In so-called high-power distance cultures (see Chapter 2) feedback tends to be just one way from the boss to the subordinate. In low-power distance cultures, 360° assessment and feedback or upward appraisal where the subordinate gives feedback to their boss may be options.

Whatever the culture, giving feedback to your boss is a sensitive issue. It is important to have a reference point for the feedback – ideally an objective (most bosses are quite results-oriented) which has not been reached or has been very difficult to achieve. Then you can show how the boss's behaviour has made it difficult.

Individualism – group-orientation

Giving feedback as practised in, say, British and US organizations, is based on the belief that performance is the result of individual effort and that individuals can be held responsible for good or bad performance. This may clash with group-oriented notions of responsibility in cultures such as Japan.

Managers need to conduct both individual and group feedback. For group or team feedback it is essential to have some framework for the feedback. This could be provided by a SWOT analysis (see Chapter 3: Best Practice). A good SWOT analysis will lead to team targets and the team can monitor these targets and give feedback on them. For example, you could identify external communication as a weakness in the team and set the target to improve understanding of the team's work in the organization. Six months later, you could review this and see if you have made progress. If not, why not? This can be the basis for team feedback.

Face and feedback

A very significant influencing factor in more group-oriented cultures (see Chapter 2) is the concept of *face* – a person's dignity and self-respect or the public self-image that a person wants to project of him/herself. Whereas in the West the concepts of 'losing', 'saving' and (to linguists, at least) 'threatening' face are familiar, Chinese face concepts are much more complex and include, for example, the notion of 'giving face'. This complexity underlines the fact that the need to protect face felt in all cultures is especially important in group-oriented cultures. A person can lose face as a result of losing his or her temper, confronting an individual, acting in an arrogant manner, failing to show appropriate respect – or indeed receiving negative feedback in the presence of others.

What consequences does the value given to face have when you are giving feedback in group-oriented cultures?

● Be sure to give negative feedback one-to-one. Face-loss results from standing out from the group or of being criticised, ridiculed or reprimanded in public.

● The wish not to stand out may also apply to positive feedback. If you give positive feedback publicly, praise the group, not an individual or individuals in the group.

● If you want feedback on your ideas from group-oriented members of your team, you probably won't get it by asking what people think of them – any negative feedback would damage your face. It may be more effective to ask what ideas they have.

● Whereas individualists are mainly concerned about their own face, it is certainly the case that group-oriented cultures are also concerned about other people's face. This means they will often act in order to protect the face of others, especially the face of members of their own group.

● Relationships are long-term and need to be cultivated. This means that damage caused to the face of someone in your group or your team may come at a very high price.

● The reputation of your family, colleagues and your organization can be affected positively or negatively by your own reputation, and vice versa. Criticism is therefore not just a matter of an individual accepting and learning from it. The criticism can be seen to affect other people and organizations.

You can never ever surprise or embarrass a Baltic manager in a meeting in front of his colleagues because then he's lost. And that's part of the culture.
Erik Hallberg (Sweden), TeliaSonera, Sweden

Personality and feedback

Feedback is also a very personal issue. Most people are sensitive about receiving critical feedback. Some people are suspicious about receiving positive feedback.

Sincerity

People need to feel the feedback they receive is sincere. The more introverted their preferred behaviour is, the more sensitive they may be about feedback. Extroverts often accept feedback at face value – it could be that the feedback is superficial but that does not matter to them. More introverted people find superficial feedback insincere and may well only welcome feedback that is properly considered. The best way of making sure this happens is to get the receiver of the feedback to reflect upon his or her own performance.

Self-reflection

The starting point for much personal development is self-reflection – holding the mirror up to ourselves. We need to see ourselves clearly and also through the eyes of others. The person giving the feedback has a vital role in helping us to see the gap between where we are and where we want to be. The feedback-giver can also help us to get there by suggesting suitable actions.

The manager who is skilled in the feedback process will rarely just say, 'That was good. I like the way you presented the issue' or 'That could have been better. I thought you should have been better prepared.' He or she will ask the team member 'How did you think that went?' or 'What do you think went well?'

In this way, the feedback comes from self-reflection and is much more powerful and much more likely to lead to change.

Building a feedback culture

Many people receive no explicit feedback at all at work. This lack becomes part of the organizational culture. Often feedback is only given when something goes wrong and then people get criticised. This leads to a 'blame-culture' that is counter-productive and can deter initiative, risk-taking and innovation.

International managers may work across a large number of cultures and will discover that attitudes towards feedback vary a great deal. However, the behaviour of the manager can be very powerful. You can set the tone for all your colleagues by selecting culturally appropriate actions from these:

- At the start of an international project, set up a framework for feedback:
  - regular team meetings (last item on the agenda: Feedback);
  - regular one-to-one meetings;
  - reporting schedule.
- At the first meeting explain why feedback is important, how it will be used to monitor and improve performance but also how it can be used to motivate people.

- Agree in the team on norms of behaviour (for example, email response time, punctuality, use of mobile phones, contribution in meetings).
- Observe mindfully the process of working, not just the outcomes (for example, behaviour in meetings as well as the follow-up actions). Give feedback on how they work as well as what they achieve.
- Follow up soon after you observe good or poor performance and give feedback.
- Ask for feedback yourself from your colleagues and so encourage your team to ask for feedback.
- When working from a distance, don't just give feedback about results or lack of them (see Chapter 12).
- Celebrate successes as a team.

Types of feedback

Q: Can we start with a basic question? What is feedback exactly?
A: For me, you give feedback when you want someone to develop, to be better. But it's only on behaviour, not personality. And if you want to give feedback, you have to check if the person really can change it or not, if it really is a behaviour.
Dani Stromberg (Sweden), management consultant, Sweden

There are two types of feedback used for increasing the performance of teams and individuals.

Affirmative feedback

In this case, the manager observes a team member contributing to the success of the team. This may be through the quality of work on a certain task or it could be through hard work and dedication over time. It is important to follow these steps in the following box.

Three-step affirmative feedback

1 Say what you have observed.
   I've noticed how hard you have been working these last few weeks.

2 Say what effect this behaviour has.
   This has meant that we have reached some demanding deadlines.

3 Show appreciation and encouragement.
   Thank you for all your efforts. Your work is really making a difference.

Clearly, you can give affirmative feedback to the team as well as the individuals.

Developmental feedback

In this case, the manager observes an individual or the team having difficulty with a task or not performing to their potential. It is important to follow the steps in the box below.

Three-step developmental feedback

1 Say what you have observed.
I noticed that the quality has dropped in this area.
2 Say what effect this behaviour has.
This means we are having to repeat a lot of tasks.
3 Say what change you want to see.
We need to focus on each step more carefully.

Balancing affirmative and developmental feedback

Over a longer period of time of several months what do you think the balance should be between these types of feedback?

1 A ratio of 50% affirmative to 50% developmental
2 A ratio of 20% affirmative to 80% developmental
3 A ratio of 60% affirmative to 40% developmental

Of course it depends on the situation – is your team doing a good job or not? However, if you want them to accept the development feedback, it is very important to recognize good performance when you see it – the 60:40 ratio is a good guideline.

Best practice: Balancing transparency and harmony

While recognizing the importance of feedback in achieving performance, mindful international managers are also aware of the implications of cultural values and norms for the giving and receiving of feedback. It is probably the most sensitive task in interpersonal terms that international managers working with numerous cultures have to deal with.

The fundamental challenge is to take account of both the need for honesty and transparency, and the need for harmonious relationships – needs which vary in degree across cultures. In every culture, you need to get a message across, but you also need to make sure that relationships remain sound. The seriousness of the damage that can be done to relationships by transparency varies from culture to culture.

In some cultures more than in others, it is difficult to separate the *transactional* from the *relational*. Where relationships are damaged by too much transparency (from the viewpoint of the feedback receiver), the feedback may lead to negative feelings and to demotivation. It may thus not only fail to improve performance but even actually have the reverse effect.

Giving individual feedback – both affirmative feedback and developmental feedback – may contribute to improved individual performance in *individualistic, task-oriented* cultures with small hierarchical differences. In very strongly task-oriented cultures, people may see affirmative feedback as superfluous and even insincere. For example, the hamburger approach of surrounding the meat of the developmental feedback with the soft roll of the affirmative feedback will not necessarily be effective. In such cultures, you can often give developmental feedback in a relatively direct and open fashion.

In more *group-oriented* cultures that value *face and harmony*, feedback needs to be given less transparently, so that the face of the individual and the harmony of the group are preserved. In the box that follows, notice that as the feedback progresses down the list, it becomes less transparent and so more likely not to be a threat to face and harmony.

Reducing transparency in the interest of harmony

Talk about a person's actions rather than about the person's shortcomings:
Don't say: *You forgot to deal with south-east Asia in the report.*
Say: *You omitted south-east Asia in the report.*

Use a negative plus a positive verb rather than just a negative verb:
Don't say: *You omitted south-east Asia in the report.*
Say: *You didn't deal with south-east Asia in the report.*

Remove the feedback receiver by emphasizing the feedback giver:
Don't say: *You didn't deal with south-east Asia in the report.*
Say: *I couldn't find the section on south-east Asia.*

Remove the feedback receiver and the feedback giver by emphasizing the message:
Don't say: *You didn't deal with south-east Asia in the report* or *I couldn't find the section on south east Asia.*
Say: *The section on south-east Asia is missing.*

Use down-toners, such as seem, appear, apparently, unfortunately, I'm afraid:
Don't say: *The section on south-east Asia is missing.*
Say: *I'm afraid the section on south-east Asia seems to be missing.*

Another way to reduce transparency in the interest of harmonious relationships is to use blurring techniques.

Blurring techniques	
Blur the receiver:	Give negative feedback to the whole group and not to the individual.
Blur the sender:	Use a third party – a friend or a colleague – to pass on the criticism.
Blur the message:	Talk about a hypothetical case to direct the feedback receiver's attention to the cause of the negative criticism.

(Adapted from Verluyten, 1999)

These techniques can also be used to make feedback more indirect and to reduce the possibility of face-loss.

CASE STUDY 7 Claudia Borges

Read the case and then consider the questions below.

The Individual

Claudia Borges is a consultant based in São Paulo, Brazil. She works for an international consultancy firm with offices in all the major capitals. The office in Brazil was set up just a year ago with a Frenchman in charge – Stephane Morrisot. Claudia had worked previously as a consultant for a local firm specializing in marketing consultancy. Her new role is to advise clients on their business development plans. She is good at her job and already has a strong local network of clients and other agencies. She thought she would be joining a very dynamic international firm with a lot of potential for her career but so far she has been disappointed. Stephane has been very busy, out of the office practically all the time and has not spent much time with her. She is feeling quite isolated and wondering whether she has made a mistake.

The Boss

Stephane has been in the consultancy business for nearly 20 years. The culture of the company is very much 'sink or swim'. He believes in hiring strong performers who can manage their clients very independently. He sees his job as primarily client acquisition and growing the business. He has a strong team who so far are getting excellent results. He is very pleased with Claudia. She has a great network of contacts which he is hoping she can introduce him to.

The Meeting

To Stephane's surprise, Claudia has asked for a meeting with him. She seems quite anxious when she enters his office and starts by nervously chatting about her journey to work that morning. He has a client-call in 10 minutes so he checks his watch. She then plunges into a fairly emotional account of how she feels totally alone and ignored. She seems very embarrassed. He reassures her that she is doing a great job and in the early days the priority is to build the business and therefore there's not much time for anything else. He says he wants to start visiting clients and contacts with her. She listens but starts to disengage and leaves the office quickly saying she is sorry to have taken his time.

Reflections

Claudia: 'He's so cold. All he's interested in is his success. Why does he think I would want to introduce him to my contacts? He needs to get to know me first and understand the culture and the business. A pity, I thought this was going to be a really great job. I need to look around for other options.'

Stephane: 'I hope she didn't mind me being in a rush. She doesn't seem very happy. It's tough, this business. You have to manage on your own. I guess she'll adapt. Head Office have given me some very ambitious targets so we've just got to focus on them.'

Questions to consider

1 Do you think it is partly Claudia's responsibility to ask for more feedback and time with her boss? How could she have handled this session better?

2 Do you think Stephane will be successful in this market?

3 What advice would you give Stephane?

Suggested answers can be found at the back of the book.

Representing

10

This chapter focuses on:

- Why international managers need to represent themselves, their teams and projects inside and outside their organization.
- How cultural factors play a role in the ways this is done.
- How we can develop competence in representing internationally through:
  - making the most of chance opportunities;
  - doing good presentations;
  - managing first contacts effectively;
  - reading body language to make sure your message comes across;
  - representing while socializing;
- Applying the insights of this chapter to a case study.

The importance of representing

Representing means talking about and publicizing the work you and your team do inside and outside your organization in order to promote yourself and the team. In small, local organizations, you don't need to do this. Your colleagues, bosses and partners can see what you do.

When working internationally, what you do can often be less visible to others in the organization. Travelling a lot, working in another culture, managing people virtually all mean that you and your teams are less visible. People do not get a chance to observe what you do. Therefore you need to make sure they know what you do and that you do it well. Of course, they can judge you by your results but it is much more memorable if they can put faces to those results and understand something about the people behind the results. For relationship-oriented cultures this may be absolutely crucial.

We have opportunities to represent when we meet formally and informally but also in the online world through social media (for example, blogs, Facebook, Twitter, etc). Because we are often communicating with people we do not know well, we need to be very skilled.

The skills of representing

Chance encounters

Having just a minute to present yourself and your work to a colleague you meet in an elevator, a contact you make at a conference or trade fair or on some other unplanned, informal occasion is an ideal opportunity to promote what lies at the heart of your work. You need to be ready at any moment to explain who you are and what you do in a few, well-chosen and convincing words.

You have to be particularly skilled at this because of the cultural factors that may make how you do it more or less appropriate. In ascriptive cultures (see Chapter 2) your audience will want to know your job title and maybe even your level in the hierarchy, while in others this would be of no interest.

In more performance-oriented (see Chapter 2), more masculine cultures (see below) you will need to focus on your own personal record of achievement and your contribution to your current project. In other, more feminine cultures you should be more modest, only representing the work of the team, the department or the company. In some cultures, you should mention a few key figures to quantify your successes – turnover, profitability, ROI. In more feminine cultures, this may be considered too pushy and too soon.

Presentations

A presentation gives you a chance to represent yourself and your team more fully. A key cultural consideration will be how long and how detailed the presentation should be. Increasingly, people expect information in small bite-sizes with lots of visualization. However, there are national cultures, for example, task-oriented or uncertainty avoiding cultures, and especially professional ones, where depth of knowledge and therefore also the depth of the content of a presentation are signs of seriousness and competence. We see this most markedly when comparing academic and business cultures. In the latter, the mantra is KISS – keep it short and simple, while academics feel evidence needs to be presented and properly explored.

One way of making your presentation connect with a truly international audience may be to share some personal information which is universally understood – for example, something about your family or private life. This will help the audience to bridge the gap that cultural difference can create. If you are presenting as the only foreigner to a task-oriented, uncertainty-avoiding audience such informality may merely emphasize the difference. Certainly, the Anglo-Saxon light-touch tendency to start with a humorous remark or story will not be appreciated in every culture.

Other opportunities

Telephone-calls and emails can also provide opportunities not only to update your colleagues but also to promote your team and yourself. Social media can also be used to keep people informed of developments in your career and the work of your team. The international manager needs to represent two aspects of his or her identity. In the first place, externally with clients and partners, the corporate identity with simpler and more generic information needs to be emphasized; and secondly, internally with colleagues, messages need to be adapted carefully for different functions and parts of the organization.

Factors that influence representing

Gender

Traditionally, men tend to want to promote themselves and their achievements. Tannen (1990) argues that men talk in order to maintain independence and status. Their focus is on demonstrating knowledge and skills or just giving important information. Women, on the other hand, she argues, talk in order to establish relationships; their focus is on finding similarities and matching experiences. While this may only be a tendency and one which individual men and women may disprove, it highlights a major difference in how the two sexes tend to represent themselves. Some men need to get better at finding what they share with others and women may sometimes need to focus more on the critical piece of information or on self-promotion.

Culture

This difference is not only to be found between the two genders. According to Hofstede (1980, 2001: 279–350) cultures may display comparable differences. He identifies the dimension of *masculinity* in order to describe 'societies in which social gender roles are clearly distinct (ie men are supposed to be assertive, tough, and focused on material success whereas women are supposed to be more modest, tender, and concerned with the quality of life)' (Hofstede, 1994: 82).

In feminine cultures, both men and women are supposed to be modest and therefore may tend to be unwilling to promote and represent themselves. Hofstede (1994: 79) himself, from the more feminine Netherlands, describes an incident in his own early life when he failed to get a job with a more masculine-based organization because of his modesty and lack of self-promotion.

With the concept of assertiveness, Den Hartog (2004: 405) also distinguishes between cultures in a similar way: more assertive cultures tend to value assertive, dominant and tough behaviour. They are cultures in which success, progress and direct and unambiguous communication are valued. They emphasize equity, competition and performance. Less assertive cultures see assertiveness as socially unacceptable and value modesty and tenderness. They tend to value warm relationships, speak indirectly and attach importance to equality and solidarity.

How differences in assertiveness may express themselves in business and management

More assertive cultures ...	Less assertive cultures ...
value assertive, dominant and tough behaviour	see assertiveness as socially unacceptable and value modesty and tenderness
value competition and equity	value cooperation and equality
value success and progress	value people and relationships
prefer low-context communication	prefer high-context communication
build trust on the basis of abilities and calculation	build trust on the basis of predictability

(Adapted from Den Hartog, 2004: 405)

These differing value orientations clearly may affect the ability and willingness of individuals to promote themselves, their work and the work of their team to key organizational influencers. International managers often find themselves sitting between these two cultures. On the one hand, they may try to get members of the team from more feminine, less assertive cultures to be more assertive and represent their achievements more loudly. On the other, they may want members of the team from more masculine, assertive cultures to step back and be less forceful.

Individualism

How far should individuals go in promoting themselves? Older generations were often discouraged from self-promotion and encouraged to be modest about their accomplishments, confident that seniority would bring recognition and respect. Today, in a far more competitive world, individuals in all societies are encouraged to exaggerate or at least not understate their achievements.

You can see this in the writing of a curriculum vitae and in job interviews where candidates identify their strengths or in seminars on 'self-marketing'. Hofstede (2001: 318) points out that job-applicants from masculine cultures tend to oversell themselves and those from feminine cultures undersell themselves too. International managers also need to be sensitive to the organizational culture they find themselves in. Signs of an individualist culture where self-promotion is applauded are 'Employee of the month' competitions or incentive schemes that openly reward individuals for high performance. On the other hand, corporate cultures that disapprove of self-promotion tend to stress the efforts of teams and departments, rather than individuals and only publicly reward individuals for length of service.

Representing internationally

Building the reputation and status of your team, department or company across the globe requires good representational skills and also a flexible approach. International managers need the following in their toolbox:

Corporate information / key facts and figures

You may think that your organization is well-known but often you will be surprised by how little people know about your business or work. You need to have at hand all the key figures such as headcount, turnover, profitability, main products and services, USPs.

Business cards

Business cards are very important when working internationally. Consider having a card with the two sides in different languages (for example, home language or target market language plus English as the language of international business). Business cards in Chinese are a must for those frequently in China. It will be necessary to include your job title and position as well as letters or abbreviations indicating qualifications before or after your name. Also consider including private as well as work contact details. In some cultures the line between private and work life is not distinct at all and private telephone numbers are shared at first meetings.

Brochure/departmental publicity

Organizations usually provide you with general brochures. Consider also producing a small leaflet that explains clearly the structure of your department or project, the main roles and the main activities. With a culturally mixed group of contacts, some will welcome the written word more than the spoken word, not least as a second chance to understand a presentation in a foreign language.

Gifts

As the intention of a gift in a business context is not always explicit – is it a gift or is it a bribe? – gift-giving can be a difficult area for international managers for compliance reasons, especially if they exceed a certain monetary value (usually determined by their organization). However, you should not underestimate the value of small promotional gifts (pens, calculators, umbrellas etc) that remind your contacts of who you are and where you come from.

Dress

How you are dressed will often send a powerful message as to how you want to be perceived. Be ready to adapt to the local culture with regard to the degree of formality of the dress code and the religious constraints on dress.

Tuning into body language

When you are working internationally, communication through language often becomes more difficult and less effective for those who are not using their first language. So, understanding body language becomes more important than at home. Mindful international managers, aware of the importance of focusing on the process of their work, must learn to read the signals communicated in other ways than through language.

Your interpretation of these signals will enrich and support your understanding of the verbal message to create clearer meaning in a complex communication situation. But remember that the non-verbal signals you notice may not have the same meaning as they do in your own culture.

Key competence:
Perceptiveness through being attuned

Being attuned to non-verbal signals is an ability of effective international managers. They are focused on picking up meaning from signals such as intonation, eye contact and body language. They can interpret such signals correctly in different cultures.

Eye contact

Be careful to observe the nature of eye contact which is common in a culture new to you. Westerners should not assume that they must make and maintain eye contact. In some cultures, people hold eye contact; in others, people make eye contact but do not hold it. Westerners should not interpret a lack of steady eye contact as a sign of untrustworthiness. In many cultures, the conventions for eye contact are different for men and for women.

Physical distance between people

Observe the distances people maintain when standing or sitting next to each other. For example, in Latin cultures people may like to stay closer to each other and to have some physical contact. In some other cultures, a greater distance can be maintained and no physical contact made at all.

Facial expression

In some cultures, it is the norm for people to show clearly what they feel – to show that they are happy or upset, by smiling, frowning, and so on. In some cultures, people maintain neutral facial expressions and the preference is for people to hide what they feel. In other cultures, people may smile a lot in order to hide their real feelings.

Greeting rituals

The mindful international manager knows that, in some cultures, rituals attached to meeting somebody for the first time and to greeting business acquaintances are important. This is especially true in settings relatively uninfluenced by international business. You should give greeting rituals time and attention here.

Observe who shakes hands with whom, and who kisses whom, and how many times. In France, for example, the morning greetings at work are important. Managers may go round the office, shaking hands with everyone in the team and perhaps kissing some of them. In some Muslim countries, men and women do not usually shake hands. The importance attached to business cards and the way we exchange them also differ across cultures.

> I'm very informal. But in the Hong Kong context one has to be a bit careful about being informal too soon. Certainly middle-aged Chinese people expect a certain degree of formality to begin with in terms of both address, how you use names, etc., and dress, what you wear and how you hold yourself and so on.
>
> *John Duncan (United Kingdom), educational consultant, Hong Kong*

Of course, as an outsider, you will not necessarily be expected to behave like a member of the culture that you are visiting. But local people may appreciate your ability to adapt to an appropriate extent to local behaviour, especially if you are a frequent or long-term visitor to the place in question.

A more difficult situation is meeting an international group: for example, members of a project team from all over the world – away from your home location – where there is no clear and established norm for greetings.

Representing through socializing and building relationships

Whether we like it or not, socializing is an important part of building relationships and a vehicle for representing ourselves and our team. People may socialize both during and after work. During work, it may be over lunch or a coffee or a birthday cake. After work, it could be a drink, a meal in a restaurant or a larger celebration. Attitudes towards interpersonal distance and therefore also socializing are culturally influenced (see Chapter 2). How much socializing takes place with colleagues and the setting chosen for it may thus differ greatly, not only from culture to culture but also from person to person. As an international manager you need to be sensitive and flexible in this area.

Peaches and coconuts

Peaches have soft outsides which are easy to bite into. Coconuts have hard outsides that can be difficult to crack. In what Zaninelli (1994) calls a coconut culture, colleagues tend to keep their public, work life and their private, non-work life separate from each other. What they regard as public may be much more limited in scope than in a peach culture. Social conversation at work may be relatively rare. People in coconut cultures feel that they should not invade your personal space, either physically or mentally. They may seem unfriendly and unapproachable to peaches but their behaviour aims to express respect for your privacy. You may have to take the initiative in showing that you want to get to know them, even if you are the visitor. 'Coconuts' may thus lose an opportunity for representing themselves and their people by failing to build a more personal relationship with their colleagues or boss.

When a peach meets a coconut

When a peach meets a coconut

Peach   Coconut

(Adapted from Lewin, 1936, Trompenaars, 1993 and Zaninelli, 1994)

On the other hand, in a peach culture, you may be expected to socialize a lot at or after work and even at the weekends. 'Peaches' may see relationships as short-term and their friendliness must not be mistaken by coconuts for a sign of lifelong friendship.

> I try to build up a sort of 'Let's do something after work' whenever possible.
> In the office I'm trying to get to know what they're doing, to get involved in their talks, and now I'm starting to talk Turkish a little bit, only a few words and always try to say a few words in Turkish.
>
> *Luis Ortega (Spain), Henkel, Turkey*

You are more likely to be invited to somebody's home in a peach-like culture. They are usually more willing to share their personal living space with you more quickly. The more peach-like the culture, the more of their lives people will share with you – for example, you may be allowed to move around their homes, sit and talk to them in the kitchen, and help yourself to a drink from the refrigerator. 'Peaches' are also more likely to share personal information about themselves and expect you to do the same – their likes and dislikes, the trouble they are having with their children, even the state of their marriages.

The ability to make small talk or social conversation is a must in peach-like cultures as it helps to build relationships and is what happens during socializing activities. You must not only talk about work.

Analyse how you make social conversation

Assess on a scale from 1 (very little) to 7 (very much) the extent to which you ...

listen for personal information that your interlocutor mentions. Do you refer to it in your contributions to the small talk as a way of connecting with the person?

1   2   3   4   5   6   7

mention personal information in passing which your interlocutor can build on in the same way.

1   2   3   4   5   6   7

seek common ground – experiences, interests, views you share – with your interlocutor.

1   2   3   4   5   6   7

integrate and connect the experiences and views of your interlocutor with your own rather than seeking contrasts.

1   2   3   4   5   6   7

remember that opinions are merely opinions, and not facts which can be right or wrong.

1   2   3   4   5   6   7

ask open questions rather than closed questions.

1   2   3   4   5   6   7

look and sound interested even if your interlocutor is a complete bore!

1   2   3   4   5   6   7

Taking turns at speaking

How individuals contribute to social conversation (and discussions in other settings) varies and is also influenced by cultural factors. Some people allow you to finish before they start to speak. Others speak at the same time. Others allow a moment of silence before speaking.

We tend to make judgements about deviations from our own way of taking turns in a conversation. To some people, interrupters seem pushy, but to others they seem lively. To some people, those who wait to speak seem polite, but to others they seem reserved and even boring.

These different ways of taking turns can be driven by personality, but also by cultural background. Our judgements about turn-taking conventions can be the product of our personality but also of our culture.

Taking turns

In which cultures do you think people tend to take turns in a conversation as shown below?

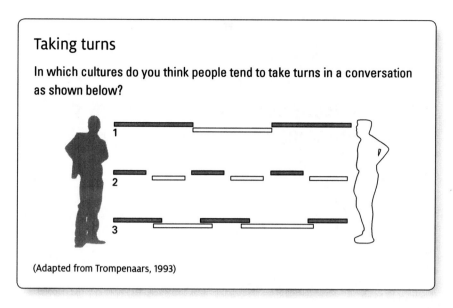

(Adapted from Trompenaars, 1993)

In the first conversation, one speaker waits until the other has finished his or her turn before saying something. Many people consider this polite and think speaking at the same time as the other person is rude. This is the norm in many north-west European cultures and in North America.

In the second conversation pictured above, there is a very short pause between turns in the conversation. People may often talk like this in Japan or parts of Finland, for instance. The third example shows how in some cultures, for example in southern Europe or Latin America, turns overlap – people may begin talking slightly before the other person has finished. People do not think this is a rude interruption.

The ways of taking turns in a conversation that are typical of a culture can lead to negative – and positive – evaluations of a person from a different culture with different turn-taking norms.

What pausers and overlappers may think of each other		
	Positive evaluation	Negative evaluation
Pausers may see overlappers as	lively, dynamic	rude, self-centred
Overlappers may see pausers as	patient, interested listeners	boring, no ideas or opinions

One influence on turn-taking styles could be how people use time. In cultures with a tendency to structure time and do one thing at a time, turn-taking may be structured more formally. In these cultures (as in example 1 above), turns tend to occur without overlapping or pausing. In cultures with a more fluid approach to time, the turns may tend to overlap and people tend to speak at the same time (see example 3 above).

Best practice: Representing yourself, your team, your company

Pushing

This means communicating a strong clear message. It does not allow for discussion or interruption. You need to push when time is short, your listeners are impatient or when you want to convince them with the strength of your beliefs.

To push well, you need a very well-prepared message of which you are totally convinced. The intention is that your audience will hear this and also be convinced.

Pulling

This means building the bridge across which your message will be transported. This bridge could be a relationship formed while socializing. But you can achieve this more simply, for example, by asking questions to understand your audience at a presentation. You need to pull when audiences are not engaged or when you need to understand them better before you communicate your message. By showing you are interested in them, they will be more interested in you.

CASE STUDY 8   Talal Hamieh

Read the case and then consider the questions below.

The individual

Talal, 38, was born in Lebanon. He is the marketing manager for Betafilms in Dubai. His job is to arrange distribution across the whole of the Middle East. He does this through a web of contacts that he and his family have built up. Whether he is in Damascus, Riyadh, Tehran or Cairo, he works with local distributors and negotiates specific deals with each of them. He travels almost constantly and only comes back to Dubai once a month for the management committee meetings.

He has a strong personality and likes to do things his way. Talal has helped make Betafilms a big player in the Middle Eastern market.

The team

Back in Dubai, Ben Matthews has been made general manager of the Middle East and Asia region. This is Ben's first job in the film industry. He has an impressive CV and has held successful positions in marketing and sales for major international companies. Betafilms wants to build on their success in the Middle East and start to break into the fiercely competitive but very extensive film distribution business in India. Ben has taken over an existing multinational team of graduates who look after marketing, sales, communication and who handle all the back-office operations for invoicing, accounting, and so on.

The challenge

Ben's job is to build on the company's success and spread the business to India. He believes that Talal can be the person to help him do this. However, he first needs to understand how Talal works and find out what the business model is that has really worked in the Middle East. He has already brought in a consultant, Rashid, who is advising on the Indian film distribution market.

The meeting

Ben calls Talal back to the office. He introduces Rashid and they present the challenges and opportunities in the Indian market. Talal is very enthusiastic about this and says he already has contacts in Mumbai and Bangalore. He suggests going there next week to talk to them. Ben tries to get him to talk about the contracts, terms and conditions that he will agree with local distributors. Talal is very vague and basically says that these will depend on the particular case. The meeting ends with Talal taking a call from a contact in Saudi.

Reflections

Ben: 'I can't just let Talal go off and start the business in India. We need to have a framework to build on. India is an enormous market. He can't do it all by himself. I need to understand what he's been doing these last five years and then we can start to train up others to support him.'

Talal: 'Ben's just a pen-pusher. He wants systems and numbers but he doesn't understand that the business is all about contacts. I didn't tell him but I've already had an offer from a major player in Delhi. So, if he won't do it my way, I think I may talk to this other fellow.'

Questions to consider

1   Talal is good at representing the company and its products externally.
    How can Ben get him to represent what he does better internally?

2   If Ben cannot persuade him to be a team player and communicate with his
    colleagues internally, should he let him go?

Suggested answers can be found at the back of the book.

Conflict

11

This chapter focuses on:

- Understanding the causes of conflict.
- Understanding personal and cultural attitudes towards conflict.
- Approaches to preventing conflict.
- Approaches to resolving conflict.
- Identifying best practices for dealing with conflict across cultures.
- Applying the insights of this chapter to a case study.

Causes of conflict

One person's conflict is another person's debate. In other words, what people see as a conflict can vary enormously. In this chapter, we mean by conflict a breakdown or turbulence in a working relationship caused by one or more people feeling strongly about an event or an on-going situation. An event could be a meeting in which someone speaks rudely or it could be a failure to do a piece of work that had been agreed on. An on-going situation could be a lack of support in a demanding role or the implementation of change of some kind. These events or situations upset us and engage our emotions. We can feel anger, hatred, resentment or jealousy.

This emotional response differentiates conflict from a misunderstanding or disagreement where it should be possible to distinguish between the reason for the misunderstanding or disagreement and your feelings. However, in some cultures and with some people, a disagreement can often provoke emotion and thus lead to conflict as we define it.

Classically, the setting of a conflict can be of various kinds. A conflict can occur between individuals (interpersonal conflict), within groups (intragroup conflict), between groups (intergroup conflict), within organizations (intraorganizational) and between organizations (interorganizational). In the following examples of conflicts that can occur when working internationally, you can see that international managers are often confronted with conflicts that arise in intraorganizational or intragroup settings.

When working internationally conflicts can be caused, for example, by:

1 Organizational change

Organizational change, in which, for example, an organization is restructured or merged with another, or in which new processes are introduced, is often the cause of a sense of threat or loss. Employees feel they are losing:

- control – as power shifts to another centre;
- professional value – as your area of competence is no longer appreciated;
- identity – as organizations are taken over, merged, renamed;
- security – as futures become more uncertain;
- tradition – as change forces a break with the past.

These feelings of loss are very powerful. They can cause a deep sense of resentment and easily lead to relationships at work being disturbed by negative emotions. International managers who are dealing with organizational change and whose relationships with their reports or superiors are marked by conflict need to show understanding and, where possible, reassure colleagues that they are not forgotten and unappreciated.

2 Cultural differences

Cultural differences can cause conflict because we may find culturally influenced differences in values, norms and behaviour difficult to handle, especially when we are under pressure to perform. Organizations want people from different cultures and professional backgrounds to work together because, as research and experience confirm, this diversity can help them to see tasks and problems from new perspectives and thus create new outcomes, opportunities and solutions.

But, this increased creativity comes at a price – the price of increased conflict. In a large-scale analysis of research into 10,000 teams, Stahl *et al* (2010) confirm that cultural diversity and task conflict (ie conflict connected to issues that are relevant to meeting team goals) go together. Different perspectives often lead to disagreement and this to all the familiar frictional losses – such as different priorities, delays, misallocated resources, withdrawal of cooperation etc. These factors may in turn cause negative emotions, such as anger, frustration and disappointment and turn an objective disagreement into turbulence in relationships and a conflict in our sense.

Surprisingly, Stahl *et al* (2010) find no evidence that cultural diversity in teams is related to relationship conflict (ie conflict stemming from personal antipathies) and process conflict (ie conflict related to methods and procedures for achieving goals). Experienced international managers may find the latter result hard to believe, as we do too.

3 Team dynamics

Tuckman and Jensen (1977) believe that teams go through different stages:

(Adapted from Tuckman and Jensen, 1977)

International managers need to guide their teams through these stages and manage the conflicts that often occur at the storming phase, when team members are struggling to commit to common objectives. In the norming phase which follows, the team should be clarifying the common processes which all team members understand and commit to.

Members of international teams often experience conflict and are therefore dysfunctional because not everybody is at the same stage. Team members miss the kick-off in the forming stage; a team member is silently upset during the storming phase; team members only pay lip-service to the common processes agreed in the norming phase because their own way of working is so different.

4 Individual differences

Much conflict is caused by two individuals having a serious disagreement that leads to emotional responses. The disagreement may be so serious that they stop talking to each other and end up even disliking each other. Perhaps most seriously they fail to trust each other.

Diversity of personality types (see Chapter 3) is considered helpful for high-performing teams but it is difficult working with someone who is different from you, especially when you are working under stress. This difficulty can lead to disturbed relationships. The notion of mindfulness reminds international managers to focus on the process and context of management in order to observe and understand their own behaviour and this insight helps to understand and be tolerant of others.

Attitudes towards conflict

If we do not address the cause of the conflict, the feelings could go away – our emotions could gradually diminish. Or they could remain, slowly eating away at our motivation, enjoyment and performance.

Avoiding conflict

Some people are very skilled at disguising their feelings so it is difficult to see that there is a breakdown in the relationship. Many people do not want to face a conflict – the thought of bringing the conflict into the open is even worse than continuing to suffer from it. Maybe they have found through experience that trying to resolve the conflict can be more damaging than pretending everything is okay. This conclusion may be based on other conflicts they have experienced or on their lack of skill in dealing with conflict.

Facing conflict

Other people believe it is always better to face a conflict and try to resolve it. While the conflict is there, they cannot work or concentrate up to their usual standard. It robs them of their motivation and focus. Even if they may know that it will be difficult or even impossible to resolve the conflict, they try to achieve this because they feel it is better than doing nothing. Unfortunately, if they try without the necessary skill, it may be difficult for them to resolve the conflict. In fact, they could make it worse.

What is your attitude towards conflict?

A colleague arrives late. You are going to miss a travel connection. You feel she has been selfish – she should have called you to keep you informed. *Do you criticize her for being late?*

One of your colleagues in the team is always dominating meetings. You have some really good ideas but you find it difficult to get them heard. You wish the project leader would shut him up. However, you don't believe this will happen. *Do you raise the issue with the dominating colleague?*

Your boss shows favouritism towards a colleague. He gives her a lot of attention and also the most interesting jobs to do. You feel undervalued and more and more resentful. *Do you raise this issue with your boss or someone else, or not at all?*

What *action* we take when we face conflicts is determined by our attitude to conflict and here four fundamental orientations exist, which are pictured in the grid below. At the heart of this picture of orientations to conflict is the question: Are you more interested in satisfying your own interests and needs (self-centred) or those of the other party (other-centred)?

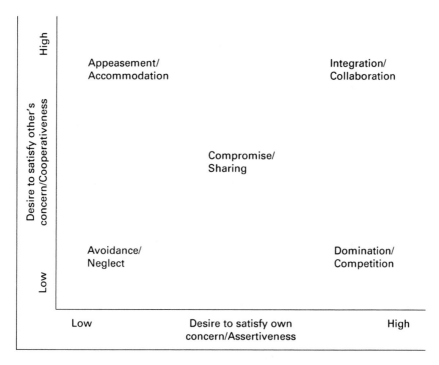

Thomas's 'grid' framework of conflict management orientations
Adapted from Thomas (1976) and Spencer-Oatey and Franklin (2009)

If you have no desire to give in to the other party to the conflict but if you are also not interested in settling the conflict in your own interest, you will be located in the bottom left-hand corner (avoidance/neglect). You will tend to take no action.

If you are prepared to give up and satisfy the other party at the expense of yourself, you can be found in the top left-hand corner (appeasement/accommodation). You will tend to give in to the other party.

Domination/competition (bottom right-hand corner) is an orientation in which you seek to get your own way at all costs and are not interested in satisfying the needs of the other party in the conflict at all. You will tend to fight.

Integration/collaboration (top right-hand corner) seeks to satisfy both parties by applying a problem-solving approach. You will tend to collaborate in the attempt to find a solution which satisfies both parties.

Constructive solutions to conflicts which satisfy strongly perceived concerns of both parties to the conflict will tend to be located between collaboration, which though difficult to achieve may satisfy both parties to a large extent, and compromise, where both parties may be satisfied but to a lesser extent.

How do you prefer to manage conflict?

Think of some work-related conflicts you have been involved in and consider how you handled them. What was your preferred approach? What was your least preferred approach?

Now consider conflicts with your family and friends. What is the order of your preferences in those cases? Is it different from that at work?

Most people have a hierarchy of orientations and choose the preferred approach depending on the particular conflict. This hierarchy may, however, be strongly influenced by culturally influenced preferences.

Culturally influenced attitudes towards conflict

Belonging to a certain culture – national, business or other grouping – helps us to define our identity and gives us the security of belonging to a group. Unfortunately, people tend to define identity in contrast to another group. Finance as opposed to marketing, German rather than American, Microsoft not Apple. This provides the context for much conflict. When cultures are closed to outsiders, they may become defensive and see difference as a threat.

The mindful international manager needs to be careful not to blame cultural preferences for conflict. Often, personality or the situation is much more to blame for a breakdown in a relationship. However, culture does have a large impact on how we *view* and *resolve* conflicts.

Group-oriented cultures tend to view and deal with conflict differently from individualistic cultures. Ting-Toomey (1999) describes how, in individualistic cultures, people usually identify the source of conflict as being personal. They tend to believe that resolution can be achieved through focusing on outcomes that will satisfy the individuals concerned as far as possible.

People from more group-oriented cultures see restraint of personal emotions as key to protecting face and maintaining long-term relationships. This has priority over achieving particular goals in the resolution of conflict. They may also attach a great deal of importance to protecting the face of others, not only their own.

In an interview conducted in Canada, an elderly Chinese man indicated that he had experienced no conflict at all for the previous forty years.

LeBaron and Grundison (1993)

| Assumptions about conflict | |
In individualistic cultures:	In group-oriented cultures:
Conflict is outcome-oriented, ie people in conflict want to achieve goals	Conflict is process-oriented, ie people in conflict want to preserve face before dealing with goals
Satisfying communication in the conflict involves bringing the conflict out into the open and sharing feelings honestly and assertively	Satisfying communication in the conflict involves both face-saving and face-giving and paying attention to both verbal and non-verbal messages
Conflict outcomes are productive when tangible solutions are reached	Conflict processes or outcomes are productive when face on both sides is preserved and substantive agreement is reached

(Adapted from Ting-Toomey, 1999: 202–12)

| Behaviour in conflict | |
In conflicts in individualistic cultures people tend to:	In conflicts in group-oriented cultures people tend to:
express strong personal opinions	express the opinions of the group
display their emotions	restrain emotions
take personal responsibility for the source of the conflict	protect members of the group from being held personally responsible

(Adapted from Ting-Toomey, 1999: 202–12)

Advice for individualists in conflict with people from a more group-oriented culture

- Be patient.
- Listen actively but also reflectively.
- Be prepared to listen to stories that do not seem relevant.
- Use questions that allow your colleagues to help or advise you ('What do you think we should do?')
- Focus on the group, not individuals.

There was a very nasty man called Habib and he found a very small palm tree growing in the desert. He didn't like to see it growing there so he put a large stone on top of it. The palm tree tried hard to survive despite the stone and pushed its roots deeper and deeper until it found water. As a result, it grew and grew to be a very large palm tree. Habib returned some years later. He didn't recognize the tree until he looked upwards and saw the stone perched on its top.

Story told by Khaltoum Feiler during intercultural conflict training

Advice for collectivists in conflict with people from a more individualistic culture

- Be assertive about personal interests and goals.
- Listen actively, especially to the content of the message.
- Clearly indicate responses (positive and negative) and also reasoning.
- Use questions to clarify in order to be more specific.
- Focus on individuals, less on the group.

Preventing conflict through effective and appropriate communication

A lot of communication is email and we all communicate in a language which is not our mother tongue. That can cause problems because you can read between the lines something that was never meant. Maybe someone writes something quickly, thinking it is good English and I read it as a command or a criticism just because of not using the right words. A lot of misunderstanding is possible.

Wibke Kuhnert (Germany), Henkel, United States

When working internationally it is necessary to be mindful of the channel of communication, the style of communication, and the language of communication.

The channel of communication

The most common channel of communication in international business is email; text-messages are also increasingly being used in work contexts. Although both are very efficient, they can also be very damaging when used carelessly. It may be acceptable to write short, sharp emails to local colleagues whom you know well. However, mindful international managers need to realize that short, sharp emails or text-messages can reach your partners abroad at a bad moment, can easily be misunderstood, and lead to negative reactions.

This misunderstanding can have two causes. Firstly, the reduced redundancy of emails and especially text-messages means that context and relationships receive too little attention in the message sent. This increases the potential for misunderstanding and decreases the opportunity for the sender to handle potential damage to the relationship. Secondly, the lack of real-time feedback by the receiver of the message sent also means that the sender doesn't have the opportunity to create understanding and repair relationship-damage as it occurs.

- Do not use email or text messages to communicate complex or sensitive messages or give negative feedback. Send an email to book a telephone call at an appropriate time.
- Never respond to an email too quickly. If you find yourself getting angry or upset on reading an email, take a break. Reply to the email the next day.
- Use the phone more often in order to build and cultivate relationships and also to make sure your messages are getting across.
- Do not send copies of your emails to other people in order to cover yourself. It may display a lack of trust in your partner.

The style of communication

In international work settings, the style of communication becomes very critical to building relationships and avoiding conflict. House (2005) and Holmes *et al* (2011) show that flexibility in communication style is critical to successful international team interaction. When managers work in their home environment, people see them and get to know them – they may be forgiven if they are sometimes very direct or rather bossy. Getting the style wrong when working internationally can be disastrous.

Personal/impersonal

If you are very personal in your style of communication, you may need to vary your style and make sure you can communicate more impersonally – or the other way round. An over-personal approach may not be appreciated by more coconut-like cultures (see Chapter 10). On the other hand, in more relationship-oriented cultures, it may be necessary to focus on the personal.

> The Turkish way of doing business means you have to be close, to know about their personal situation. Then people will listen to you and are open to accepting proposals.
>
> *Luis Ortega (Spain), Henkel, Turkey*

Direct/indirect

If you tend to be direct in your style of communication, you may need to vary your style and make sure you can communicate more indirectly. An over-direct approach may not be appreciated by more indirect cultures (see Chapter 2) and can lead to loss of face, to disharmony and damage to the relationship. On the other hand, in a more direct culture, as an indirect communicator you may need to overcome your default-setting for communication and say more exactly *what* you are thinking and *how* you are thinking it.

> Q: Well, what does 'yes' mean in a Pakistani context?
>
> A: Yes doesn't necessarily mean yes. I don't really know what it means but there are no guarantees. People think the important thing is to have the client and take the problems later on. I was in Pakistan two weeks ago and everywhere in any kind of business they deal like this. They say 'Yes we can do it'. They never say no.
>
> *Sherri Warsi (Pakistan), Integrico, Sweden*

The language of communication

We saw in Chapter 7 some of the problems connected with using English as a lingua franca. Both native and non-native speakers need to realize how powerful language can be. Just one word can set off a conflict.

Compare 'We expected better results' with 'We forecast better results'. 'Expect' is more personal and may suggest that somebody is responsible for 'poor' results.

When using English as an international language, managers cannot afford to be too sensitive about language. They need to use English as a tool but not as a weapon.

Preventing conflict through understanding the context

The mindful international manager needs to understand the often conflicting interests which may exist in any business situation in order to prevent conflict arising.

You may find that in hierarchical cultures, you need to involve bosses directly but discreetly. If these cultures also have a strong group-orientation, they will not want their employees singled out. In international projects it is important to open these channels from the start. The project manager needs to speak to the line managers of all project members before the project starts.

Conflict can often arise as a result of a clash in local and international priorities. A local manager can be pulled in both directions – by his local boss to achieve local targets and by his project leader to achieve international results. If you establish contact with local bosses, this can help avoid conflict arising later.

Resolving conflicts: Some options

There are various ways of handling conflicts, all of which have advantages and disadvantages and which may be more or less appropriate when managing conflicts in particular cultures:

Approach	Advantages	Disadvantages	Appropriate in what kinds of culture?
Ignore	cooling-off possible time heals outward harmony preserved	things may get worse	face-saving high-context group-oriented relationship-oriented
Confront directly	clarity and understanding created those involved find the solution and thus are more committed to it	commitment to process may be incomplete process can be emotional and subjective	low-context task-oriented individualist small power distance
Involve a third party	harmony preserved conflict addressed, even solved	possibly incomplete understanding of the conflict	face-saving high-context group-oriented relationship-oriented
Involve the team	more and better solutions a decision made by a team is strong and not authoritarian	loss of face is possible really critical issues avoided in the group	low-context task-oriented individualist small power distance
Escalate/ appeal to authority	may be effective and efficient in urgent cases	win-lose outcome loser may feel devalued and lose face	large power distance

(Adapted from Bennett, 1995, and Spencer-Oatey and Franklin, 2009)

Approaches to managing conflicts

Ignore

This approach may be the best option if you are working in a culture where this is the usual practice in order to maintain harmony and save face. Consider the advantages and disadvantages of this option. If you feel the conflict is affecting performance, you may need to move on to one of the other options.

Confront directly

This technique is often the first instinct of US or German managers and members of other cultures which value low-context communication. Bring the conflict out into the open and deal directly with the person. Don't involve intermediaries. You may expect people to be frank but in many cultures, people will be unwilling to be so.

Involve a third party

The third party – a colleague or a superior – will talk to the parties individually but not together. This means that the two people who are in conflict do not have to meet together initially. This saves face and maintains harmony.

> So people often try to calm the waters, to do things through a third party or behind the scenes, or just sitting down and talking and trying to solve problems in a spirit of understanding.
>
> *Brian Cracknell (United Kingdom), Language Works, Malaysia*

Involve the team

This approach is used by some Western managers. The group discusses the conflict and together the members offer support to both parties and suggest solutions. People need to handle this option very sensitively. It would not work if individuals feel exposed in the group. There is some risk of loss of face.

Escalate the issue and appeal to authority

This means taking the issue higher up in the organization in order to involve someone with more power and authority. This person then settles the conflict by imposing a solution. People in more hierarchical cultures, where decision-making is always pushed upwards, may favour this approach.

> As soon as there was a conflict, instead of dealing directly with the person, they take it to the boss. And I think they should come and talk to me first and I will try to explain why. The reason they do it is that they want to be on the safe side. They send lots of mails up just to show later on that this wasn't our fault.
>
> *Sherri Warsi (Pakistan), Integrico, Sweden*

Which is the best option?

It is important not to think that there is a single right way to solve a conflict. There are some underlying skills (see below) but there is no universally appropriate approach. You need to reflect on your preferences and those of the people you are working with, observe how others deal with conflict, and extend your range of approaches.

Best practice: Yourself, the others and trust

Reflect on yourself

Effective and mindful conflict management starts with yourself. If you know how others see you, this helps you to understand them and take their perspective.

Key competence: Perceptiveness through reflected awareness

Being aware of how members of other cultures see them is a quality of effective international managers. They understand how their culture influences their attitudes and behaviour and that this may be strange and difficult for the people they work with internationally. They are sensitive to how their behaviour is interpreted by their business partners.

Q: Were the conflicts you experienced related to culture, personality or working styles?

A: It's a good question because you can't always say that the problem is due to the fact that this is an American or a German. It depends so much more on the personality. And so self-awareness, of your own personality, is really important. You need to know how you are perceived, what aspects of your culture you exhibit, and what kind of impact that it might have on other people, and to be open to these things.

Wibke Kuhnert (Germany), Henkel, United States

Display an ability to take the perspective of the other party to the conflict

It may be possible for each side to demonstrate that it understands the position of the other party to the conflict. This does not mean the two sides agree but they must show that they can see why the other side has arrived at this position. Understanding of this kind is the basis of much conflict resolution.

Preserve face – theirs and yours

It is very important to separate the person from the issue – if this is possible, because sometimes the person *is* the issue. If either party feels that the conflict is an attack on him or her personally, it will be very difficult to resolve. In some cultures, indirect and implicit communication is necessary, as we have seen, to maintain face and harmony, especially in public. In more direct cultures, it is possible to be more explicit, but even so, it is important to be aware of *individual* sensitivities.

Build trust

It is possible to resolve a conflict if both parties believe that the other side will keep to the agreed resolution of the conflict and that this will make a difference in the future. The strength of this belief depends on the existence of trust among the parties to the conflict. Trust reduces the uncertainty that naturally occurs in any kind of cooperation or interaction. This uncertainty is all the greater if people come from different cultures or work in virtual teams – or are in conflict!

Ideas about trust vary across cultures: competence, benevolence, integrity, predictability and openness with information are some of the things that can lead to the creation of trust (see Chapter 12). Work at finding out what kind of trust is important for your international partners. If you have built the right kind of trust, it will be easier to resolve conflicts when they occur.

CASE STUDY 9   Gisela Schaefer

Read the case and then consider the questions below

The Individuals

Gisela Schaefer has worked for nearly 20 years for a US company based in Boston. Gisela comes from Hamburg in Germany and moved to the United States to work as an au-pair. She trained as a secretary and is now office manager for a firm of accountants. She is unmarried and lives a very private life that she does not share with her colleagues. She is in charge of five office assistants and reports to the six partners in the business. She is very efficient and has always been central to the success of the firm. She does not have any close relationships at work.

Bernard George is currently the managing partner. He has been with the firm for 30 years. Bernard has always got on well with everybody except Gisela. He finds her very efficient but unfriendly. Bernard wants the admin team to become more client-focused and has recently appointed two new members of the team who accompany the partners to client meetings and look after certain key accounts. He has also reorganized the workplace so the whole admin team now work in one open space. He has noticed that Gisela has become isolated in the office. She sits in her corner, working hard, but without interacting with the rest of the team. She ignores Bernard, does not reply to his emails and avoids meetings when he is present.

The Meeting

Bernard wants to improve the working atmosphere so calls a meeting for all the staff plus two other partners. During this meeting Gisela criticizes him personally for not listening to the staff when they have concerns. She gets upset and walks out of the meeting. The rest of the staff are surprised but put it down to Gisela not feeling well. She does not come into work the following two days.

Reflections

Gisela thinks: 'I can't work there any more. They do not respect me. I have been a loyal employee for 15 years and then they go and appoint two young women to do client relations – we all know what that means! Bernard has never liked me. He just ignores me. He's reorganized the office so that I have a desk in the corner. No respect for me. I am the office manager. I should be in charge of the office, not him. I just can't face work anymore.'

Bernard says to Susan, one of the other partners, after the meeting: 'How can she behave like that? You see what I have to put up with. She doesn't respect me and she sits in her corner all day plotting and upsetting the rest of the team. To be honest, it would be better if she doesn't come back but I fear she will.'

Questions to consider

1 What do you think are the causes of this conflict?

2 If you were Susan, one of Bernard's colleagues, how would you try to resolve it?

Suggested answers can be found at the back of the book.

12

Cooperation

This chapter focuses on:

- Understanding the basis for cooperation.
- Approaches to building and maintaining cooperation.
- Identifying best practices for cooperating in virtual teams.
- Summarising international cooperation best practice.
- Applying the insights of this chapter to a case study.

The basis for cooperation

Cooperating with colleagues from the same culture – be it a national, ethnic or organizational culture – is rooted in a shared context and is usually based on a shared interest, often unspoken. For example, in an organization, this shared interest may be in making that part of the organization successful.

When people cooperate across cultures, it may well be necessary for them to work hard to define a shared context and to develop and maintain this shared interest, especially if local interests compete or conflict.

Building cooperation can be broken down into three phases:

Pre-contractual / establishing contacts

Before you start to work together formally, for example in a joint venture or in a project team, you are likely to meet the people you are going to work with. Your judgements about people can sometimes be made very quickly – you like them or you don't like them; you think they are trustworthy or not, competent or not.

People tend to form these judgements very quickly on the basis of knowledge and experience they have gained – very often largely in their own cultural context. This might be a good guide when judging people from that context but it can easily let you down when you work internationally.

In an unfamiliar context you need to be more flexible in your judgements. It can be wise to wait quite a while before you make up your mind about people who have very different backgrounds from your own.

Key competence: Flexible judgement

Not only flexible behaviour but also flexible judgement is a quality of effective international managers. They are flexible enough not to draw rapid and final conclusions about people and situations they don't know in cultures they don't know. They are willing to question assumptions and stereotypes and revise their first impressions.

Relational

Having made contact with new people, we establish a basis for trusting cooperation through building relationships. And we build trusting relationships to a greater or lesser extent upon, for example, judgements about a person's:

- *Integrity.* Can I trust that the person will behave in accordance with a moral code?
- *Competence.* Can I trust that the person will do his/her job or perform a task well?
- *Consistency.* Can I trust the person will behave in a way I can predict?
- *Openness with information.* Can I trust that the person will share information with me in the same way as I share information with him or her?
- *Reciprocity.* Can I trust the person will help me in the same way as I help him or her?
- *Hospitality.* Can I trust that the person will look after me in the same way as I look after him or her?

In some national cultures, for example, in group-oriented or relationship-oriented cultures, these last two elements may be key. Trust comes when you join the 'in-group' and this may only happen if you show reciprocity and hospitality. However, this kind of behaviour – returning favours, inviting people to lavish dinners, for example – may well cause compliance issues for international managers working in accordance with universalist (see next section) concepts of good corporate governance. You need to be able to adapt flexibly to local expectations while still adhering to ethical management practice, the code of conduct of your organization and the law.

> And you have to allow time for people (in the Middle East) to get to know you, your personality, if they can trust you or not. But when you are accepted you are very rapidly taken into the circle and then you are invited to lunch and dinner... and things really speed up. When you are a member of the circle, it's at a very emotional level that you deal with people. Decisions are then emotionally based, not fact-based as we are used to.
>
> *Thomas Ruckdäsche (Germany), T-Systems, Germany*

Structural

This third basis for cooperation is formal and has a mandatory character. The basis for cooperation on this level is, for example, a contract, the authority of the law and organizational procedures and processes. Members of some cultures share a strong belief in this element of cooperation. They believe that rules and contracts regulate behaviour in a relationship and are there to be followed for the good of everyone.

On the other hand, members of some cultures do not share such a strong belief in the supreme authority of law: perhaps there is no adequate legal system in place or maybe it is corrupt. They tend to believe that there are times when you must obey the letter of the law or a contract but that there are other times when you can ignore it, try to modify it or get round it. These cultures rely much more strongly on relationships based on trust – a handshake rather than a legal contract.

Regulating cooperation

Parsons (1937) describes how in universalist cultures, there is a shared belief that codes and rules – for example, the rule of law, a moral or ethical code, a code of conduct or a contract – should regulate behaviour in relationships and society. These are seen as definitive and exceptions are not really acceptable as they tend to weaken the fundamental system that regulates behaviour. Examples of universalist cultures are the United States and North-West European countries.

The consequences of a universalist tendency in business are predictable. Contracts have great significance, as do lawyers when business people draw up the contracts, and law courts when things go badly. For universalists, the contract regulates expectations and behaviour.

In international management, the desire to systematize becomes stronger and stronger as a company grows larger and more complex: universal, standardized processes are the result. Codes of conduct describing a model of behaviour to be followed in an organization acquire great importance –

not least because they may also embody aspects of the law. Rules governing expected behaviour generated by an international project team also take on mandatory status for universalists.

In particularist cultures, the obligations people have to each other tend to regulate their behaviour towards each other. What Trompenaars (1993) describes as 'the exceptional nature of present circumstances' becomes more important than impersonal codes and rules. Examples of particularist cultures can be found in Southern Europe, the Middle East and Asia.

> Chinese people understand that normally the written rules are not the real rules; the real governing rules are unspoken rules, eg rule of exchanging favours with other people.
>
> *Manager (China), car manufacturer, China*

To particularists, relationships are extremely important in business and management because cooperation takes place most reliably with somebody you know and trust. From a particularist standpoint, a reliable business person is one who is prepared to take account of changing circumstances in a personal business relationship, for example by more readily modifying agreements and contracts.

Universalist cultures	Particularist cultures
Trust placed in codes, systems and models	Trust placed in networks of relationships
People are assigned to tasks	Tasks are assigned to people
Core business focus	Flexible customer focus
Standardization and globalization	Customization and localization
Fairness and consistency	Particular circumstances
Transparency and simplification	Appropriateness and contextualization
Objective measurement of performance	Subjective measurement of performance
Facts convince	Opinions convince
The science of management	The art of management

(Adapted from Trickey and Ewington, 2003)

Building a common culture to leverage diversity

When you start working internationally, in a project team or perhaps on an assignment, you need to start by exploring the diversity – the differences between members of the team. As you go on, you need to establish a common culture (see the mapping, bridging, integrating process described in Chapter 1). This new team culture provides an orientation system that should not view the differences in the team merely as difficulties to be managed but as a potential to be harnessed for the success of the task.

Leadership

The most influential factor in forming a common culture is the behaviour of management. International managers must demonstrate through their behaviour what they believe in. This means that they need a strong set of values that support their behaviour and are communicated to everybody they meet. The values of honesty, transparency and modesty are key values that need to shine out.

Of course, leaders need to have other qualities such as drive, intelligence and an ability to build successful relationships. These help leaders to convince their colleagues that they have the competence to do the job. We look in more detail at the qualities of people leading internationally in the next chapter.

Key competence: Personal autonomy through inner purpose

Effective international managers often have a clear set of beliefs and values which gives them support in cultural environments which may be difficult to handle. These personal values can make them self-disciplined, confident and determined in achieving their goals. They provide them with a sense of purpose and direction, which they pass on to others.

Communication

Leaders need to put in place a strong platform for communicating across cultures. The first step is to agree on a common language – usually English. Whatever language the company or the team chooses as a lingua franca, learning and using a few sentences in other languages demonstrates openness and respect for other cultures and people. It will help you in your relationship building in the team. Do not worry about not being fluent or feel embarrassed by your mistakes.

> **Key competence: Learning languages**
>
> Effective international managers have often been able to learn a number of different languages – especially when they are not native speakers of English. They win the appreciation of their local partners by learning and trying out a few sentences in their language. They enjoy learning and using their foreign languages.

You should never underestimate the barriers that language can create. Some unpublished research of our own at an international company has shown that about a third of problems encountered by international managers can be ascribed to language, a third to culture and a third to task-complexity. Investment in a professional language learning programme is therefore essential for cooperating internationally. Another helpful step is to create a glossary of key terms used in the company (financial, technical, commercial, etc).

> In the past we had some meetings where we gave some clear definitions, a clear terminology. Depending on different countries we have different names for our products, so nobody knew which product people were talking about. So we decided that for this product we use this name. For this reporting, we all use this format. So when people do market research and gave information on market share, etc, to avoid the problem of comparing different types of data, it's important to specify the issue, market share in volumes or percentages, which columns for figures, etc. This makes communication clearer.
>
> *Camillo Mazzola (Italy), Henkel, Germany*

However, even when people have attained an adequate operational level in the common language, there can still be many communication breakdowns. The cause? People are often not willing to admit that they don't understand. Leaders need to work hard to optimize communication – for example, agreed best practice for email, telephone, video conferencing and meetings helps to make communication more effective.

Exchange

People working internationally need to see what it is really like to work in another country. Only when we live abroad do we really start to understand the host culture, our own culture, and other cultures too. Many companies have moved away from traditional expatriation – from head office to local markets – because of the expense and instituted global exchange or rotation policies. These policies transfer employees from one local market to another, from a local market to head office and still sometimes head office to local market. This demonstrates an attempt to take advantage of the diversity that is present in their workforce – as does working in cross-functional and cross-border teams. It can also promote cultural hybridity and the ability to take multiple perspectives in the people who are moved in this way around the world.

Exchange is not just a question of physically moving location. It also provides opportunities for knowledge exchange. Knowledge about markets, products and cultures needs to be shared if an organization is to take advantage of the diversity. Developing a knowledge transfer process, supported by a company intranet, is another key building-block in constructing a common culture.

Best practice: Cooperating in virtual teams

International teams work virtually most of the time. Although the team shares a common goal, it does not share the same office, building or even country. The absence of face-to-face contact means that it is potentially more difficult for team members to cooperate. So what are the challenges of working virtually?

Time

Being based in different time zones from your colleagues is an obvious obstacle to good cooperation but perhaps even more of an obstacle is the different approaches to managing time. We saw in Chapter 2 the big differences between those who manage time in a very structured and linear way and those with a looser and less time-dominated approach. This, in our opinion, creates the biggest challenge for virtual workers. Synchronized online diaries will help but, above all, the international manager needs to agree and get commitment to key milestones and deadlines.

Relationships

There are some people who like to work very independently and autonomously but many more who appreciate the support and encouragement of close colleagues. You don't normally have close working relationships when you work virtually. So, you have to be satisfied with more distant and more functional relationships. This does not mean you should not get to know your virtual colleagues. On the contrary: it is essential for virtual teams also to have at least a minimum of face-to-face contact during the lifetime of the team. However, the relationships that you form will never be the same as those that arise when you work face-to-face.

Very often the virtual world competes with the physical world. In other words, we prioritize the things we need to do for our colleagues who are physically present and put the virtual tasks to the bottom of the list. You should try to avoid this.

Context

When you work together face-to-face, the context is shared as well. We are familiar with the immediate context, for example, with the layout of the offices, but also the external context, for example the weather, the news of the day, the television programme last night. This shared context is like glue in that it binds people together, gives them topics of conversation and a chance to laugh and moan.

When you are working virtually, you should work hard to understand your colleagues' context, at least where they work but maybe even outside in their everyday life. The more you share and understand the context, the more you understand each other and the more you can work well together.

Communication channels

People need to be much more disciplined about how and when they communicate virtually. This means scheduling and preparing for conference calls regularly but it also means keeping more informal channels open such as text messages. For more formal, written communication, email is still the default mode because it is the easiest to handle. It is often not the most effective or appropriate because it can gradually degrade the quality of relationships. Good virtual managers will use all the tools available.

Face to face

Communicating in person is clearly not virtual in character but virtual teams can still and indeed should arrange occasional opportunities to meet. Maximize any opportunity for face-to-face contact. Use it to meet socially as well as professionally as this will cement relationships. It will make for better communication once you are back in your local offices. The kick-off meeting is a particularly important moment in the life of a virtual team. It may be one of the few moments when team members can spend time face to face. It is vital to maximize the use of this time.

Q: How important is the kick-off phase for an international team?
A: It's very, very important. When a team is not performing 100 per cent, the main reasons are lack of time, lack of commitment and a badly prepared kick off. And yet sometimes we don't give enough focus to this.

Camillo Mazzola (Italy), Henkel, Germany

Email

Make sure you do not rely too much on email. Use email for information exchange but not for communication on sensitive topics; use it to book telephone calls – as members of task- and time-oriented cultures may not cope well with unannounced telephone calls. Specify what is the expected response-speed to emails (eg within 24 or 48 hours).

Think about opening the message with some ice-breaking remarks and closing with something more personal, especially when you are communicating with people from relationship-oriented cultures.

Be careful who you copy emails to – do not assume that your colleagues have the same idea of who should be informed (eg your boss, your colleagues) as you do. People can see copying an email to your boss as an escalation of a difficult matter rather than a mere passing on of information.

Telephone

Use the telephone as your main one-to-one relationship-building medium. Especially with members of relationship-oriented or particularist cultures, it is important to telephone regularly and not just when you have something specific to say. This may be difficult for members of task- and performance-oriented cultures to understand and fit into their busy schedules. But telephone calls are vital in keeping channels open.

Before you call, maybe send an email describing some or all of the topics you want to talk about. At the start of a call you haven't arranged in advance, check whether you are calling at a suitable time, perhaps follow with some social conversation and then establish the purpose of the call. Members of task-oriented cultures may assume that an unannounced phone call is very urgent and so may find relationship-building small-talk inappropriate. In such cases, it is better to do without the small-talk and get down to the reason for your call quickly.

Structure the call clearly and end by summarizing any actions or further steps. Send a follow-up email to confirm things in writing if you have any doubts about understanding or commitment.

Audio and video conferences

The skill of facilitating an audio or video conference is very similar to that of chairing a face-to-face-meeting. The difference is that you will need to pay more attention to clear and structured communication:

- **Before the conference:** Prepare carefully making sure you send out documentation and the agenda before the meeting. Connect earlier than the set starting time so that you are already present to handle any issues before the conference starts.

- **During the conference:** Do not assume everybody is prepared and has read the documentation and the agenda you sent out. Go through the objectives and agenda again. Be very precise about the process you are going to use (for example round the table first or listen to one expert first). Use names to invite people to contribute to the discussion and comment on what others say. Actively summarize important contributions and the progress made on topics, for example, highlighting points of agreement and disagreement and underlining decisions made and actions agreed on. Encourage participation and also use the tools the conference platform offers – whiteboard, voting, text box etc. Close the conference with clear action steps.

- **After the conference:** Write any minutes promptly. Email participants with summary of actions.

The quality of video conferences is improving all the time. Use this facility for top-down messages to the team with a chance for response and reaction from those taking part.

Social media

Many virtual teams use a teamspace to post photos and more personal stories. You can also carry out surveys on team development issues – for example planning a trip together.

The team leader could encourage colleagues to write a blog about their work and life on the project. This will help to share the context more but may not be popular with those who see it as too time-consuming.

Feedback

Although you cannot observe your team members working, this does not mean you should not give them feedback. When they reach a milestone, congratulate them; when they write a helpful email, thank them; when they clearly work extra hours, show your appreciation. On the other hand, when they miss a deadline, contact them and get a promise to catch up; when they don't bother to attend conference calls, telephone afterwards to ask why; when they are apparently not putting in much effort, ask them why, tell them what you expect and give them a target to improve.

Make sure you set up formal and informal feedback processes. It is very easy for motivation to drop or for priorities to change when people working virtually don't have the feeling their work (or lack of it!) is being noticed.

Best practice: Cooperating in international teams

Whether you are a team-member or a team-leader you will need to be mindful not only of your tasks but also of the other people in the team.

Tasks

Giving direction (see Chapter 5)

A key driver for cooperation is the commitment to common goals. Sometimes the immediate objective – for example, to reduce costs in your region – can be very difficult to accept. You will only get commitment from local managers if they understand and are part of the larger goal – for example, to build market share in their region.

Organization and change (see Chapter 6)

In many organizations, projects are the main tool for driving through change. International project managers cannot assume that a head-office project will be well accepted locally. They need to address local resistance to change and to involve and engage all parties in a process which is SMART – Specific, Measurable, Achievable, Relevant and Timely.

Clarifying roles (see Chapter 7)

It is very important for everybody to be clear about their role and that of other team members. So it is vital to invest time at the start of an international project in specifying and clarifying roles. You cannot give support or ask for support unless you know what people do and what knowledge they have.

Understanding networks (see Chapter 7)

To get cooperation, team members also need to understand the networks that operate in the different parts of the world. This is not easy as it takes time. Drawing up a network diagram to show your colleagues who are the key members of your network is a good starting point. If you all do this, you should start to see where the networks overlap and also major gaps in the network.

People

Support (see Chapter 8)

Team members can feel very isolated when working internationally. They may also feel they are a long way from where the important decisions are being made. As a result, they may start to think of themselves as small pawns in a much larger game of chess. Leaders need to work hard to communicate clearly, openly and frequently with their team and extended network. They need to understand the high probability of misunderstandings and use all means possible to make sure that people *do* understand each other. They need to recognize that some team members may find some of their work difficult. Be ready to coach them so that they can close the skill gap.

Representing (see Chapter 10)

International teams and especially virtual teams are not very visible. International managers need to promote the work of their teams within the organization. They also need to encourage team members to represent the work of the team locally. Increasing visibility is good for the project and also good for the careers of the team members. Senior management need to know about the challenges and successes of the team. In this way, your efforts can be rewarded.

Handling feedback (see Chapter 9)

We have identified feedback as a basic human need. So you need to establish how you are going to build this into your daily practice. When working internationally it is difficult actually to observe people working and then comment on their work. So you need to encourage your team-members to reflect on their work and to ask your team-members what is going well and what is not. Involvement with the local management team will help in making feedback relevant to the local situation.

Dealing with conflict (see Chapter 10)

Mindful international managers need to be prepared for conflict that will inevitably arise when working under such complex conditions and consider their own attitude towards it. You need a set of strategies to deal with conflict which you can apply according to the situation, the person and the culture.

Effective cooperation consists not only of working together well but also of seeing the benefit of being open to sharing different knowledge, experience and also difficulties.

Key competence: Valuing differences

Effective international managers enjoy working with people different from themselves. They find cultural diversity interesting and valuable and are sensitive to the different perspectives on the world that it creates. They are actively interested in understanding others' values, beliefs and practices and are able to communicate respect for them.

Having understood your differences, you then need to build a common culture that allows you to cooperate successfully and leverage the differences. Your empathy enables you to see things from other viewpoints and to recognize that the cultural diversity present in a group offers the potential for high performance and is not regarded negatively as a threat.

And what is more, you have the ability to tap into this diversity to help the group create new synergetic solutions and options which amount to more than the sum of the parts: 2 + 2 = 5!

Key competence: Synergy through creating new alternatives

Effective international managers are aware that it is necessary to take a systematic approach to getting the most out of international teams. It doesn't just happen by itself! They work at bringing out, understanding and reconciling the different cultural perspectives in the group and at using this potential to create genuinely new alternatives.

CASE STUDY 10   Bracken International

Read the case and then consider the questions below.

The project

Bracken International has set up an international project to increase innovation and speed-to-market for new products. The first phase of the project is finished. Two new products have been developed and test-marketed. In the second phase, these two innovative products will be launched in much bigger markets.

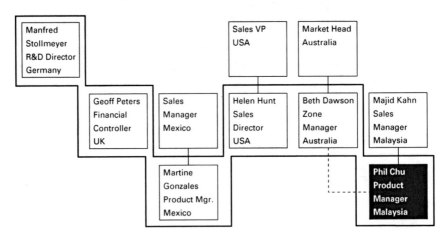

DPI Story ©York Associates 2007

The team

Manfred Stollmeyer: Project Leader. Head of R&D in Mainz, Germany. He is a very good scientist and has learnt quickly to manage this project. He has kept the project on track and has good relations with a couple of the team members – Martine and Phil. However, the more senior team members do not seem to respect him.

Helen Hunt: Head of sales, United States. Helen is a forceful personality. She will be in charge of launching one of the products in the US this year. At times abrasive and self-centred, she has not really made any friends in the project. However, she is good at her sales job and is the only one who can lead this part of the project.

Beth Dawson: Head of Operations in Australia. Zone manager for Phil Chu in Malaysia. She does not get on with Helen.

Geoff Peters: Head of Controlling, United Kingdom, responsible for overseeing the launch of the other innovative product in France this year. Mentor of Phil.

Martine Gonzales: Product Manager, Mexico. Needs to work with Helen in the second phase to support the launch. She ran the test-market in Mexico last year. She does not get on with Helen.

Phil Chu: Product Manager, Malaysia. Needs to work closely with Geoff in the next phase. He ran the test-market for the product which will be launched in France. He works well with Geoff and other members of the team, although he also clashed with Helen in the first phase.

The challenge

They all need to cooperate well if the next phase of the project is to work. Manfred arranged a kick-off meeting at the beginning of the project and this helped the team to get to know each other. He has suggested another face-to-face meeting to celebrate the end of phase 1 and to plan phase 2. Unfortunately both Helen and Beth have said they cannot attend, claiming they have too much work. Helen has told Manfred that she just needs to work with Martine for this next phase and does not need anybody else in the project. Manfred knows that Martine is already not comfortable working with Helen. He feels that the best solution would be for himself to lead this phase so that he can make sure Helen and Martine cooperate successfully. He is very worried about the success of the project.

Questions to consider

1 Should Manfred reschedule the face-to-face meeting so that Helen and Beth can attend?

2 If the face-to-face meeting is not possible, how should he run an audio-conference for the whole team? What would the agenda look like? What should be his objectives for the conference?

3 How present should he be in the United States to help support Helen and Martine? What type of virtual support can he offer them?

Suggested answers can be found at the back of the book.

Leading

13

This chapter focuses on:

● What leaders and managers do and how they differ.

● How different kinds of power lead to different kinds of leader and leadership.

● The nature of leadership.

● 'Doing' leadership and being a leader.

● How leadership may vary from culture to culture.

● What leaders have in common in all cultures.

● Applying the insights of this chapter to a case study.

Managers and leaders – managing and leading

Somebody once said that managers run the shop while leaders change it (or try to). Or to put it another way: managers produce *order and stability in the present* by *handling processes and people*; leaders bring about *change for the future* by *influencing people and organizations*.

These snapshots of managers and leaders show the influence of Kotter's famous distinction between management and leadership, which is described in the exercise which follows.

Managing and leading

Are you more of a manager or more of a leader? Do you do more managing or more leading?

Looking at the full range of your activities at work, indicate the extent to which you do the things listed by circling the appropriate number (1 is to a small extent, 7 is to a large extent).

Managing for stability and consistency

Planning and budgeting:

allocate resources	1	2	3	4	5	6	7
establish agendas	1	2	3	4	5	6	7
set timetables	1	2	3	4	5	6	7

Organizing and staffing:

provide structure	1	2	3	4	5	6	7
assign staff	1	2	3	4	5	6	7
establish processes	1	2	3	4	5	6	7

Controlling and problem-solving:

develop incentives	1	2	3	4	5	6	7
generate solutions	1	2	3	4	5	6	7
put things right	1	2	3	4	5	6	7

Leading for change and movement

Establishing direction:

create a vision	1	2	3	4	5	6	7
clarify big picture	1	2	3	4	5	6	7
decide strategies	1	2	3	4	5	6	7

Aligning people:

communicate goals	1	2	3	4	5	6	7
build teams	1	2	3	4	5	6	7
seek commitment	1	2	3	4	5	6	7

Motivating and inspiring:

inspire and energize	1	2	3	4	5	6	7
empower subordinates	1	2	3	4	5	6	7
satisfy unmet needs	1	2	3	4	5	6	7

(Based on insights from Kotter, 1990, and Northouse, 2010)

Power as the basis for leadership

Some managers may become leaders because their organization gives them *positional power*. That is to say, they take on a particular role in an organization or acquire responsibility for a particular task. For example, they may become head of some functional department. With that they gain the right to reward and sanction the behaviour of others with lower status than themselves in order to fulfil that role or perform that task.

On the other hand, many people who see themselves mostly as managers, perhaps like many readers of this book, may occasionally or often find themselves acting as leaders or being expected to act as leaders. They *emerge* as a leader; they are not necessarily formally *assigned* to be a leader. *Emergent leaders* use this *personal power* to get something done in a team or a project or in permanent work group in a department. They gain this power not through any formal position but through being respected as a good role model or through being liked. Or their superiors and peers see them as competent or knowledgeable.

This kind of leader acquires power as a result of the people he or she leads, their *followers*. Followers recognize over time and through experience and interaction that somebody without formal positional power can nevertheless be influential. Research by Smith and Foti (1998) indicates that followers tend to ascribe personal power to people who are intelligent, dominant and confident about their own performance. Being informed, seeking others' opinions and initiating ideas are activities typical of emergent leadership. These are activities that the mindful international manager may find easier at home than in the international work setting.

The heart of leadership

Leadership is a process aimed at influencing the interaction or the joint, goal-oriented activity of a group of followers. Leaders exert this influence through the actions they perform and through the relationships they build up. This influencing process – how leaders get people and organizations to act in certain ways – varies in nature from individual to individual and especially from culture to culture. Mindful international managers are aware that the cultural values and preferences of the cultures they are working with may mean that leadership in these cultures is very different from their own preferred way of leading. Culturally influenced values may have a significant effect on the exact nature of the influencing process leaders and followers engage in.

'Doing' leadership

So what are the actions leaders take which make up this process? Various models have been suggested to describe what leaders do. The *style approach* suggests a repertoire of styles which are intended to support either task achievement or relationships. The *situational approach* describes styles that are appropriate in certain situations or in interactions with certain kinds of people (see Chapter 7). *Path-goal theory* describes leadership behaviours which are directive, supportive, participative or achievement-oriented. *Transformational leadership* emphasizes idealized influence, inspirational motivation, intellectual stimulation and individualized consideration.

These approaches are just a few examples of many which give an impression of the kind of actions and relationships that may be expected of leaders in the influencing process which is at the heart of leadership.

Being a leader

Although the view of leadership as an influencing process consisting of actions and relationships suggests that anybody doing the 'right' things can be a leader, followers in fact often identify an effective leader as somebody who has a set of personal characteristics or traits which make him or her a good leader. The research, theorizing and experience of many decades – most of it stemming from the United States and the United Kingdom – have produced often unhelpfully long lists of traits which a good leader should have.

Being a leader

To what extent would you say you possess any of the following leadership traits? (1 means to a small extent, 7 means to a large extent)

Achievement	1	2	3	4	5	6	7
Alertness	1	2	3	4	5	6	7
Cognitive ability	1	2	3	4	5	6	7
Confidence	1	2	3	4	5	6	7
Conservatism	1	2	3	4	5	6	7
Cooperativeness	1	2	3	4	5	6	7
Dominance	1	2	3	4	5	6	7

Drive	1	2	3	4	5	6	7
Extroversion	1	2	3	4	5	6	7
Influence	1	2	3	4	5	6	7
Initiative	1	2	3	4	5	6	7
Insight	1	2	3	4	5	6	7
Integrity	1	2	3	4	5	6	7
Intelligence	1	2	3	4	5	6	7
Masculinity	1	2	3	4	5	6	7
Motivation	1	2	3	4	5	6	7
Persistence	1	2	3	4	5	6	7
Responsibility	1	2	3	4	5	6	7
Self-confidence	1	2	3	4	5	6	7
Sociability	1	2	3	4	5	6	7
Task knowledge	1	2	3	4	5	6	7
Tolerance	1	2	3	4	5	6	7

(Adapted from Northouse, 2010, Stodgill, 1948, Mann, 1959, Stodgill, 1974, Lord *et al*, 1986, and Kirkpatrick and Locke, 1991)

Five traits seem to appear regularly in such lists: intelligence, self-confidence, determination, integrity and sociability. Such traits may well be intuitively reasonable, also in the international context, but are not especially insightful. Would you want a leader to be the opposite of these things: unintelligent, diffident, easily discouraged in the face of difficulty, lacking in integrity and a loner?

Such lists of traits are also not useful for people who want or have to develop leadership competencies. The traits mentioned are just that – personality characteristics rather than learnable behaviours. This approach to leadership competence is particularly problematic when we consider what we know about leader-effectiveness across cultures. They also don't take account of the variety of situations in which leadership has to be exerted.

How leadership may differ from culture to culture

Organizational culture clearly influences leadership behaviour but in this chapter we want to focus on how national and ethnic culture may impact on preferred leadership approaches.

The GLOBE Study on Global Leadership & Organizational Behavioural Effectiveness (House *et al*, 2004) investigated the value orientations (what should be) and practices (what is) among 17,000 middle-managers in 62 societies. In particular, the study found out what attributes caused individuals to accept and respond to others as leaders. The investigators were guided by the theory that people have implicit beliefs about what makes leaders different from non-leaders and effective leaders from ineffective leaders.

The study generated six global leadership dimensions, which mindful international managers need to be aware of because their own 'default' preferred leadership style may well be different from that of their followers.

The GLOBE Study leadership dimensions:

- *Charismatic/value-based:* inspirational, motivating, expecting high performance based on core values. Being visionary, self-sacrificing, trustworthy, decisive, performance-oriented.
  Valued most in Anglo cultures and least in Middle East cultures.

- *Team-oriented:* emphasizes common purpose. Being collaborative, integrative, diplomatic, not malevolent, administratively competent.
  Valued most in Latin American cultures and least in Middle Eastern cultures.

- *Participative:* involves others in making and implementing decisions. Being participative and non-autocratic.
  Valued most in Germanic cultures and least in Middle East cultures.

- *Humane-oriented:* emphasizes supportiveness, consideration, compassion, and generosity. Being modest and sensitive.
  Valued most in south Asian cultures and least in Nordic cultures.

- *Autonomous:* independent and individualistic. Being autonomous and unique.
  Valued most in Eastern Europe and least in Latin American cultures.

- *Self-protective:* Ensures the safety and security of the group and leader. Being self-centred, status-conscious, conflict-inducing, face-saving and procedural.
  Valued most in Southern Asian cultures and least in Nordic cultures.

(Adapted from House et al, 2004)

These leadership dimensions are motivated or driven by a set of different values or preferences, many of which we have elaborated on in earlier chapters. In the table that follows a plus sign indicates a significant positive relationship between the leadership dimension and the value mentioned, and a minus sign a significant negative relationship. That is to say, in the first line of the table the plus signs would suggest that charismatic/value-based leadership, participative leadership and autonomous leadership may tend to be found in cultures that attach importance to performance-orientation whereas the minus sign in the second line would suggest that autonomous leadership would tend not to occur in a culture in which group-orientation is valued.

The connection between culturally influenced values and preferred leadership dimensions established by the GLOBE Study scholars makes it possible to place leadership dimensions in the order of their preference in particular clusters of cultures.

> For example, hierarchy plays a big role. In Scandinavian countries it is no problem that a direct report of the CEO becomes his project leader, whereas in African countries where I have been working recently, this is impossible.
>
> *Torsten Weber (Germany),*
> *Management Consultant HLP, Germany*

> The man who is at the top gets our support because he is at the top. Whether he's wrong doesn't come into it. We must follow him. That would be the first thing I would say. The leader is everything, so get to know the leader, his approach, his thoughts and so on.
>
> *Brian Cracknell, (UK),*
> *MD of Language Works, Malaysia*

> I would say that in Germany it's easier to create a team with a solid hierarchy. For Germans, if there is a hierarchy, there is a push to work in that team because the authority has more influence in German guys. In Latin guys, hierarchical pressure is less important so you must have more and more charismatic leadership because the hierarchy is not enough.
>
> *Camillo Mazzola, (Italy),*
> *Marketing Director Henkel, Italy*

Unsurprisingly, the GLOBE Study (Dorfman *et al*, 2004: 678) found that leaders who are irritable, egocentric, loners, non-explicit, asocial, dictatorial, ruthless and uncooperative are disliked and regarded as ineffective. These are attributes to be found. Amongst others in the *self-protective* and the *autonomous* leadership dimensions.

More interestingly, there was considerable disagreement on what attributes were regarded as desirable. This list of attributes is important as it contains quite a number which many people would intuitively regard as likely to be attributes of an effective leader in every culture, for example compassionate, enthusiastic, orderly, sincere. But the study showed that this is not the case.

The value drivers of the GLOBE leadership dimensions

	Charismatic/ value-based	Team-oriented	Participative	Humane oriented	Autonomous	Self-protective
Performance orientation (see Chapter 2)	+		+		+	
In-group collectivism (see glossary)	+	+				
Institutional collectivism (see glossary)					−	
Gender egalitarianism (see Chapter 2)	+		+			−
Uncertainty avoidance (see Chapter 5)		+	−	+		+
Humane orientation (see glossary)			+	+	−	
Assertiveness (see Chapter 10)				+		
Power distance (see Chapter 2)	−		−			+

(Adapted from Javidan et al, 2004: 46–48)

Order of preference for the GLOBE Study leadership dimensions in selected cultural clusters

	Charismatic/ value-based	Team-oriented	Participative	Humane oriented	Autonomous	Self-protective
Anglo	1=	2=	1=	1=	2=	3
Confucian Asia	2=	1=	3	2=	2=	1=
Eastern Europe	2=	2=	3	2=	1=	1=
Germanic Europe	2=	2=	2=	2=	1	3
Latin America	1=	1=	2=	2=	3	1=
Latin Europe	1	2=	2=	3=	3=	2=
Middle East	3=	3=	3=	2=	2=	1
Nordic Europe	1=	2=	1=	3=	2=	3=
Southern Asia	2=	2=	3	2=	2=	1
Sub-Saharan Africa	2=	2=	2=	1	3	2=

1 indicates first-preference leadership dimension, 2 indicates second-preference leadership dimension etc.
(Adapted from House et al, 2004 and Northouse, 2010)

These so-called culturally contingent attributes, which some cultures regarded as positive and some as negative, are to be found in the *participative*, *humane-oriented* and *autonomous* leadership dimensions.

Leadership attributes that some cultures regard positively and some regard negatively		
Anticipatory	Habitual	Risk-taker
Ambitious	Independent	Ruler
Autonomous	Indirect	Self-effacing
Cautious	Individualistic	Self-sacrificial
Class-conscious	Intragroup competitor	Sensitive
Compassionate	Intragroup conflict avoider	Sincere
Cunning	Intuitive	Status-conscious
Domineering	Logical	Subdued
Elitist	Micromanager	Unique
Enthusiastic	Orderly	Wilful
Evasive	Procedural	Worldly
Formal	Provocateur	

(Adapted from Dorfman *et al*, 2004: 679)

What leaders have in common across cultures

The GLOBE Study also discovered what attributes are regarded in all cultures investigated as desirable. We have reproduced them in the exercise that follows. These attributes are to be found in the *charismatic/value-based* and the *team-oriented* leadership dimensions. So it could be said that these two leadership dimensions are those that are likely to be welcomed by most followers regardless of their culture of origin.

Leadership attributes which are regarded positively in all the GLOBE Study cultures

To what extent would you say your foreign colleagues, superiors, reports, etc see you as the following?

Administratively skilled	1	2	3	4	5	6	7
Communicative	1	2	3	4	5	6	7
Confidence builder	1	2	3	4	5	6	7
Coordinator	1	2	3	4	5	6	7
Decisive	1	2	3	4	5	6	7
Dependable	1	2	3	4	5	6	7
Dynamic	1	2	3	4	5	6	7
Effective bargainer	1	2	3	4	5	6	7
Encouraging	1	2	3	4	5	6	7
Excellence-oriented	1	2	3	4	5	6	7
Foresight	1	2	3	4	5	6	7
Honest	1	2	3	4	5	6	7
Informed	1	2	3	4	5	6	7
Intelligent	1	2	3	4	5	6	7
Just	1	2	3	4	5	6	7
Motivational	1	2	3	4	5	6	7
Plans ahead	1	2	3	4	5	6	7
Positive	1	2	3	4	5	6	7
Team-builder	1	2	3	4	5	6	7
Trustworthy	1	2	3	4	5	6	7
Win-win problem-solver	1	2	3	4	5	6	7

(Adapted from Dorfman et al, 2004: 677)

There are a number of problems with the implicit conclusions of this study. Firstly, the results describe what leaders across cultures should *be* like rather than *how* leaders should *behave* or what they should *do*. This is not very useful for managers wanting to develop a portfolio of international leadership behaviours and competencies. Secondly, even if they can know, for example, how to build confidence or display trustworthiness in behaviour in their own culture, doing these things there may be very different from how it is done in another culture.

So in their influencing role as leaders, mindful international managers may very well be best advised to develop those competencies that are crucially connected with influencing effectively and appropriately in international contexts: developing a wide *range of styles* to communicate in (see Chapter 7), *rapport* competencies (see Chapter 3) to build and cultivate relationships and a *sensitivity to context* (see Chapter 5).

Key competence: Influencing by using a range of communication styles

One aspect of influencing that is important for effective international managers is the ability to select from a range of styles an approach which best suits the situation, the people and the cultures in question. They are able to analyse their interlocutors' preferred communication style and tune into their wavelengths. They can thus use a style that their interlocutor feels comfortable with. They have a broad repertoire of communication styles with the result that they can communicate effectively and appropriately with people from different cultures and backgrounds.

Key competence: Influencing through rapport

One aspect of influencing which is important for effective international managers consists of the ability to express warmth and attentiveness when building relationships. They make the other person feel comfortable and at ease. They are able to build personal as well as professional connections with the people they work with. This helps them to empathize with their interlocutors and to understand their perspective better. With time they are thus better able to enlist the cooperation and support of their colleagues in achieving their professional goals.

CASE STUDY 11   Leila Mehmet

Read the case and then consider the questions below.

The individual

Leila Mehmet is Lebanese by birth. However, she was brought up and educated in Switzerland. After studying natural sciences at university she joined a pharmaceutical company based in Geneva. For four years she worked in their clinical trials department organizing international trials for new drugs. Three months ago she was promoted to be a team leader. She is now in charge of a team of people who were her colleagues. This is a difficult transition for her but she is ambitious and keen to be an effective leader of the team. Leila is considerate, quietly spoken, clear thinking, determined and demanding of herself and her team members. Most of the team have accepted her but one, Regina Sasser, who does not accept Leila's authority.

Her team member

Regina Sasser is Swiss and the same age as Leila – 29 years old. She is also ambitious. When they were just colleagues in the same team, they got on. They were not friends but they worked well together. Regina cannot understand why Leila was promoted. In her opinion, Leila is too quiet and not assertive enough to lead the team. Leila is very well liked by the rest of the team and in fact by most people in the company. Regina, on the other hand, is a more abrasive individual. She is well respected but not liked by quite a few people.

The culture

The company is the Swiss subsidiary of a German company. The leadership style in the head office is traditional – classic command and control. However, in the Swiss office the style is much more participative, encouraging employees to take responsibility and in the belief that they can work autonomously, without direct supervision. Business is not going well and the German head office has recently 'parachuted' in some senior managers to take over key departments in Geneva.

The incident

During a team meeting, which Klaus Kinsky, the German head of department (Leila's boss) is also attending, Regina behaves disrespectfully towards Leila. She ignores Leila's attempts to facilitate the meeting in an ordered and considerate way. She takes over and presents a strong argument for reorganizing the department. The head of department seems impressed by her ideas. Leila feels very disappointed by both her boss and Regina.

Reflections

After the meeting:

'That was humiliating. Regina showed no respect for me and just took over. She clearly did it to impress the boss... he seemed quite impressed. I must talk to Regina.' (Leila)

'That went well. I'm glad I got the opportunity to present my ideas. I know I jumped in but the meeting was going nowhere so I thought I should just take the chance while Klaus was there.' (Regina)

'That was a strange meeting. Leila was in charge doing things well and then suddenly Regina took over. She had some interesting things to say but Leila should have interrupted and made her wait till the right time.' (Klaus)

Questions to consider

1 If you were Leila, how would you deal with Regina – during the meeting and after?

2 Does Leila have to adapt her leadership style to this situation – a tough economic climate, a German boss and a disrespectful team member? If so, what should she change?

Suggested answers can be found at the back of the book.

Case study answers

Case study 1: Nora Lundquist

Possible answers

1. Nora has her way of doing things but this is not working in this new international environment. When she started on the project, she needed to keep an open mind and observe how the others behave and communicate. Then she needed to adapt her quiet and thoughtful style to this new environment. This does not mean changing her character but learning some skills which help her to be more proactive in her communication. She is suffering from a sort of culture shock where she can't find her place. If she can be less demanding of her role in the project, she can still appreciate the experience and learn from it. She could speak to Sam about him actively involving her more.

2. Sam doesn't seem to have gone through the 'mapping' stage at the start of the project. It is very important for all to understand who they are working with, their backgrounds and their strengths. In the first face-to-face meeting, he needed to spend time mapping the diversity in the group in terms of knowledge, experience, culture and personality. He needed to sell this diversity to the group so they all see it as an advantage. He could also establish some best practice during virtual and face-to-face meetings where there is an opportunity for all to contribute. He seems to be saying that it is up to the participants to find their place in the team but this is his responsibility as well. Now that they are some way into the project, he could include a 'feedback and lessons learnt session' during the next meeting. He will need to structure the feedback so there is a chance to recognize the positives as well as the areas for development. Following this team feedback, he can then more actively manage the communication in the team.

Case study 2: Laurence Berger

Possible answers

1. Barry is obviously a key obstacle. It only takes one person in a team to make cooperation difficult. Laurence has two choices: she can confront the issue or hope that it goes away in time. We suggest that she discuss the best course of action with her boss. She may find a bridge to Barry once she gets to know him. Certainly she needs to involve him in the objectives of the team and also to help him to recognize and take the opportunities he still has for promotion and success in the company. He seems to feel at a disadvantage because he doesn't have a command of foreign languages and doesn't have international experience. If Laurence picks up on this, she could downplay the importance of languages in the company but stress the importance of engaging with the bigger picture in Frankfurt.

2. She could do a SWOT analysis with the whole team to give them all a shared perspective on where they stand and what they need to improve. This will be a chance to build on their strengths but perhaps also highlight their lack of understanding of the international dimension. This dimension may be seen as a threat by some members of the team. Laurence has to convince them it is an opportunity. Once they can see the opportunities, holding the next meeting in Frankfurt (subject to budget) would help to reinforce her vision of what the team can achieve and also contribute to the work of the rest of the finance department.

Case study 3: Phil Carey

Possible answers

1. Phil needs to reflect on his own personality. His friendliness is a great asset but maybe he needs to adapt to the 'colder', more coconut-like culture of WFC. He also needs to reflect on the differences between his way of doing things and the norm in WFC. His up-beat, can-do style may clash with the more neutral style of WFC. He should make the bridge between the Matty CRM system and WFC's and show how they can be integrated.

2. Judging by the feedback, Phil needs to develop more transparency and a wider range of communication styles. More transparency means remembering that he is a native speaker of English; none of the rest of the team are. So he needs to be very careful in his use of language and in the way he communicates: he may need to speak more slowly and clearly, structure what he says, highlight important points and also check that his listeners

have understood. His range of styles could extend to more engagement with the group as he talks rather than waiting until he has finished.

Case study 4: Pierre Menton

Possible answers

1. Fred will not be able to make these changes successfully without engaging with the people in the French plant. This means visiting them, getting to know them and planning the changes together. Otherwise, he is likely to find himself and the company in a major industrial dispute. Pierre could be the one to help him but again he needs to get to know him so that Pierre can start to trust him. He also needs to understand how difficult it is for Pierre to speak in English over the phone. Perhaps Fred should adapt the way he speaks. Maybe he could even try out a little of his largely forgotten French!

2. Pierre needs to buy more time to consider the offer and the plan. He should persuade Fred to visit and then start to build a relationship with him. He needs to show Fred what the French plant does well and involve his colleagues in a discussion with Fred about the best way forward.

Case study 5: Sun Mei Ling

Possible answers

1. Sun Mei Ling needs to observe and reflect on the differences between Helga's way of working and hers. Sun Mei Ling is used to working in a very top-down bureaucratic government lab where initiative was not encouraged. She is used to following orders and delivering results day to day. She is not used to working towards longer-term objectives and to being given lots of autonomy. She could start by talking to Chinese colleagues with more experience of working internationally and get more insights into Helga's more bottom-up management style.

2. Helga needs to demonstrate to Sun Mei Ling that she is interested and committed to China and not just another expat here to make her mark and move on. She needs to demonstrate a willingness to learn about the Chinese way of doing things. She needs to make Sun Mei Ling feel part of a team and not leave her so much on her own. This may compromise or delay her objective to be out doing external networking, but she needs to invest time in getting the right balance between direction and support for Sun Mei Ling. She also needs to get the message across to Sun Mei Ling that she (Helga)

has Sun Mei Ling's best interests at heart. She wants to help her grow and develop new skills so that she can work successfully in a Western company in China and feel content there.

Case study 6: Nguyen Binh

Possible answers

There are a number of options for Zhang to consider:

1 Training course on sales administration.
2 External local coach to support Nguyen.
3 Ask Malik to act as a mentor to Nguyen.
4 Visit Nguyen as soon as possible and restart the coaching process.

Zhang needs to spend time with Nguyen before he takes any further action. He needs to show that he appreciates Nguyen's success and to ask Nguyen about the market and the types of customers he is dealing with. Then they can talk about why the reports are so important. Maybe he can tie Nguyen's bonus partly to the reliability and quality of the weekly reports. He needs to coach Nguyen about the completion of the reports, so they should sit together and complete a report. This face-to-face coaching session then needs to be followed up with regular calls to give feedback on the weekly reports. It may also be a good idea to ask Nguyen whether he would like Malik to mentor him for the next year.

Case study 7: Claudia Borges

Possible answers

1. Claudia will meet many bosses like Stephane. She either has to live with their style or change it. She needs to help Stephane set up a framework for more involvement and therefore motivation. She could start by requesting a regular individual feedback-session every month to discuss clients and difficulties. It won't help if she shows her emotion. She needs to be professional at all times with him and confront him with some clear steps to get better performance.

2. Stephane may get good results in the short term but he will demotivate and lose team members over the medium term. Consultancy companies are notoriously performance-oriented but this does not mean they can ignore the sources of long-term performance – loyalty, commitment, involvement etc.

3. He needs to support and give feedback to his team, Claudia especially. He needs to build a culture of feedback where he encourages feedback all round. He does not seem very mindful. In other words, he pays little or no attention to the processes of work. He needs a structure of team meetings and one-to-one meetings in which he can gauge performance and motivation.

Case study 8: Talal Hamieh

Possible answers

1. Ben needs to persuade Talal that there are two sides to his job. To represent the company with customers and partners but also to represent what he does internally. The latter is important if they are going to grow the business as knowledge and competence must be shared. Talal may not accept this but Ben needs to try. Perhaps he can incentivize Talal by giving him not only sales targets but internal development targets. The question is whether Talal wants to be more than a one-man band.

2. This is a very difficult decision. How does he manage someone who does not want to be managed? Talal is obviously good at representing the company and it would be a pity to lose this expertise. On the other hand, Ben's job is to build up expertise in the team so that they can develop the market more systematically. Maybe Talal could have a role as a consultant, rather than an employee.

Case study 9: Gisela Schaefer

Possible answers

1. Gisela is feeling a strong sense of loss – loss of control, power and respect. She feels ignored. Her isolation from the rest of the team means she feels alone and unsupported. She is resentful of the new young women who have been appointed to do client-relations. She does not like Bernard because he does not talk to her and listen to her advice. Even though she has been in the United States a long time, the difference between how she was brought up to work – maintaining some distance, not getting too close to colleagues (see peach and coconut in Chapter 10) – creates a lot of tension with the way her colleagues like to work.

Bernard cannot understand why Gisela won't fit in and be one of the team. He wanted to create the open space to make sure the team interacted better. In fact, it seems to have made Gisela remove herself even more. Bernard feels

Gisela does not show the respect that is due to him as a partner. As far as he is concerned, the firm needs to get rid of her.

2. Susan needs to reflect on the cause of this conflict and also the best outcome that can be achieved. Gisela has been a loyal employee and deserves to be given the chance to find a place at work that satisfies her and the rest of the team. On the other hand, Susan herself cannot tolerate a long-term conflict between a member of staff and one of the partners. She needs first to talk to Gisela, listen to how she feels (if she is prepared to tell her). Then she needs to talk to Bernard so that she understands how he feels and give him a chance to better understand Gisela. She could then go back to Gisela and explain what the firm needs to continue operating successfully. When Gisela and Bernard are ready, she needs to sit them together and give each a chance to talk positively about the future and how they are going to work together. Bernard may need to open up a more regular channel for communication. Gisela needs to participate more positively in the work of the team.

Case study 10: Bracken International

Possible answers

1. Organizing face-to-face meetings for virtual teams can be almost impossible. Manfred is not Helen's and Beth's line manager so he cannot insist. He can only try to influence them. With time short, he might be best advised to kick off with an audio conference and then make sure he visits the US and meets with Helen and Martine as soon as possible.

2. The audio conference would be a chance to capture the lessons learnt from the first phase of the project and make sure they follow agreed best practice in the second phase. He should email all members of the team and ask them to identify what went well and what did not go well in the first phase. He can then collate these and present them on a slide. He needs also to state clearly the objectives of the conference:

- To celebrate the successful test-market results and in particular work on Martine and Phil.
- To learn lessons from the first phase which will help guide them through the second phase.
- To agree on the direction, organization and roles for the second phase and also to put in place effective support and feedback processes.

3. He needs to schedule regular trips to the United States (perhaps once every two months). In-between, he can have regular calls with the two individuals and also conference calls with all three. Given the history of the first phase, he needs to develop Helen's ability to work internationally. She probably needs incentives to see the benefit of this project to her career.

Case study 11: Leila Mehmet

Possible answers

1. Leila is in charge of the process of the meeting – she is the facilitator. In this case, she needs to insist on respecting this process. Therefore she should make Regina wait her turn. After the meeting, she needs to speak to Regina one-to-one. She should outline her expectations of team performance and behaviour and ask Regina if she is prepared to meet these expectations. Regina may agree or simply not engage on this issue. In any case, Leila needs to set a deadline with Regina at which the team cooperation will be discussed again. If there is no improvement, she will need to move towards a more formal warning.

2. Leila certainly needs to respond to the changing context. If business is not going well, she and her colleagues will be under more pressure to perform. She needs to emphasize the task orientation so that everybody can see a clear way forward. However, it would be a mistake to stop supporting and listening to her team members. We would suggest more frequent communication with team members to keep them informed and involved. With her new German boss, more formal reporting on a regular basis will probably be appreciated.

Situational judgement commentaries

1. Poor performance

a. Meet him individually and set him some clear targets for improved performance and then, if he does not achieve them, give him a formal warning of proposed dismissal?

This action fits with a culture that has a high performance-orientation and is more individualistic than collectivist. You are seen to be following the rules and applying them fairly. However, you may find that this straightforward approach backfires if Doug is protected by the unions or will respond with claims of discrimination because of his disability.

b. Organize a team meeting in which the whole team commits to annual objectives and tasks, including Doug and wait to see if he fulfils his tasks?

This approach is still performance-oriented but tries to use the strength of the collective to oblige Doug to conform to the behaviour and performance of his colleagues. It leaves the outcome open which gives you the flexibility to respond as the situation develops.

c. Talk to your boss about Doug, agree on a joint strategy for dealing with his poor performance?

This option presupposes you have a supportive boss who is happy to be consulted on these issues. The culture of your organization may encourage this 'escalation' in difficult situations or your boss may feel it is up to you to deal with it.

d. Follow the advice of your predecessor and do nothing?

This is a poor decision, inviting more problems and indicating to Doug and your other team members that you do not have the strength of mind to face up to the issue.

e. Talk to your HR department about the legal requirements for dealing with poor performance and then follow them strictly?

This option is advisable in cultures in which labour relations are guided by laws and importance is attached to the rule of law. It is a hands-off approach passing responsibility to another department.

2. A rude boss

a. Wait some more weeks to observe and reflect on how he is working?

This is a good option in that you may find that you are wrong about how you have judged this situation. It could be that this sort of direct critical communication is expected in this culture. This still raises the issue of a company code of good leadership but maybe you need to accept a local variation.

b. Talk to other colleagues in the department to see what they think? This will be difficult as they are all Chinese and only a few speak English.

This option is full of risk in that the boss may feel undermined if you do this. The colleagues may also be embarrassed to be asked to comment on their boss.

c. Talk to your boss back in the head office about the behaviour and ask for his advice?

This option depends on the culture of your organization. If it is a 'sink or swim' culture, your boss back home may see this as a sign of weakness or insecurity on your part. On the other hand, in a supportive culture, this request for advice would be appreciated.

d. Talk to Liu and ask him why he seems so upset with his workers?

This is a high-risk option as he may feel a loss of face. He may also feel it is not for you to judge him. Perhaps there will be a chance to have less threatening discussion about leadership at some time.

e. Accept the behaviour as different and the way things are done locally?

This may be acceptable but it is a passive option that may not help you to establish a clear framework for international leadership.

3. Corruption

a. Explain to Igor that there are strict ethical guidelines and so you can no longer invite him and his family?

This is a very direct and low-context approach. It probably takes no account of the way Igor is used to communicating with your company.

b. Ask Igor to join your company's annual skiing trip for employees but make it clear he will have to pay?

This approach downgrades the personal relationship that your predecessor had with Igor. It could be that Igor particularly appreciated the joint family holiday. However, you may want to distance yourself from this very personal relationship. Are you going to go on the company's annual skiing trip and look after Igor and his family?

c. Take Igor out to lunch and offer him better price incentives but don't mention the skiing holiday?

This seems like a good balance between maintaining a good relationship but also keeping the focus on business.

d. Talk to the director in charge of sales and ask for his advice on how to deal with this situation?

Finally, it is you who has to manage this business. The advice could be helpful but you need to maintain the business and the relationship.

e. Do nothing but continue to provide good products at good prices?

This approach presupposes that you can do business without having a close relationship. The evidence of the past suggests this is not the case.

4. Divided loyalties

a. Inform Helga of the approach you have had from Ahmed?

This is very straightforward and would be appreciated by Helga. It ignores the confidentiality of the conversation you had with Ahmed and places your loyalties firmly with the head office of your customer.

b. Inform Helga of the threat posed to both your businesses by this regional luxury-goods chain, without telling her about the plans Ahmed has?

This is quite a clever option in that it lifts the issue away from the personalities to focus just on prospects for the business. In the end, it is likely that Helga and maybe Ahmed will understand that you are caught between the two of them.

c. Continue to focus on your business and relationship with Helga without mentioning any developments in Dubai?

This is a 'wait and see what happens' option and again could be appropriate in that you cannot be sure what will develop over the next few months.

d. Hint that Helga needs to talk to Ahmed about his future plans?

This depends on your skill in doing this. If you can do this well, this is not a bad option in that it respects the current hierarchy of your customer's organization.

e. Call Ahmed and tell him to tell Helga about his plans before you do?

Ahmed may be very disappointed if you do this and there is a good chance that, in so doing, you will make it difficult to build any future relationship with him.

5. Close relationships

a. Ask her colleague, the other local project member, to talk to her and explain that she can't continue getting so emotionally upset at work?

This seems like a weak option in that you are avoiding facing the issue yourself. Both project members may conclude that you are a weak leader.

b. Talk to Martine yourself and explain that she needs to separate her private and professional life in future?

This is the direct approach and imposes your preferred behaviour on her. It is also typical of the parent telling the child how to behave. You need to remind yourself that she is doing a good job and the risk is that by speaking to her like this you will demotivate her.

c. Talk to the whole team about the need to focus on key deliverables and not be distracted over the next few months?

This is a safe option and communicates the result-driven behaviour you are expecting from all the team. Martine may not get the hidden message about her emotional behaviour.

d. Accept that Martine is an emotional person and needs to have the opportunity to express herself sometimes?

This shows total acceptance and tolerance but does not give Martine the chance to develop and also adapt to working with people like you.

e. Accept Martine's behaviour for this project but determine to never let yourself get so close to a colleague in future?

This would be a sad conclusion to reach. Balancing results and relationships is at the heart of international management. You need to develop yourself so that you can get the best out of more emotional team members as well as people like yourself.

Profiles of the managers quoted

The authors would like to thank all the interviewees for their contributions to this book. We have managed to collect short profiles of some of them. Our apologies go to those whose profiles are missing. We would also like to thank these managers we have quoted who have preferred to remain anonymous.

Brian Cracknell is the Director of Language Works, Malaysia, where he has lived for the last 29 years. He designs and delivers innovative learning experiences for clients throughout South East Asia.

John Duncan is a business language and communication teacher of many years' standing. He has worked in Libya, Egypt and Finland, and spent eight years as a teacher-trainer in Hong Kong. He has written 12 English language and communication textbooks.

Birgitta Gregor worked internationally in human resources management positions in industry for many years. As a management consultant her projects include change processes and organization development in Europe and Africa.

Erik Hallberg presently heads the Swedish Broadband Services operations of the Swedish telecoms company TeliaSonera. During his nine years with the company, Erik also headed up its Baltic operations. Earlier in his career, Erik worked as CEO of a European telecoms company and established a new operation for alternative telecom in 8 countries.

Ulrich Hansen is currently Manager Process and Plant Safety at Henkel in Düsseldorf. In his career he has worked in Milan, Paris and Saudi Arabia. In his current role he acts as an internal consultant travelling worldwide to support production sites.

Dr Frank Kühn worked in the electrical industry and in research institutions, where he was responsible for labour economics and organization. As a partner at HLP Hirzel Leder & Partner he supports executives and teams in developing their international organizations in the areas of project management, process management and interaction.

Wibke Kuhnert worked for five years in consulting before she joined Henkel in 2004. There she led an international team responsible for design and implementation of standard finance processes in the US and Europe. She has recently moved to the operational business and is leading the Business Controlling department of Henkel Cosmetics Retail in Germany.

Camillo Mazzola is currently Marketing Director at Henkel Italy Consumer Adhesives Sector. He has considerable international experience not only in Henkel but also with Loctite, Duracell and Nestlé.

Washington Munetsi is an international human resources practitioner, working for Nestlé, the largest food and beverages company in the world based in Vevey, Switzerland.

Luis Ortega has held different positions in Purchasing at Henkel. After an assignment in Turkey he was appointed Corporate Manager of Plastic packaging for the Personal Care Division.

Lorenzo Pestalozzi is a director of CRPM, a leading training organization in western Switzerland. He is a Swiss citizen, with international experience in sales and marketing and executive management positions.

Tim Taylor has worked in consumer products R&D for Unilever, Reckitt-Benckiser, and Henkel (both in Germany and at their subsidiary, The Dial Corporation, in Arizona). Tim is currently a Director in the R&D department at Dial.

Peter Wollmann has worked in numerous international projects in the last few years in Zurich Financial Services, one of the leading international insurance companies. Since 2005 he has been Head of Strategic Business Development at Zurich Group Germany with functions in the worldwide Zurich matrix organization. He is also co-publisher and author of several books on 'project management'.

GLOSSARY

This glossary is intended in particular to help readers for whom English is a foreign language and who might have problems with understanding some of the less frequent words used in the book. It describes the meaning of the words listed as they are used in the book and not in all their possible meanings. The glossary also includes many of the technical terms used in the text. These entries may be useful to all readers. Words in bold type within a glossary entry are also explained in the glossary.

360° feedback   Feedback on an employee from a wide variety of sources, such as your bosses, subordinates, and colleagues. Sometimes it also includes feedback from the person herself. The feedback is usually given anonymously.

accommodation   Giving up your own interests to satisfy those of the other person in a conflict. See also **appeasement**.

achievement   A term used by **Trompenaars** to describe the basis upon which certain **cultures** assign status to members of that society: a person has to be acknowledged to have achieved something valued by that society before status is given. Achieved status and respect in business **cultures** are assigned on the basis of judgements about the effectiveness with which a person does a job and about the extent of this person's knowledge. This contrasts with **ascription** as the other foundation for status. Typical **achievement**-oriented **cultures** are the USA, Canada and Britain. People from **achievement**-oriented **cultures** may appear knowledgeable (though with few titles!), young and uninfluential to more **ascription**-oriented people, who might be puzzled to find they are dealing with somebody so clearly different from themselves.

affective   A term used by **Trompenaars** to describe the tendency in a particular **culture** to show emotions in relationships with other people and to express them in the communication **behaviour** typical of that **culture** – both verbally and non-verbally, for example by laughing, smiling, frowning, touching or gesturing. In the communication **behaviour** of 'affectives', emotions are very obvious and conversation can thus be lively, uninhibited and even heated. Members of **affective** cultures may appear over-excitable, uncontrolled and theatrical to people who are more **neutral**, the term given to those at the opposite end of the spectrum. According to **Trompenaars'** research, countries such as Italy and France are among the most **affective** in Europe, with the USA following closely. **Affective behaviour** contrasts strongly with **neutral behaviour** in communicative style.

affirmative feedback   Affirmative feedback tells people what they did well, often also involving praise and even rewards.

ambiguity   A state or situation which can be viewed and interpreted in several ways and is therefore unclear and confusing.

appeasement   A strategy which gives in to demands or orders in order to maintain good and harmonious relationships at the expense of your own interests. See also **accommodation**.

appraisal   An assessment or judgement of something; an evaluation of the abilities of an employee; a formal process of giving feedback on an employee's performance.

appropriate   Suitable for a particular situation.

ascription   The term used by **Trompenaars** to describe the basis upon which certain cultures ascribe status to members of that society: a person must be acknowledged to *be* something valued by that society rather than to *have done* something valued before status is assigned. Ascribed status may be assigned on the basis of age, gender, social class, connections and function in a **culture**. Status is conferred by position rather than by proficiency. The Middle East and Southern Europe are examples of areas in which there is a greater tendency towards the conferring of status through **ascription** rather than **achievement**. People from **ascription**-oriented **cultures** may appear to be rather middle-aged, high in formal position and perhaps lacking in knowledge to more **achievement**-oriented people.

assertive   Very self-confident, direct and confident when interacting with others; determined in a conflict situation.

assertiveness   A **GLOBE Study** dimension which may be defined as the degree to which individuals in organizations or societies are **assertive**, confrontational, and aggressive in social relationships.

assumption   Something which is taken for granted, something which is believed without requiring proof; an idea of how things or people are like without really knowing whether that idea is true.

attitudes   The ways in which a person or a group of persons regard certain phenomena, including other persons and themselves, and they are the result of the application of **values** and **norms** to concrete cases. As such, they may be culture-specific. **Behaviour**, including communication, is the concrete manifestation of **values, norms** and **attitudes**.

autonomy   Being independent of others, making decisions by yourself and not being influenced by others.

avoidance   In terms of conflict management strategies, if you use an avoidance strategy you are not interested either in giving in to others or in satisfying your own interests.

behaviour   The way a person acts. **Behaviour** is not only the expression of a person's individuality but also the perceptible bearer of **culture** in a person in that it is the concrete manifestation of culture-specific **values, norms** and **attitudes**.

benevolence   Being kind, nice and caring to people, wanting to help people and care for their well-being, wanting to do good to others.

blocker   Something which blocks and hinders a process, eg change; something which prevents a process from being carried forward and which weakens the process. See also **driver** (antonym).

to blur   Making it difficult to see the clear lines and boundaries of a situation or thing; to become unclear and indistinct.

bottom-up   Interaction or processes starting at the bottom of the hierarchy in an organization and moving upwards; employees giving suggestions and other input to leaders which is then transported up the organizational hierarchy and finally judged by those leaders. See also **top-down** (antonym).

boundary   The borders or limits of something; a concept defining your responsibilities and task within a team or organization.

buy-in Everything that somebody can contribute to a team or organization and its success; acceptance, for example, of the value statement of an organization and being willing to act according to that statement.

to cement Cementing a position or relationship means to emphasize or strengthen it.

code of conduct Rules and regulations on how to act and behave in a certain situation or in a certain organization.

collectivism A term used by many interculturalists and in particular by **Hofstede**, **Trompenaars** and the **GLOBE Study** to describe a dimension of cultural variation in **values**. For **Hofstede**, extreme **collectivism** refers to 'societies in which people from birth onwards are integrated into strong, cohesive in-groups, which throughout people's lifetimes continue to protect them in exchange for unquestioning loyalty.' Based on answers to a ranking question concerning work goals which brought out training opportunities, physical working conditions and opportunities to use one's abilities and skills at work as the most important work-related aims, **Hofstede**'s index shows the most collective **cultures** to be found in East and West Africa, Central and South America and in Asia, although Argentina, Brazil and Japan, being located in the middle, are notable exceptions to this generalization. **Trompenaars** seems to adopt Parsons and Shils's (1951) definition of **collectivism** as 'a prime orientation to common goals and objectives'. **Trompenaars** suggests that Latin Catholic cultures together with those on the Pacific Rim tend to be more collectivist than others and also places Japan higher than does **Hofstede**. Both **Hofstede** and **Trompenaars** describe the greater significance attached to 'we' which people dealing with collectivists might expect. **Trompenaars** points to the possibility of people consulting with superiors and referring a decision back to the organization and claims that building lasting relationships in business is a prime goal. Here, we see a feature in common with **Trompenaars' particularism** and with the diffuse cultures he describes, a feature which **Hofstede** also refers to when he describes the communication style of collectivist cultures as being typically **high-context** and aimed at **face**-saving. The **GLOBE Study** distinguishes between institutional collectivism and in-group collectivism. Institutional collectivism is the degree to which organizational and societal institutional practices encourage and reward collective distribution of resources and collective action. In-group collectivism is the degree to which individuals express pride, loyalty and cohesiveness in their organizations or families. **Collectivism** contrasts with **individualism**.

conform To follow and act according to the rules, **norms** and regulations set by an organization; to act as you are expected to act.

conservation Conservation is a set of value orientations originated by Shalom H Schwartz which is made up of the values of conformity, security and tradition. Scoring high on conservation means that it is likely that you follow rules, avoid danger, and find religion and customs important.

consistency Acting or behaving in a similar way in similar situations and contexts over time, without strong changes in behaviour or performance.

context The circumstances in which a particular event takes place; the setting and a set of characteristics of a particular event; the set of characteristics that form the setting for a situation and therefore enables people to interpret it in a particular way. **Context**, as the term is used in the expressions **low-context** and **high-context**, is described by ET **Hall**, the scholar who coined them, as 'the information that surrounds an event' (**Hall** and **Hall**, 1990). Its meaning becomes clearer when it is contrasted with **text**, which **Hall** describes as 'the coded, explicit, transmitted part of the message' (**Hall**, 1976). **Context** is therefore the implicit, assumed and understood information and meaning shared by those communicating. Unspoken and unwritten information and meaning make up the **context**. Shared experience and personal relationships built up over time contribute to the creation of **context**.

contextualize   To place something in a particular **context** in order to understand it better. See also **context**.

culture   In this book, culture is regarded as what is common to a group of people within national or regional boundaries in terms of **values, norms** and **attitudes**. These are manifested in shared patterns of **behaviour**. Particularly important examples of these manifest forms of culture in international management are communication styles, the management of relationships, **time** and work, business practices and etiquette but they also include more generally artefacts, art, habits, rituals and heroes. Culture, which is specific to a group, is learned through interaction in that group. It is distinguished from basic human characteristics (which are universal) in that culture is not inherited through one's genes, and from personality (which is specific to the individual) in that it is not both inherited and learned. See also professional culture.

culture-blind   Not being able to see the characteristics of a culture other than your own; not being aware that people of a different culture communicate or act differently. See also **culture-sensitive** (antonym).

culture-sensitive   Being capable of seeing the characteristics of a culture other than your own; being aware that people of a different culture communicate or act differently. See also **culture-blind** (antonym).

deep-seated   Firmly established. Deep-seated ideas, concepts and feelings are very difficult to change or adapt. Sometimes, people are unaware of these deep-seated ideas, concepts and feelings.

defensive   If the members of a group become defensive towards others, they try to exclude them and may not share information freely with them. They may try to hide their weaknesses and protect their own interests.

deference   Openly showing respect to people more powerful than yourself; showing submission and respect to others because of their age, status or position.

to delayer   If you delayer an organization, you get rid of some of the hierarchical levels in order to make the whole system flatter, thereby making interaction between people from various levels easier and more direct.

detriment   To the detriment of something or somebody means that somebody or something suffers a disadvantage; at the expense of something; the state of being damaged or made worse.

developmental feedback   Feedback from a manager who evaluates an individual or a team which is not performing as well as expected, with the aim of helping the individual or team to perform better and reach their objectives; feedback which aims to lead to a change of behaviour and performance for the better.

directness   The explicit and open communication of meanings and intentions. It is one of the chief characteristics of **low-context** communication and is highly valued by **low-context** cultures because it is regarded as displaying honesty and a valuing of the truth. **Directness** is one of the communicative features most likely to cause problems for people coming from higher-**context** cultures: the directness of **low-context** communicators is frequently perceived as unsophisticated and blunt or even rude and aggressive, whereas the **indirectness** and vagueness of higher-**context** communicators may be perceived as evasive, even dishonest and often slightly annoying to people unfamiliar with this phenomenon.

discreet   Carefully communicating or doing something with the aim or keeping it confidential and trying to avoid embarrassing others.

diversity   Within a **culture**, the full range of **values, norms, attitudes** and **behaviour**s, from which a number are consciously or unconsciously selected and accepted to make up the dominant **culture**.

domination   In conflict management, domination is an orientation in which somebody who is involved in a conflict tries to succeed and get his/her own way at all costs.

down-toner   A word or expression which takes away some of the **directness** and strength of what is communicated – the meaning of the message is not changed, but it is seen as less imposing by the receiver of it.

driver   Something which helps and supports a process, eg change; something which carries a process forward and strengthens it.

to embody   To include, to contain; to be an expression of an idea, concept or feeling.

to escalate   To make more intense and serious.

explicit   Clearly expressed, formulated or stated; not hidden. See also **implicit** (antonym).

to exploit   To make full use of something; to use something as well as possible in order to get the most out of it.

extrovert   A person who is confident, relaxed and at ease in a social environment. See also **introvert** (antonym).

face   If you lose face, you lose your dignity and you feel embarrassed or ashamed. **Face** in intercultural communication may be defined as the exterior dignity of a person. If a person saves **face**, he or she does or says something in order to preserve this exterior dignity and thus what he or she sees as the immediate respect of those involved in the communication situation. White lies and euphemisms for 'no' (such as 'This is going to be very difficult' and 'I'll see what I can do') are examples of **face**-saving devices. The need to 'save one's own **face**' and to try to 'save the **face** of others' is present in all **cultures** but to very different degrees: a **low-context** culture tends to have a smaller need to save **face** whereas a **high-context** culture has a great need to do so. The communication **behaviour** of low **face**-saving **cultures** will typically tend to be characterized by **directness**, which is considered as unthreatening and honest, a higher degree of verbal self-disclosure and by precision. Typical high **face**-saving communication **behaviour** will tend to be indirect and polite, with less verbal self-disclosure and more tentativeness and vagueness. The concept of 'giving face' is rarely familiar to members of Western **cultures**.

face value   If you take a comment or feedback at face value, you accept the apparent and obvious meaning, even though the real and hidden meaning may be different.

femininity   A term used by **Hofstede** to describe a dimension of cultural variation in work-related **values**, which has **masculinity** at its opposite extreme. Criticised by some as relying on outdated and/or discriminatory sexual role attributions, **Hofstede** defines **femininity** as pertaining 'to societies in which social gender roles overlap (ie both men and women are supposed to be modest, tender, and concerned with the quality of life)'. Based on answers to a ranking question concerning work goals, which brought out the importance attached to a good relationship with one's superior, good co-operation with one's colleagues, living in a desirable area and employment security, **Hofstede's masculinity** index shows the highest **femininity cultures** to be those in Scandinavia and the Netherlands, some but not all in South America, those in East Africa and West Africa and a small number in Asia. High **femininity** may correlate with a greater willingness to resolve conflict through negotiation, consensus and compromise rather than fighting.

feudal   Referring to the system of feudalism in a figurative sense, it means here that lower-ranking people support higher-ranking people without questioning whether what the higher-ranking people do is right or wrong.

fit in   If you fit in easily in a group, you are accepted and considered to be a valuable member of this group, and you and your **values** are unlikely to cause any conflict within that group.

future-oriented   A term used by Kluckhohn and Strodtbeck (1961) to describe a culture which sees a better future for itself and which sets out to achieve it. As to be expected, the international business person interacting with members of **future-oriented cultures** can expect to encounter talk of the future – strategy and plans are important and interesting. The young are valued as representatives of the future.

gate-keeper   A person who controls access to something or someone.

gender egalitarianism   A **GLOBE Study** dimension which may be defined as the extent to which an organization or a society minimizes gender role differences while promoting gender equality.

generalist   A generalist education is an education that strongly values a general and broad education; a person who is competent in many areas and who can do a lot of different things but at a lower level of competence than a specialist.

GLOBE Study   The Global Leadership and Organizational Behavior Effectiveness Research programme (GLOBE) investigated the relationship between culture and societal, organizational and leadership effectiveness. 170 scholars questioned more than 17,000 middle managers in 62 cultures. The study expanded and refined Hofstede's dimensions distinguishing two types of **collectivism** (societal collectivism, and in-group collectivism), and added **gender egalitarianism, assertiveness, performance orientation** and **humane orientation** to the **uncertainty avoidance, power distance** and **long-term orientation** familiar from Hofstede's work. Though based on a much smaller sample than Hofstede's work, it meets some of the criticism levelled at his pioneering work: the data was collected in companies in three industries (financial services, food processing and telecommunications) and not just one; the study was the work of a multi-cultural team of investigators bringing with them all the benefits of multiple, culturally influenced perspectives; the study's insights are more recent than Hofstede's: work began on the investigation in 1994 and was published in 2004, 24 years after the publication of Hofstede's *Culture's Consequences*.

glue   In a figurative sense, something which holds various parts together; a common understanding between people which holds these people together and connects them more.

guanxi   A concept in Chinese society which describes the social network of friends, acquaintances, colleagues and others who have various responsibilities and roles in that network.

Hall   Edward T Hall was an anthropologist and scholar who made a significant contribution to the science of intercultural communication through his studies of **non-verbal** communication, the first of which, *The Silent Language*, appeared in 1959. This was followed in 1966 by *The Hidden Dimension*, *Beyond Culture* in 1976 and *Understanding Cultural Differences*, a study of German, French and US business **culture** published together with his wife in 1990. Although sometimes criticised for his overgeneralizing and outdated comments on particular business **cultures**, not least the German one, by those who obviously know them better than he does, ET **Hall** has shaped the entire field of intercultural communication by his coining of the bipolar terms '**monochronic**' and '**polychronic**' and '**high-context**' and '**low-context**', which, despite the dangers of simplification connected with all scholarly bipolarities and dichotomies, are of genuine usefulness to the manager working internationally.

hands-off   Having a hands-off role means that people are not directly involved in working with their colleagues and staff. They leave their staff to do the job alone without detailed instruction.

harness   Using something for a particular advantageous purpose.

hearsay   Rumours or something which you have heard from somebody but the truth of which you cannot check; information about somebody which you have received from others and not from that person directly.

hedonism   An attitude which aims at getting as much fun and pleasure as possible in life and trying to enjoy it.

hierarchy   A system in which members of an organization are ranked according to their status; a hierarchy reflects the power relationships within an organization.

high-context communication   According to ET **Hall**, who first used the term and described its significance, high-context communication is characterized by large amounts of stored information shared by the parties to the communication, which is not transmitted explicitly but assumed and understood in the communication process. This is known as **context** and this **context** in addition to or rather than **text** plays a large part in **high-context** communication. Extreme **high-context** communication is located at one end of a continuum occupied at the other end by extreme **low-context** communication, in which large amounts of explicit, verbal information (**text**) are transmitted between the parties to the communication. Examples of regions typically displaying greater or lesser degrees of **high-context** communication **behaviour** are Arabic countries, Asia and Latin America. Knowing that a particular business associate comes from a **high-context** culture allows the international manager to prepare for certain typical features of **high-context** communication. These are likely to include: a low reliance on explicit messages consisting of words; a correspondingly greater reliance on **non-verbal** signals; vagueness and tentativeness; a resulting tendency to interpret intentions of the other party to the communication; low self-disclosure and **indirectness**, which are valued as showing consideration of the other party. As far as agreements in business are concerned, **high-context** cultures attach much importance to personal promises, which offer security because they are based on sound interpersonal relationships and are guaranteed by the need to save **face**.

Hofstede Geert Hofstede, formerly professor of organizational anthropology and international management at the University of Limburg in the Netherlands, and sometime employee in different capacities for various multinationals, including IBM, can genuinely be said to have done ground-breaking work in the field – and, given his success, to have brought about a paradigm change in intercultural studies. His original empirical research, published in 1980 in his book *Culture's Consequences: International Differences in Work-Related Values* and based on a matched sample of many thousands of IBM employees from more than 50 countries, together with subsequent smaller surveys, provide the interculturalist, whether scholar or international manager, with reliable insights into differences in work-related **values** and the ways in which these **values** are reflected in the organizations and societies, and by inference, in the communication styles to be found in various **cultures**. The usefulness of his findings is that they are expressed in the form of bipolar dimensions or, as **Hofstede** defines them, aspects of a **culture** that can be measured relative to other **cultures**. Hofstede names the four basic dimensions he ascertained in his research: **power distance** (from small to large); **collectivism** v **individualism**; **femininity** v **masculinity**; **uncertainty avoidance** (from weak to strong). In subsequent research, **Hofstede** adds a fifth dimension, namely, **long-term orientation** v **short-term orientation**. Since the publication of his work, no discussion of an intercultural issue in business or management is complete without at least a mention of **Hofstede**. His quantitative approach has gained many supporters – it offers empirical security in a field notoriously subject to the perverting effects of anecdote and prejudice – and a few imitators, all of whom, including **Trompenaars**, pale in comparison with the real thing. Criticism of his insights has grown in the last decade, for example, for being based on data derived from one organization, suggesting a no longer current cultural homogeneity and promoting stereotypes. The Hofstedian dimensions were refined by the more recent **GLOBE Study**.

hospitality/gift-giving The condition of being friendly and welcoming to others; in a business context, entertaining business partners or clients in order to promote harmonious relationships. Hospitality and gift-giving are two ways in which a company or an individual in a company can show gratitude for the business relationship which exists or is about to begin. Every international manager is certain to be confronted with these phenomena, which can vary greatly from **culture** to culture. Being invited as the visiting business person to lunch or dinner or returning the compliment on a later visit would seem to be a cultural universal. **Hospitality** can of course be much more elaborate and what is appropriate to offer and accept will vary not only across cultural borders but also between companies (many will have their own codes of ethical conduct) and individuals. The same can be said for gift-giving: whereas the giving of small gifts, sometimes bearing the name or logo of the company, or of something typical of the present-giver's home-country is nothing exceptional and even expected, the giving of larger presents may cause difficulties, especially if the receiver is not familiar with the gift-giving conventions of the giver's **culture**. Even the giving and accepting of normal business gifts may be surrounded by an etiquette unknown to one of the parties involved. For example, in Japan, gifts must always be wrapped, cannot be refused (unless it appears to be a bribe), are belittled by the giver and are often not opened while the giver is present (because of the risk of loss of **face**).

humane orientation   A **GLOBE Study** dimension which may be defined as the degree to which individuals in organizations or societies encourage and reward individuals for being fair, altruistic, friendly, generous, caring, and kind to others.

humour   The ability of a person to perceive a situation as amusing and funny and to create such situations in words. As **Trompenaars** rightly says, 'Cultures also vary on the permissible use of **humour**'. For example, the British value **humour** on all occasions, including in serious business and work situations, and **Trompenaars** speculates that this allows the release of emotions, which in Britain's **neutral** culture tend not to be expressed openly. The typical British understatement, he points out, is both a controlled expression of emotion and at the same time a trigger for emotional release in the form of laughter. The Japanese use exaggerated deference for similar purposes. **Humour** is particularly **culture**-specific so even if a relationship has been built up which makes the use of **humour** permissible, seeing the funny side of something or telling jokes may backfire. Verbal **humour** is naturally very problematical if one of the parties to the communication is speaking a language which is not his/her own.

implicit   Understood but not directly expressed, clear or observable. See also **explicit** (antonym).

indirectness   The **implicit**, oblique and tentative communication of meanings and intentions. It is one of the chief characteristics of **high-context** communication and is greatly valued by **high-context cultures** because it is regarded as displaying consideration for the person addressed and as a way of reducing the risk of losing **face** for both parties. **Indirectness** is one of the features of **high-context** communication style which people from **low-context** cultures are likely to find difficult to deal with: the **indirectness** of **high-context** communicators with their vagueness and tentativeness is frequently perceived as evasive or even dishonest and can be frustrating to more direct **low-context** people, who in turn may be perceived as blunt or even rude and aggressive.

individualism   The concept of people seeing themselves as individuals acting independently of others without feeling that strong obligations exist between people. It is a term used by **Hofstede, Trompenaars** and the **GLOBE Study** to describe a dimension of cultural variation in **values**, which has **collectivism** at its opposite extreme. For **Hofstede, individualism** refers to 'societies in which the ties between individuals are loose: everyone is expected to look after himself or herself and his or her immediate family.' Based on the answers to a ranking question concerning work goals, which brought out personal **time**, freedom at work and challenge as the most important aims at work, **Hofstede's individualism** index places the USA, Australia and Great Britain as clearly the most individualist cultures followed some considerable way behind by Canada, the Netherlands, New Zealand, Italy, Belgium, Denmark, Sweden and France. **Trompenaars'** defines **individualism** as 'a prime orientation to the self' and demonstrates that Protestant influenced north-west Europe (Britain, Scandinavia, the Netherlands, Germany) and the North America it settled are the most individualist **cultures**. He also points out the fact that the first person singular pronoun 'I' is not only very frequent in the speech of people from individualist cultures but also spelled with a capital letter! Such people are frequently empowered to act without reference back to the organization. They are likely to have a **low-context** communication style and the corresponding **attitude** to the preservation of **face**.

in-group   A group of people sharing similar interests and similar characteristics; people with whom you are in close contact because you share a similar identity. See also **out-group** (antonym).

integrity   The condition of being honest and having strong moral convictions.

interdependent   Being dependent on each other; feeling that you have strong obligations towards other members of a group and that your identity is shaped by the interaction with other members of a group.

interplay   The way in which several things or people depend and have an effect on each other.

introvert   Person who is not confident and not at ease in a social environment and somebody who is primarily concerned with their own feelings rather than the world about them. See also **extrovert** (antonym).

kick-off   The start of an event or meeting, often allowing time for team members to get to know each other.

line function   The function that an employee has in an organization in his/her day-to-day job as opposed to the particular role and function he/she plays while working in a specially formed project team.

lingua franca   A language that is used by members of an organization who work together but who speak different languages – in international business, English is very often the lingua franca.

long-term orientation   LTO, according to Bond and **Hofstede**, is a tendency in certain **cultures** to value persistence, the regulation of relationships through status, thrift and the possession of a sense of shame. Named by Bond as dynamic Confucianism because these **values** may all be seen in the teachings of the Chinese philosopher, **long term orientation** is most common (in descending order) in China, Hong Kong, Taiwan, Japan, South Korea, Brazil, India and Singapore. The Netherlands is the only European country listed in the top ten positions (of 23 altogether). LTO correlates strongly with economic growth rates. The international business person interacting with members of LTO **cultures** can expect an interest in long-term business relationships and perseverance and tenacity in pursuing goals coupled with a reliability in keeping commitments (brought about by the valuing of the possession of a sense of shame).

low-context communication   According to ET **Hall**, who first used the term and described its significance, low-context communication is characterized by the transmission of large amounts of explicit, verbal information. This leads to the creation of spoken or written **text**. Extreme **low-context** communication is located at one end of a continuum occupied at the other end by extreme **high-context communication**, in which much information is not transmitted but assumed and understood by those involved in the communication process. This **context** in addition to or rather than **text** plays a large part in **high-context** communication. Examples of cultures typically displaying **low-context** communication **behaviour** are Germany, the USA, the Scandinavian countries (except Finland) and the Netherlands. Knowing that a particular business associate comes from a **low-context** culture allows the international manager to prepare for certain typical features of **low-context** communication. These typical features are likely to include: a great reliance on words rather than **non-verbal** signals to communicate; a great emphasis on detail and exactness; a resulting literalness; and verbal self-disclosure and **directness**, which are valued as showing honesty and straightforwardness. As far as agreements in business are concerned, **low-context** cultures attach much importance to the written word of laws, regulations and contracts (a tendency also seen in the value attributed to written documents such as minutes, memos, procedure handbooks): **low-context** USA has 279 lawyers per 100,000 inhabitants as opposed to **high-context** Japan with only 11.

loyalty   The quality of showing strong and constant support to others, usually over a long period of time.

majority culture   A **culture** that dominates or is very powerful; a **culture** whose members make up the majority of the number of people in a society. See also **minority culture** (antonym).

mandatory   Required and not optional; compulsory.

masculinity   A term used by **Hofstede** to describe a dimension of cultural variation in work-related **values**, which has **femininity** at its other extreme. **Hofstede** defines **masculinity** as pertaining to 'societies in which social gender roles are clearly distinct (ie men are supposed to be assertive, tough, and focused on material success whereas women are supposed to be more modest, tender, and concerned with the quality of life)'. Based on a ranking question about work goals, which brought out the importance attached to high earnings, recognition, advancement and challenge in a job, **Hofstede's masculinity** index lists Japan as the highest **masculinity culture** by a long way, followed by some European countries (Austria, Italy, Switzerland, Ireland, Great Britain and Germany) and a number of countries around the Caribbean, with the USA in 15th position. People from high **masculinity cultures** may tend to be ambitious and tough and, where other cultural **values** do not prevent it as in the case of Japan, **assertive**. An expected approach to conflict is combative rather than conciliatory.

mentor   An experienced person in an organization who helps new employees and guides them in their career and their work and gives them advice on both work-related and personal issues.

to micro-manage   To manage in a very detailed manner.

mindset   The set of **attitudes** and ways of **behaviour** typical of a group.

minefield   In a figurative sense, a minefield is a potentially dangerous and unclear situation; in a cultural minefield, people do not know where there may be potential problems in communicating or interacting with others and whether they may even insult others without being aware of it.

minority culture   A **culture** which is more open to outer influences than members of the **majority culture**. See also majority culture (antonym).

mission statement   A formal and written statement of the aims, **values** and **attitudes** of an organization; it outlines what the organization wants to do and achieve and how it wants to do and achieve this.

modesty   **Behaviour** in which you avoid talking about your knowledge and skills; not boasting about your skills.

monochronic   A term used to describe a conception of **time** (and also cultures which identify with this conception of **time**) which means dealing with one activity at a **time** (a meaning related to the Greek from which the word is derived) and which regards **time** as an almost tangible and limited resource. First made famous in intercultural studies by ET **Hall**, **monochronic** cultures are also characterized by adherence to schedules and deadlines, **punctuality** and promptness. **Monochronic** cultures are typically **low-context** in their communication style. Classic examples of **monochronic cultures** are the USA,

Germany and Switzerland. Knowing whether his/her opposite number in the international work setting comes from a **monochronic** or **polychronic culture** can help the international manager to be prepared for these and other business **behaviours**.

neutral A term used by **Trompenaars** (and others before him) to describe the tendency in a particular **culture** not to show emotions in relationships with other people and not to express them in the communication **behaviour** typical of that culture. Members of **neutral** cultures control the verbal expression of their feelings in their interaction with others and their **non-verbal behaviour**, such as facial expression, gesture and touching, is restrained. They may appear cold, unfeeling and repressed to members of **cultures** which are **affective**, the term given to those **cultures** at the opposite end of the spectrum. According to **Trompenaars'** research, the most **neutral** cultures are Japan, Indonesia and Britain. The potential for puzzlement and annoyance when representatives of these two tendencies encounter each other is obvious. Contrasts with **affective**.

non-verbal Non-verbal communication is communication without using words or speech; smiling, nodding and other features of body language are examples of ways to communicate in a non-verbal way. **Non-verbal communication** may be defined as the conscious or unconscious exchange of information through the use of unspoken or unwritten signs. Such communication may vary widely across cultures and in an intercultural interaction, a situation which in any case may be accompanied by unfamiliar features, **non-verbal** communication may be puzzling and difficult to deal with. Indeed, research has shown that for western European business people, it was the second most frequent source of difficulty in their interactions after dealing with conflict. Victor (1992) divides **non-verbal** communication into active and passive categories, active being those **behaviours** which can be consciously controlled and passive those which are less easy to control. The category of active **non-verbal** communication contains: kinesics, or movement (including gestures); appearance; oculesics, or eye **behaviour** (including eye contact); haptics, or touching **behaviour**; proxemics, or space usage; and paralanguage (or all sounds produced by the vocal organs which are not words). The category of passive **non-verbal** communication includes: colour; counting signs; non-kinesic emblems, or symbols; and olfactory communication, or smells.

norms Those **values**, **attitudes** and **behaviours** which are consciously or unconsciously selected and most commonly accepted by the members of a **culture**, ie those **values**, **attitudes** and **behaviours** which are considered most 'normal' for that **culture** by that **culture**.

organizational culture The particular **culture** to be found in a company, perhaps including its subsidiaries at home and abroad. It may exist in a group which is at the same time also influenced by national and **professional culture**. Hofstede suggests that corporate culture is created by practices in a company which can be placed on the following dimensions: process oriented vs. results oriented; employee oriented vs. job oriented; parochial vs. professional; open system vs. closed system; loose control vs. tight control; and normative vs. pragmatic.

other-centred Attaching more importance to the interests of other people than to your own.

outcome Result.

outgoing Friendly and confident in a social environment.

out-group A group of people with which you do not share similar interests; people with whom you are not in close contact. See also **in-group** (antonym).

to overlap   If two systems, actions or ideas overlap, they involve some of the same periods of time, topics or people; taking place at the same time.

pace   The speed or rhythm at which an organization works and at which organizational processes take place; a single step when walking.

particularism   The term made famous by **Trompenaars** to describe the **value** orientation which tends to allow **behaviour** in relationships to be guided by the needs of that unique relationship or what he describes as 'the exceptional nature of present circumstances', rather than rules and regulations as is the case in **cultures** which are oriented to **universalism**. Typically particularist **cultures** are those in southern Europe or the Middle East. According to **Trompenaars**, Catholic-influenced cultures will tend to be particularist. For people working internationally the particularist orientation will show itself in the importance attached to **relationship-building**: business should be done with somebody known and trusted and so part of the interaction will be devoted to this possibly time-consuming process. To a **particularist**, a reliable business person is one who is prepared to take account of changing circumstances in a personal business relationship, for example by modifying contracts.

particularist   For a particularist, personal relationships are very important for doing business, because they emphasize the importance of trust in a business setting; for particularists, a particular relationship in a business context is more important than abstract rules according to which an organization functions. See also **universalist** (antonym).

past-oriented   The term used by Kluckhohn and Strodtbeck (1961) to describe a **culture** which aims to maintain and restore traditions in the present. In intercultural interaction, members of **past-oriented** cultures may tend in the **relationship-building** phases to talk about the origins of their family, company and country, to show respect for predecessors and more senior people and generally to take an approach which honours tradition and history.

path-goal theory   States that a leader's behaviour is contingent to the satisfaction, motivation and performance of her or his subordinates. A later version of the theory also argues that the leader engages in behaviours that complement subordinate's abilities and compensate for deficiencies. It distinguishes between directive, supportive, participative or achievement-oriented leadership behaviours. Directive behaviour provides guidance and structure; supportive behaviour shows concern for the followers' well-being; participative behaviour involves leaders consulting followers before making a decision; and achievement-oriented behaviour sets challenges combined with the expectation that followers will perform at their highest level and shows confidence in their ability to fulfil these expectations.

to peer coach   To train or advise colleagues.

performance orientation   A **GLOBE Study** dimension which refers to the extent to which an organization or society encourages and rewards group members for performance improvement and excellence.

polychronic   A term used to describe a conception of **time** (and also **cultures** which identify with this conception of **time**) which means dealing with several or many activities at a **time** (a meaning related to the Greek from which the word is derived) and which regards **time** as fluid and flexible. Originally coined by **ET Hall**, the term **polychronic** describes **cultures** which regard personal relationships as more important than timetables and deadlines (and as such has something in common with **particularism**). The consequences for the international manager are obvious. **Punctuality**, also for business appointments, is less important in **polychronic** cultures and work **time** and personal **time** tend to flow into each other, with work subject to distraction and interruption. **High-context** in their communication style, people from **polychronic** cultures like to derive information from non-explicit sources, are more concerned with family, friends and close acquaintances (cf. **particularism**) and have a tendency to form long-term business relationships. Classic examples of European **polychronic cultures** are Spain, Italy and Greece.

power distance   One of the five dimensions of cultural variation identified by **Hofstede** in his research into work-related **values**. It also features in the **GLOBE Study**. **Hofstede** defines **power distance** as 'the extent to which the less powerful members of institutions and organizations within a country expect and accept that power is distributed unequally'. The power distance index shows high power distance values (ie a great expectation and acceptance of the unequal distribution of power) for Asian, African, Latin American and Latin European countries like France and Spain; and lower values for North America and the remaining European countries, among which the Scandinavian countries score very low. Features of management to be expected in high **power distance cultures** include: steep hierarchies with much supervisory personnel; centralized decision-making; subordinates expect instructions; status symbols and privileges for managers are expected; broad salary differentials. Features of management to be expected in low **power distance** cultures include: flat hierarchies with less supervisory personnel; decentralized decision-making; subordinates expect consultation; status symbols and privileges for managers are disapproved of; narrow salary differentials.

predictable   Able to be foreseen; if something is predictable, people can assume that it will happen as they expect it to happen, even if they cannot be sure of this.

prejudice   An unreasonable dislike of something, an opinion or assessment that is not based on actual experience and first-hand knowledge or insights. See also **stereotype**.

present-oriented   The term used by Kluckhohn and Strodtbeck (1961) to describe a **culture** which is **time**less and traditionless and which is not concerned with the future. The international manager interacting with a person from a present-oriented culture may expect importance to be attached to present matters rather than the future, whether they are relationships or actions. Plans, which necessarily refer to the future, are of less importance.

prevent   To keep something from happening; to stop someone from doing something.

professional cultures   Are **cultures** to be found among people who have a similar educational or vocational qualification and, probably more importantly, who have similar jobs. These **cultures** may well transcend companies and national borders.

psychometric   Relating to measuring mental processes or capacities; relating to measuring an individual's personality or **behaviour**.

punctuality   The occurrence of something, eg a business appointment or the delivery of goods, at the **time** named and agreed upon by those involved. It is **behaviour** particularly valued in **monochronic cultures**, such as the USA, Germany, the Netherlands and Britain, where business **punctuality** is expected. The more important the person or the occasion, the more importance is attached to **punctuality**. Unpunctuality at business appointments by members of such **cultures** is accompanied by profuse apologies and detailed excuses and explanations whereas being 'late' in **polychronic** cultures such as Spain, Greece and Italy is tolerated and felt not to require such expressions of regret and explanations.

reciprocity   The practice of helping each other so that there is benefit for everyone involved.

relational   Concerning the relationship between people interacting together rather than the task-related aspects of their interaction.

relationship-building   For some **cultures** relationship-building contributes to the creation of a basis which is a prerequisite for doing business. It will include at the very least **small talk** of a minimal kind and research has shown that in western and central Europe it will often extend to the classical business lunch or dinner. In other **cultures, relationship-building** may well be much lengthier and more elaborate. **Relationship-building** is particularly important in **particularist, polychronic** and **high-context** cultures.

reliable   If somebody is reliable, you can trust that that person will act as you expect him/her to act; performing consistently well.

to reprimand   To express disapproval and dissatisfaction with somebody in a formal way.

resentment   A feeling of bitterness and anger towards others.

to resolve   To find a solution to a problem or conflict.

to restrain   To keep under control; to keep from getting out of control.

to ridicule   To make fun of somebody, to make others laugh at somebody.

to root   To come from; to base something on; to originate from.

rudimentary   Not strongly developed or basic; relatively simple or even too simple.

rungs on the ladder   Steps of a ladder; in a figurative sense, each rung on the ladder symbolizes one hierarchical level within an organization: if you go up the ladder step-by-step, you rise in the organizational hierarchy.

sceptical   Not being convinced easily, having doubts about something.

self-centred   Attaching more importance to your own interests than to those of others.

self-reliant   Counting on yourself and your own capabilities rather than on others; wanting not to be dependent on others.

short-term orientation   According to Bond and **Hofstede**, short-term orientation is a tendency in **cultures** to value personal steadiness and stability, the protection of **face**, respect for tradition and the reciprocation of greetings, favours and gifts. As with **long term orientation**, these **values** are also essentially Confucian and so **short-term orientation** can be said merely to embody a different range of Confucian **values**. The last ten positions in **Hofstede's** LTO index, ie moving from the most extreme short-term to a less **short-term orientation**, are occupied by: Pakistan, Nigeria, the Philippines, Canada, Zimbabwe, Great Britain, the USA, New Zealand, Australia and Germany. **Hofstede** states that these findings are expressed in western countries in a desire to 'keep up with the Joneses' and, of interest to the international manager, and to achieve quick results.

silo mentality   The characteristic way of thinking of the members of an organization that categorizes people or procedures into boxes, denying that it is important to take into account the relationships and interactions between these boxes.

sincerity   The quality of being honest with people; the quality of not deceiving people; the quality of not manipulating people to your own advantage.

small talk   Also referred to in this book as social conversation. Light conversation on more or less unimportant topics, frequently in a social setting, such as a restaurant. It contributes to **relationship-building** and is therefore particularly important with members of **high-context** cultures and **particularist** cultures. Appropriate topics for **small talk** vary to a certain extent – for example, research has shown that Poles avoid talking about religion more than Germans but a rule of thumb for all **cultures** is: avoid the taboo topics of your own culture (they'll probably be taboo elsewhere,) plus politics, religion, death, gossip and money if they are not among them, although **neutral** information questions on these topics might be acceptable and show openness and interest in a **culture** unfamiliar to you.

stereotype   An image or idea of a particular person or group of people which is fixed and not easily changed and which oversimplifies the characteristics of that person or group of people. See also **prejudice**.

substantive   Important and meaningful; not superficial.

subtle   Relatively precise, varied and detailed rather than relatively unfocused or general.

to surface   To make explicit and not allow to remain hidden and unspoken; to describe or articulate something.

to take for granted   If you take something for granted, you assume it just has to be like that and that it cannot be otherwise.

to take turns   To begin to speak in a conversation.

to talk down   If you talk down to people, you give them the impression that you are more important or knowledgeable than they are.

tangible   Real; having the quality of being seen or recognized; considerable.

text   A term used in intercultural communication to describe any explicit verbal (written or spoken) message or, as **Hall** describes it, 'the coded, explicit, transmitted part of the message' (**Hall**, 1976). The creation of text through the transmission of explicit information and the status of text as the dominant vehicle of communication are the main characteristics of **low-context** communication. Text is embedded in more or less **context**, which in **low-context** communication plays a small role and in **high-context** communication a much greater one.

to throw off   To abandon something; to discontinue something; to leave something behind; to get rid of something.

to tick the box   If you tick the boxes, you complete something or you do something because you are required to do it rather than because you see a real need to do it; following a particular process because you have to rather than because you believe in it.

time   A concept which is commonly valued and viewed differently across **cultures** and hence affects the **behaviour** of the members of a particular **culture**. **Hall** wrote repeatedly and at length on **polychronic** as opposed to **monochronic** cultures, a contrast which at least to a large extent is based on a fundamentally different view of **time**. **Trompenaars** uses a different pair of words to bring out the same difference, namely *synchronic* and *sequential*. Kluckhohn and Strodtbeck identified three types of **culture: past-oriented, present-oriented** and **future-oriented**. In his empirical research, Bond discovered a dimension of variation in cultural **values** relating to **time**, which he describes as Confucian dynamism, a term **Hofstede** paraphrases as a tendency towards either a **long term orientation** or a **short-term orientation** in life.

top-down   Interaction or procedures starting at the top of the hierarchy in an organization and moving downwards; the leader decides without taking into account suggestions from employees and then communicates his/her decision down the hierarchy. See also bottom-up (antonym)

transactional   Concerning the task-related aspects of people's interaction rather than the relationship between the people interacting together.

transformational leadership   The process by which leaders improve followers' performance and develop them to their fullest potential. A number of factors are important in this process, among which are: *idealized influence* (leaders are a role model for high ethical behaviour, instilling pride in followers, gaining respect and trust and perhaps making followers want to emulate them), *inspirational motivation* (leaders communicate high expectations and express a vision that is appealing and inspiring to followers), *intellectual stimulation* (leaders challenge assumptions, encourage followers to be creative and innovative and solicit followers' ideas) and *individualized consideration* (leaders create a supportive climate, attend to the follower's needs and act as a coach to the follower).

transversal   Cutting across the usual hierarchical or functional lines. If people from various hierarchies and from various departments work together for a particular purpose, often in project teams, you speak of a transversal structure.

Trompenaars   Fons Trompenaars, co-author of *Riding the Waves of Culture* and more recently co-author of a series of books on cross-cultural business and management topics, has become a sought-after management guru and star of the management seminar circuit. Although possibly justified criticism of the soundness of his data and of the conclusions he has drawn from it has been made by some people, his insights into the dimensions of cultural variation to be found in business and management have established themselves firmly in the field: **neutral** versus **affective** in the disclosure of feelings, **ascription** versus **achievement** in the assigning of status, diffuse versus specific in the range of involvement, **collectivism** versus **individualism**, **universalism** versus **particularism** in relationships with others, the management of **time** (past, present and future; sequential and synchronic) and the management of nature (internal control v. external control), together with his family, Eiffel Tower, guided missile and incubator corporate **cultures** are all concepts which the cross-cultural manager will find at least interesting and sometimes useful in his/her work.

trustworthy   If somebody is trustworthy, you can rely on them to be honest. If a person is trustworthy, we trust him/her and believe he/she will do what he/she has promised to do.

uncertainty   The state of doubt or being unsure about the future and about what is the right thing to do; the state of feeling threatened by unclear or unknown situations.

uncertainty avoidance   One of the five dimensions of cultural variation that Hofstede ascertained in his research into work-related **values**. It also features in the **GLOBE Study**. Hofstede defines uncertainty avoidance as 'the extent to which the members of a culture feel threatened by uncertain or unknown situations'. His uncertainty avoidance index lists 53 countries and regions according to whether they tend to be high or low uncertainty avoiders. The areas with the greatest subjective need to avoid uncertainty tend to be located in Latin America and southern Europe with Japan and South Korea in Asia; medium high uncertainty avoiders are the German-speaking countries; medium to low uncertainty avoiders are the USA, the other Asian countries, the African countries and those of north-west Europe. As far as intercultural communication and cooperation are concerned, high to medium uncertainty avoiding **cultures** will tend to favour formalized conceptions of management, attaching greater importance to plans, procedures, structure, the written word and to specialists and expert knowledge. They will often be more task-oriented. Low to medium uncertainty avoiding **cultures** will tend to tolerate change, improvization and ambiguity in communication and cooperation with greater ease and to believe in common sense and generalists. They will often be more relationship-oriented.

to underpin   To support and strengthen something by providing a robust foundation.

universalism   The term made famous in international management by **Trompenaars** to describe the value orientation which tends to rely more on legal, moral or ethical codes, codes of conduct, contracts, processes etc for governing **behaviour** in business relationships and society generally, than the circumstances and special nature of the individual relationship. (This orientation is known as **particularism**.) Typically universalist **cultures** are the USA and North-West European countries; Protestant cultures tend to be universalist. For **universalists**, a reliable business person is someone who keeps his/her word and honours the contract.

universalist   For a universalist, codes, formal rules and regulations determine **behaviour** and interaction with others – these codes and rules are seen as definitive and exceptions are not really considered to be acceptable, not even with close and trusted business partners. See also **particularist** (antonym).

values   Consciously or unconsciously held moral principles or beliefs that a person considers important and according to which he/she tends to live his/her life. A group of people sharing the same or similar **values** can be described as a **culture**. **Values** help to shape **behaviour** and thus shared **values** in a **culture** lead to **behaviours** conventional in and typical of one **culture**. **Values** do not necessarily completely predict **behaviour** as they merely suggest **behaviour** which is desired or hoped for rather than that which actually occurs. Inasmuch as **values** determine preferred **behaviours**, the international manager will be confronted by the **values** of the various groups with which he/she comes into contact – professional cultures, corporate cultures and, not least, national cultures, the main focus of the study of intercultural communication. The fact that **values** are frequently unconsciously held may mean that the international manager will only become aware of his/her own **values** when intercultural communication becomes problematical. For this reason an understanding of **values** and a sensitivity to their **behavioural** expression – both in others and himself/herself – can help the international manager beyond measure.

virtual   Virtual teams are teams which are not located in the same office or in nearby buildings – such teams are spread geographically and often work together using e-mail and other internet applications.

work-life balance   The principle that work should be in proportion to private life in order to take into account the need for rest and recreation of employees and thus support their well-being.

REFERENCES

Adler, N (2002) *International Dimensions of Organizational Behavior, 4th edn*, South-Western College Publishing, Cincinnati

Bennett, M (1995) Critical incidents in an intercultural conflict-resolution exercise, in *Intercultural Sourcebook: Cross-cultural training methods, Vol 1*, ed S M Fowler and M G Mumford, 147–56, Intercultural Press, Yarmouth

Blanchard, K H, Zigarmi, P and Zigarmi, D (1986) *Leadership and the One-Minute Manager*, Collins, London

Burgess, S and Steenkamp, J-B E M (1999) Value priorities and consumer behaviour in a transitional economy, in *Marketing Issues in Transitional Economies*, ed R Batra, pp 85–105, Kluwer, Boston

Carl, D, Gupta, V and Javidan, M (2004) Power distance, in *Culture, Leadership, and Organizations. The GLOBE Study of 62 Societies*, ed R J House *et al*, pp 513–63, Sage, Thousand Oaks, CA

Cottle, T J (1967) The circles test: an investigation of perception of temporal relatedness and dominance, *Journal of Projective Technique and Personality Assessment*, 31 (5), pp 58–71

Davidov, E (2008) A cross-country and cross-time comparison of human values measurements with the second round of the European social survey, *Survey Research Methods*, 2 (1), pp 33–46

Den Hartog, D N (2004) Assertiveness, in *Culture, Leadership, and Organizations. The GLOBE Study of 62 Societies*, ed R J House *et al*, pp 395–436, Sage, Thousand Oaks, CA

Distefano, J J and Maznevski, M L (2000) Creating value with diverse teams in global management, *Organizational Dynamics*, 29 (1), pp 45–63

Dorfman, P W, Hanges, P J and Brodbeck, F C (2004) Leadership and cultural variation: the identification of culturally endorsed leadership profiles, in *Culture, Leadership, and Organizations. The GLOBE Study of 62 Societies*, ed R J House *et al*, pp 669–720, Sage, Thousand Oaks, CA

Earley, P C (1997) *Face, Harmony and Social Structure*, Oxford University Press, New York

Emrich, C G, Denmark, F L and Den Hartog, D N (2004) Cross-cultural differences in gender egalitarianism: implications for societies, organizations, and leaders, in *Culture, Leadership, and Organizations. The GLOBE Study of 62 Societies*, ed R J House *et al*, pp 343–94, Sage, Thousand Oaks, CA

Flytzani, S and Nijkamp, P (2008) Locus of control and cross-cultural adjustment of expatriate managers, *International Journal of Foresight and Innovation Policy: IJFIP*, 4 (1/2), pp 146–59

French, W L and Bell, C H (1979) *Organization Development*, Prentice Hall, Englewood Cliffs, NJ

Gelfand, M J *et al* (2004) Individualism and collectivism, in *Culture, Leadership, and Organizations. The GLOBE Study of 62 Societies*, ed R J House *et al*, pp 437–512, Sage, Thousand Oaks, CA

Gudykunst, W B (2004) *Bridging Differences: Effective intergroup communication*, 4th edn, Sage, Thousand Oaks

Hall, E T (1959) *The Silent Language*, Doubleday, New York

Hall, E T (1966) *The Hidden Dimension*, Doubleday, New York

Hall, E T (1976) *Beyond Culture*, Anchor Press/Doubleday, New York

Hersey, P (1985) *Situational Selling: An approach for increasing sales effectiveness*, Center for Leadership Studies, Escondido

Hersey, P, Blanchard, K H and Johnson, D E (2001) *Management of Organizational Behavior: Leading human resources*, 8th edn, Prentice Hall, Upper Saddle River

Hofstede, G (1980, 2001) *Culture's Consequences: Comparing values, behaviors, institutions, and organizations across nations*, 2nd edn, Sage, Thousand Oaks

Hofstede, G (1994) *Cultures and Organisations: Software of the mind*, McGraw-Hill, London

Holmes, J, Marra, M and Vine, B (2011) *Leadership, Discourse and Ethnicity*, Oxford University Press, Oxford

Honey, P and Mumford, A (1992) *Manual of Learning Styles, 3rd edition*, Honey, Maidenhead

House, J (2005) Politeness in Germany: politeness in GERMANY?, in *Politeness in Europe*, ed L Hickey and M Stewart, pp 13–28, Multilingual Matters, Clevedon

House, R J et al (eds) (2004) *Culture, Leadership, and Organizations. The GLOBE Study of 62 Societies*, Sage, Thousand Oaks, CA

Javidan, M (2004) Performance orientation, in *Culture, Leadership, and Organizations. The GLOBE Study of 62 Societies*, ed R J House et al, pp 239–81, Sage, Thousand Oaks, CA

Javidan, M, House, R J and Dorfman, P W (2004) A non-technical summary of GLOBE findings, in *Culture, Leadership, and Organizations. The GLOBE Study of 62 Societies*, ed R J House et al, pp 29–48, Sage, Thousand Oaks, CA

Kirkpatrick, S A and Locke, E A (1991) Leadership: do traits matter? *Academy of Management Executive*, 5, pp 48–60

Kluckhohn, F R and Strodtbeck, F L (1961) *Variations in Value Orientations*, Harper & Row, New York

Kolb, D A (1984) *Experimental Learning: Experience as the source of learning and development*, Prentice Hall, Englewood Cliffs, NJ

Kotter, J P (1990) *Force For Change: How leadership differs from management*, The Free Press, New York

Lane, H W et al (2009) *International Management Behavior: Leading with a global mindset*, Wiley, Chichester

Langer, E J (1989) *Mindfulness*, Addison-Wesley, Reading, MA

Langer, E J (1997) *The Power of Mindful Learning*, Addison-Wesley, Reading, MA

Laurent, A (1986) The cross-cultural puzzle of international human resource management, *Human Resource Management*, 25 (1), pp 91–102

LeBaron, M and Grundison, B (1993) *Conflict and Culture: Research in five communities in British Columbia, Canada*, University of Victoria Institute for Dispute Resolution, Victoria

Lewin, K (1936) Some social-psychological differences between the US and Germany, *Journal of Personality*, 4 (4), pp 265–93

Lord, R G, De Vader, C L and Alliger, G M (1986) A meta-analysis of the relation between personality traits and leadership perceptions: an application of validity generalization procedures, *Journal of Applied Psychology*, **71** (3), pp 402–10

Luft, J and Ingham, H (1955) The Johari window, a graphic model of interpersonal awareness, in *Proceedings of the Western Training Laboratory in Group Development*, UCLA, Extension Office, Los Angeles

Mann, R D (1959) A review of the relationship between personality and performance in small groups, *Psychological Bulletin*, **56**, pp 241–70

Margerison, C and McCann, D (1992) *Team Management Profile Handbook*, Prado Systems, York

Margerison, C and McCann, D (1995) *Team Management: Practical new approaches*, Management Books 2000 Ltd, Chalford

Margerison, C and McCann, D (1997) *High Energy Teams Workbook*, Team Management Systems, Milton, QLD

Markus, H and Kitayama, S (1991) Culture and self: implications for cognition, emotion, and motivation, *Psychological Review*, **2**, pp 224–53

Markus, H and Kitayama, S (1994) A collective fear of the collective: implications for selves and theories of selves, *Personality and Social Psychology Bulletin*, **20**, pp 568–79

Northouse, P G (2010) *Leadership: Theory and Practice*, 5th edn, Sage, Thousand Oaks, CA

Parsons, T (1937) *The Structure of Social Action*, McGraw-Hill, New York

Parsons, T and Shils, E (1951) *Towards a General Theory of Action*, Harvard University Press, Cambridge

Rotter, J B (1954) *Social Learning and Clinical Psychology*, Prentice Hall, Englewood Cliffs, NJ

Ruhly, S (1976) *Orientations to Intercultural Communication*, Science Research Associates, Palo Alto, CA

Schein, E (1985, 2004) *Organizational Culture and Leadership*, 3rd edn, Jossey-Bass, San Francisco

Schwartz, S H (1992) Universals in the content and structure of values: theoretical advances and empirical tests in 20 countries, in *Advances in Experimental Social Psychology, Vol 25*, ed M P Zanna, pp 1–65, Academic Press, San Diego

Schwartz, S H (1994) Beyond individualism/collectivism: new dimensions of values, in *Individualism and Collectivism: Theory, methods and applications*, U Kim *et al*, Sage, Thousand Oaks, CA

Schwartz, S H (1999) A theory of cultural values and some implications for work, *Applied Psychology: An international review*, **48** (1), pp 23–47

Schwartz, S H and Bardi, A (2001) Value hierarchies across cultures, *Journal of Cross-Cultural Psychology*, **32** (3), pp 268–90

Schwartz, S H, Lehmann, A and Roccas, S (1999) Multimethod probes of basic human values, in *Social Psychology and Cultural Context: Essays in honor of Harry C Triandis*, ed J Adamopulous and Y Kashima, pp 107–23, Sage, Newbury Park

Schwartz, S H *et al* (2001) Extending the cross-cultural validity of the theory of basic human values with a different method of measurement, *Journal of Cross-Cultural Psychology*, **32** (5), pp 519–42

Smith, J A and Foti, R J (1998) A pattern approach to the study of leader emergence, *Leadership Quarterly*, **9** (2), pp 147–60

Spencer-Oatey, H and Franklin, P (2009) *Intercultural Interaction. A multi-disciplinary approach to intercultural communication*, Palgrave Macmillan, London

Stachowicz-Stanusch, A (2009) Cultural diligence based on HP/Compaq merger case study, *Journal of Intercultural Management*, 1 (1), pp 66–81

Stahl, G K *et al* (2009) Unraveling the effects of cultural diversity in teams: a meta-analysis of research on multicultural work groups, *Journal of International Business Studies*, 41 (4), pp 690–710

Stogdill, R M (1948) Personal factors associated with leadership: a survey of the literature, *Journal of Psychology*, 25, pp 35–71

Stogdill, R M (1974) *Handbook of Leadership: A survey of theory and research*, Free Press, New York

Sully de Luque, M F and Sommer, S M (2000) The impact of culture on feedback-seeking behavior: an integrated model and propositions, *Academy of Management Review*, 25 (4), pp 829–49

Sully de Luque, M F and Javidan, M (2004) Uncertainty avoidance, in *Culture, Leadership, and Organizations. The GLOBE Study of 62 Societies*, ed R J House *et al*, pp 602–53, Sage, Thousand Oaks, CA

Tannen, D (1990, 2010) *You Just Don't Understand*, William Morrow, New York

The Chinese Culture Connection (eds) (1987) Chinese values and the search for culture-free dimensions of culture, *Journal of Cross-Cultural Psychology*, 18 (2), pp 143–74

Thomas, D C and Inkson, K (2003) *Cultural Intelligence: People skills for global business*, Berrett-Koehler, San Francisco

Thomas, K W (1976) Conflict and conflict management, in *Handbook of Industrial and Organizational Psychology*, ed M D Dunnette, pp 889–935, Rand NcNally, Chicago

Ting-Toomey, S (1999) *Communicating Across Cultures*, The Guilford Press, New York

Trickey, D and Ewington, N (2003) *A World of Difference: Working successfully across cultures*, Capita Learning and Development, London

Trompenaars, F (1993) *Riding the Waves of Culture: Understanding cultural diversity in business*, Nicholas Brealey Publishing, London

Trompenaars, F and Hampden-Turner, C (1997) *Riding the Waves of Culture: Understanding cultural diversity in business*, Nicholas Brealey Publishing, London

Tuckman, B W and Jensen, M A C (1977) Stages of small group development revisited, *Group & Organization Management*, 2, pp 419–27

Verluyten, S P (1999) Conflict avoidance in Thailand, paper presented at 11th ENCoDe Conference: *International Negotiation: Communication across business cultures*, Barcelona

Victor, D (1992) *International Business Communication*, Harper Collins, New York

Weaver, G and Uncapher, P (1981) *The Nigerian Experience: Overseas living and value change*, Paper presented at the Seventh Annual SIETAR Conference, Vancouver, BC

Zaninelli, S (1994) Vier Schritte eines integrativen, Trainingsansatzes am Beispiel eines interkulturellen Trainings: Deutschland – USA, *Materialien zum internationalen Kulturaustausch*, 33, pp 5–8, Institut für Auslandsbeziehungen, Stuttgart

INDEX

360° feedback 124, **206**

ABC competencies 113–14
accommodation 153, **206**
achievement 10, 137, 139, **206**
achievement orientation 28
acquisitions 89–90
active listening 54, 120–21
activists 117–18
Adler, N 48
adventure 86
affective cultures 114, **206**
affirmative feedback 130, 131, **206**
ambiguity 3, 57, 112, **206**
appeasement 153, **206**
appraisal 38, 124–25, **207**
ascription orientation 28, 136, **207**
assertiveness 138–39, **207**
assumptions 4, 6, 14, 59, 165, **207**
attitudes 84–86, 113, 152–56, **207**
audio conferences 172–73
autonomy 20, 53, 57, 92, 168, **207**
avoidance 153, **207**

behaviour 21, 49–50, 64, **207**
belief-orientation 57
Bell, C H 14
best practice
    building a common culture 43–45
    communicating direction 79–81
    conflict resolution 161–62
    cooperating in international teams
        173–76
    cooperating in virtual teams 170–73
    defining roles 108–9, 174
    focus and flexibility 20–22
    leadership 59–61
    organization: the four Ps 92–94
    relationship-building 58–59
    representing 146
    transparency and harmony 131–33
big picture 73, 81
Blanchard, K H et al 97
blurring techniques 133, **207**
body language 53, 114, 140–42
bosses 66–67, 202
bottom-up communication 79–80, **207**
bridging 12
brochures 140
business cards 140, 142

case studies 8
    Bracken International 176–78, 199
    Claudia Borges 133–34, 197–98
    Gisela Schaefer 162–63, 198–99
    Laurence Berger 61–62, 195
    Leila Mehmet 191–93, 200
    Nguyen Binh 122–23, 197
    Nora Lundquist 22–23, 194
    Phil Carey 81–83, 195–96
    Pierre Menton 94–95, 196
    Sun Mei Ling 110–11, 196–97
    Talal Hamieh 146–48, 198
    see also scenarios
challenges 3, 12
change 2
    attitudes towards change 84–86
    best practice: the four Ps 92–94
    case study 94–95, 196
    and conflict 150
    conservation values 84–85, **208**
    cross-cultural mergers and
        acquisitions 89–90
    international projects 90–92, 174
    making it happen 87
    openness to change 85–86
    organizational structure 87–88
    working without a leader 91–92
Chen, L 37
Chinese Culture Connection 75
co-construction of meaning 5
coaching 118
    active listening 120–21
    leadership style 97
    managerial difficulties 118–19
    peer coaching 92, **218**
    stages 119–20
codes of conduct 14, 166–67, **208**
collaboration 154
collectivism 156, 186, **208**
communication 5–6, 14
    bottom-up communication 79–80, **207**
    in building a common culture 168–69
    clarity and transparency 54, 57, 91–92,
        93, 105–8
    and conflict 156–58
    feedback 126–27
    language 158
    style 32–34, 73, 74, 75, 157–58,
        160, 190
    top-down communication 79, 80, **222**

communication channels 157, 171
    audio and video conferences 172–73
    email 72, 93, 137, 156, 157, 172
    face to face 171
    non-verbal communication 53, 114,
        140–42, 217
    social media 137, 173
    telephone 73, 93, 137, 172
    text messages 73, 157, 171
competence 165
    ABC competencies 113–14
    core competence 10–13
    see also key competences
complexity 3, 57, 112
compromise 154
conflict
    attitudes towards 152–54
    best practice 161–62
    case study 162–63, 198–99
    causes 149–51
    cultural differences 150, 175–76
    culturally influenced attitudes 154–56
    individual differences 151
    organizational change 150
    preventing through communication
        156–58
    preventing through understanding
        158–59
    resolving conflicts 159–61
    team dynamics 151
conformity 85, 208
Confucius 75–76
connecters 103–5
conservation 84–85, 208
consistency 165, 208
    context 2–3, 5, 11, 103, 158–59, 171,
        191, 208–09
contracts 166
cooperation 164
    best practice: international teams 173–76
    best practice: virtual teams 170–73
    building a common culture 168–70
    case study 176–78, 199
    pre-contractual basis 164–65
    regulating cooperation 166–67
    relational basis 165–66
    structural basis 166
core competence 10–13
Corporate Coach U programme 119
corporate information 139
corruption 65, 67, 202–3
Cracknell, B 31, 59, 79, 160, 185, 205
creation of understanding 5
creativity 11, 57
cross-cultural mergers 89–90
cultural icebergs 14–15, 17, 18

cultural intelligence 16–20, 39–42
cultural knowledge 43, 55, 114
cultural practices 42
culture 209
    building a common culture 43–45,
        168–70
    communication style 32–34
    competing values 24–25
    and conflict 150, 175–76
    individualism and group-orientation
        35–37
    performance orientation 37–39
    power and status 26–29
    profiling other cultures 42–43
    and representing 137–39
    time 30–32
    values 24–25, 65
    your own cultures 15–20, 39–42
culture-blindness 45, 209
culture-sensitivity 45, 209
curriculum vitae 139

decision making 57, 65
deference 26, 27, 209
delegating 97
Den Hartog, D N 138
departmental publicity 140
Developing People Internationally
    (DPI) model 9, 12–13
developmental feedback 131, 209
direction
    best practice 79–81
    case study 81–83, 195–96
    communicating direction 73–81, 174
    communication style 73, 74, 75
    leadership style 97
    long- and short-term orientation 75–76
    past, present and future 77–79
    pushing or pulling 74–75
    results and relationships 72–73
    and uncertainty 69–71
    and vision 71–72
directness 32–33, 34, 49, 57, 209–10
Distefano, J J 11
diversity 168, 210
domination 152, 153, 210
Dorfman, P W et al 188, 189–90
down-toners 132, 210
dress 140
Duncan, J 142, 205

effectiveness 7
email 72, 93, 137, 156, 157, 172
emotional expression 114–15
emotional intelligence 16, 53
emotional strength 53

Emrich, C G *et al* 29
English as the lingua franca 54, 106–8, 158, 168
ethical behaviour 65, 67, 165–66
ethnic culture 17
exchange 169–70
expectations 10–11, 14–15
expert knowledge 99–101
explicitness 5, 32, 33, 34, 38, 93, 210
extroverts 55–56, 129, 210
eye contact 141

face 33, 155, 162, 210, 213
    and feedback 119, 126, 127–28, 133
facial expression 141
facilitators 105–8
feedback
    360° feedback 124, 206
    affirmative feedback 130, 131, 206
    best practice: transparency and harmony 131–33
    building a feedback culture 94, 129–30, 175
    case study 133–34, 197–98
    and culture 125–27
    developmental feedback 131, 209
    and face 119, 126, 127–28, 133
    formal feedback 124–25
    informal feedback 125
    and personality 128–29
    self-reflection 129
    sincerity 129, 220
    virtual teams 173
Feiler, K 156
femininity 42, 136, 138, 210–11
flexibility 21–22, 52–53, 57–58, 165
Flytzani, S 87
followers 181
Foti, R J 182
four Ps 92–94
French, W L 14
functional culture 17
future-oriented cultures 77–79, 211

Gandhi, M 53
gate-keepers 102–3, 211
gender 42, 137–38
gender egalitarianism 29, 211
generalists 100, 211
gift-giving 65, 140, 213
global nomads 1
GLOBE Study 26, 29, 37, 184–90, 211
goals 20–22, 69
greeting rituals 142
Gregor, B 81, 98, 205
group-orientation 36–37, 44, 127–28, 154–56

Grundison, B 155
guanxi 102, **211**
Gudykunst, W B 4

Hall, E T 30, 32, 209–10, **212**
Hallberg, E 16, 21, 59, 128, 205
Hampden-Turner, C 28, 77, 114
Hansen, U 127, 205
harmony 44, 131–33
hedonism 86, **212**
Hersey, P *et al* 97
hierarchy 26–27, 79, 88, 158, 160, 185, **212**
high-context communication 33, **212**
Hofstede, G 26, 35, 70, 75, 137–38, 139, 209, 211–12, **213**
holidays 42
Holmes, J *et al* 157
honesty 24–25, 44, 131–32, 168
Honey, P 117
hospitality 65, 67, 165–66, **213**
House, J 157
House, R J *et al* 35, 70, 184–85, 187
humane orientation 184, **214**
humour **214**

implicitness 32, 33, 34, 38, 162, **214**
in-groups 27, 47, 165, 209, **215**
indirectness 33–34, 49, 57, **214**
individualism 35–37, 44, 116, 127, 139, 154, 155–56, **214**
individuals
    behaviour 49–50
    and change 94
    and conflict 151, 175
    and culture 47, 52–55, 175–76
    and feedback 175
    international profiles 55–58
    personality 49–52, 55–58
    representing 175
    stereotypes 46–49, **221**
    supporting 114–15, 174
influencing 55, 58, 75, 101–3, 181, 190–91
information handling 57
Ingham, H 48
Inkson, K 4
integrating 12, 153
integrity 165, **215**
interdependence 35, 37, **215**
international managers 1–2
    core competence 10–13
    expectations 10–11, 14–15
    your own cultures 15–20, 39–42
    see also best practice; case studies; key competences

international profile 52–55
  and personality 55–58
International Profiler, The 8, 52
international projects 90–92, 174
international teams 11
  cooperation 173–76
  mapping, bridging, integrating 12
  people 174–75
  route map 12–13
  tasks 174
interpersonal (physical) distance 141
introverts 55–56, 129, **215**

Javidan, M *et al* 126, 186
Jensen, M A C 151
job interviews 139
Johari window 49–50
judgement 63–65, 165
  see also scenarios

key competences 8
  active listening 54, 120–21
  cultural knowledge 43
  flexible behaviour 21–22
  flexible judgement 165
  influencing and communication styles
    75, 190
  influencing through rapport 58, 191
  influencing through sensitivity to
    context 103, 191
  learning languages 169
  openness 45, 56, 104
  perceptiveness through being
    attuned 141
  perceptiveness through reflected
    awareness 161
  personal autonomy 20, 168
  spirit of adventure 86
  synergy through new alternatives 176
  transparency in communication 93, 108
  valuing differences 175
Key Performance Indicators (KPIs) 3–4
kick-off phase 171, **215**
Kitayama, S 35
Kluckhohn, F R 77
Kolb, D A 117
Kotter, J P 180
Kühn, F 92, 119, 205–6
Kuhnert, W 91, 98, 156, 161, 206

Langer, E J 4
language and speaking
  barriers 169
  building a common culture 168–69
  clarity and transparency 54, 93,
    106–8, 158
  key terms 169

learning languages 168–69
  turn-taking 144–46, **221**
  see also English as the lingua franca
Laurent, A 99
leadership
  best practice 59–61
  building a common culture 168
  case study 191–93, 200
  influencing 181, 190–91
  managers and leaders 179–80
  path-goal theory 181, **218**
  power as basis for leadership 181
  situational approach 181
  style 97
  style approach 182
  SWOT analysis 59–60
  traits 182–84
  transformational leadership 181, **222**
  see also bosses; leadership:
    cultural differences
leadership: cultural differences
  desirable attributes 188, 189–90
  leadership dimensions 184–88
  values 185, 186
learning types 117–18
LeBaron, M 155
lingua franca 54, 106, 158, 168, **215**
listening orientation 54, 120–21
locus of control 87
long-term orientation 75–76, **215**
low-context communication 32–33, 34,
    160, **215–16**
loyalty 67–68, 203, **216**
Luft, J 49

McCann, D 50–51
majority cultures 104, **216**
management styles 97–98
managers
  as experts 99–101
  and leaders 179–80
mapping 12
Margerison, C 50–51
Markus, H 35
masculinity 42, 117, 136, 138, **216**
Maznevski, M L 11
Mazzola, C 16, 58, 88, 92, 96, 169, 171,
    185, 206
meaning 5
meetings 105–6
mentoring 121–22, **216**
mergers 89–90
mindful interaction 4–5
mindful working 3–4
mindfulness 4
mindsets 21, **216**
minority cultures 104, **216**

mission statements 71, **216**
modesty 168, **216**
monochronic cultures 30, **216–17**
Mumford, A 117
Munetsi, W 43, 206

national cultures 17, 26
  communication style 32–34
  group-orientation 36–37
  individualism 35–37
  perfomance orientation 37–39
  power and status 26, 28
  time orientation 30, 32
negotiation of meaning 5
networks 36, 101–2, 174
neutral cultures 114, **217**
Nijkamp, P 87
non-verbal communication 53, 114,
    140–42, **217**
Northouse, P G 180, 187

objectivity 57
openness 45, 52, 56, 85–86, 104, 165
opportunities 3
organization 57–58, 92–94
organizational culture 14, 18, **217**
  communication style 32–34
  group-orientation 36–37
  individualism 35–37
  perfomance orientation 37–39
  power and status 26–29
  time 31–32
organizational structure 87–88
Ortega, L 102, 143, 158, 206
out-groups 47, **217**

pace 57, **218**
Parsons, T 166
particularist cultures 167, **218**
past-oriented cultures 77, 78–79, **218**
path-goal theory 181, **218**
peer coaching 92, **218**
Pena, A 58
people *see* individuals; international teams
perceptiveness 53, 141, 161
performance: managing poor performance
    66, 201
performance orientation 37–39, 44, 126, **218**
performance review 124–25
personality 50
  and behaviour 49–50, 64
  and feedback 128–29
  and international profile 55–58
  preferences 50–51
  profiles 50–52
Pestalozzi, L 85, 94, 206
physical (interpersonal) distance 141

polychronic cultures 30, **218–19**
power and status 26–29, 44, 79, 100,
    102, 181
power distance 26, 27, 116, **219**
power orientation 127
pragmatists 117–18
prejudice 14, **219**
preparation 93
present-oriented cultures 77, 78–79, **219**
presentations 136–37, 146
process 6, 93–94
psychometric tools 50–51, **219**
purpose 93, 168

qualifications 100

rapport 58, 72–73, 78–79, 191
reciprocity 165–66, **220**
reflectors 118
relational aspects 132, **220**
relationship-building 55–56, **220**
  best practice 58–59
  peaches and coconuts 142–44
  rapport 58, 72–73
  turn-taking 144–46, **221**
relationship orientation 126, 135
relationships
  case study 61–62, 195
  and professionalism 68, 204
  and results 72–73
  in virtual teams 170–71
religious culture 17
representing
  best practice 146
  body language 140–42
  case study 146–48, 198
  chance representation 136
  importance of representing 135
  influencing factors 137–39
  international representation 139–40
  international teams 175
  presentations 136–37, 146
  skills 136–37
  socialising and building relationships
    142–43
roles
  best practice: defining roles 108–9,
    174
  case study 110–11, 196–97
  connecting 103–5
  facilitating 105–8
  influencing 101–3
  international and local roles 98–99
  management roles and styles 96–98
  manager as expert 99–101
  supportive and directive styles 97–98

Rotter, J B 87
Ruckdäschel, T 36, 102, 166
Ruhly, S 14

scenarios 65
  close relationships 68, 204
  corruption 67, 202–3
  divided loyalties 67–68, 203, **216**
  poor performance 66, 201
  a rude boss 66–67, 202
Schein, E 14
Schwartz, S H 84–85
sectoral culture 17
self-reflection 129
short-term orientation 75–76, **220**
silo mentality 103–4, **220**
sincerity 129, **220**
situational judgement 63–65
  see also scenarios
skills 114, 136–37
small talk (social conversation) 143–44,
  172, **221**
Smith, J. A. 181
social media 137, 173
social relationships 42, 58, 142
  peaches and coconuts 142–44
  turn-taking 144–46, **221**
  see also relationship-building
socio-economic culture 17
speaking *see* language and speaking
Stachowicz-Stanusch, A 89
Stahl, G K *et al* 11, 150
status *see* power and status
stereotypes 46–49, **221**
stress 53, 90
Strodtbeck, F L 77
Stromberg, D 130
support 92
  case study 122–23, 197
  developing your team 116–22, 174
  developing yourself 113–14
  importance of support 112–13
  leadership style 97
  supporting your colleagues 114–15
  see also networks
SWOT analysis 59–60, 127
synergy 55, 176

tall-poppy syndrome 26
Tannen, D 137
task orientation 56, 125–26, 174
Taylor, T 16, 27, 36, 80, 100, 126, 206
team development 174
  coaching 118–21
  mentoring 121–22, **216**
  training 116–18

  see also international teams; team
    dynamics; virtual teams
team dynamics 151
Team Management Profile® 50–51, 52
telephone 73, 93, 137, 172
text **221**
text messages 73, 157, 171
theorists 118
Thomas, D C 4
Thoral, F 16, 26, 34
time 30–32, 44, 105, 170, **221**
Ting-Toomey, S 4, 154, 155
top-down communication 79, 80, **222**
training 116–18
transactional aspects 132, **222**
transformational leadership 181, **222**
transparency
  in communication 54, 57, 91–92, 93, 108
  in feedback 131–33
  in leadership 168
Trompenaars, F 28, 77, 114, 167, 207,
  208, 209, **222**
trust 162, 165, 166
Tuckman, B W 151
turn-taking 144–46, **221**

Uncapher, P 14
uncertainty 2–3, 69–71, 112, **222**
uncertainty avoidance 116, 126, **222–23**
understanding 5, 158
universalist cultures 65, 166–67, **223**

values 8, 24–25, 65, 84–85, 168, 185,
  186, **223**
  see also corruption; direction
Victor, D 218
video conferences 172–73
virtual teams 170, **223**
  communication channels 171–73
  context 171
  feedback 173
  relationships 170–71
  time 170
vision 71–72
volatility 2, 112
VUCA (volatility, uncertainty, complexity,
  ambiguity) 2–3, 112

Warsi, S 16, 158, 160
Weaver, G 14
Weber, T 43, 48, 79, 99, 125, 185
Wollman, P 69, 121, 206
work-life balance 36, 42, **223**
working day 41–42
Worldwork International Competency Set 8

Zaninelli, S 142–43

CPSIA information can be obtained at www.ICGtesting.com
Printed in the USA
BVOW03s1045090414

350183BV00007B/252/P

9 780749 469825